THOUGH THERE BE GIANTS

THOUGH THERE BE GIANTS

The Ghetto Pastoral Mode in Black Migration Novels

Donald M. Shaffer

University Press of Mississippi / Jackson

Margaret Walker Alexander Series in African American Studies

The University Press of Mississippi is the scholarly publishing agency of
the Mississippi Institutions of Higher Learning: Alcorn State University,
Delta State University, Jackson State University, Mississippi State University,
Mississippi University for Women, Mississippi Valley State University,
University of Mississippi, and University of Southern Mississippi.

www.upress.state.ms.us

The University Press of Mississippi is a member
of the Association of University Presses.

Publisher: University Press of Mississippi, Jackson, USA
Authorised GPSR Safety Representative: Easy Access System Europe -
Mustamäe tee 50, 10621 Tallinn, Estonia, *gpsr.requests@easproject.com*

Library of Congress Cataloging-in-Publication Data available

Print LCCN 2025047195
ISBN 9781496855978 (hardback)
ISBN 9781496855985 (trade paperback)
ISBN 9781496855992 (EPUB single)
ISBN 9781496856005 (EPUB institutional)
ISBN 9781496856012 (PDF single)
ISBN 9781496856029 (PDF institutional)

British Library Cataloging-in-Publication Data available

CONTENTS

ACKNOWLEDGMENTS

I gratefully acknowledge all those who supported my research at the University of Chicago, as well as the faculty and Sisters of Dominican University, and my dear friend and mentor, Illya Davis. And of course, I must thank Dr. Ken Warren, whose grace and guidance were invaluable.

I owe a debt of gratitude to many others who contributed to this book's existence. Thank you, Gerald Graff, for your early mentorship. You are the reason I attended the University of Chicago, the place where the world opened up for me. Thank you, David Bevington, for believing that an African American kid from Jackson, Mississippi, who studied race and literature could be a graduate teaching assistant for the leading Shakespearean scholar in the world. Thank you, Drs. Tommy Anderson, Ted Atkinson, and Matthew Hughey, for reading and improving my roughhewn prose. Thank you, Bria Young, for assisting me on this and other projects as my talented graduate assistant. Thank you, Brian Pugh, for your friendship, and for exemplifying scholarly and professional excellence. And lastly, I want to thank my "second reader," who made me realize that this book could be (ahem) much better than the initial draft, and who outlined in agonizing detail all the ways I could achieve that goal. You were right, mostly.

This book is dedicated to my family—to my wife, Vanessa, who pushes me toward excellence in more ways than she realizes; to my sons, Brandon and Donovan, who someday I hope will write their own books; to my grandmother, Mamie Ruth Burnett, who asked me every day after school, "What did you learn?"; and to my mother, Ruby Jean Shaffer, who made me possible. Finally, to my cousin and childhood companion, Tommy Ian Williams, I remember you every day.

THOUGH THERE BE GIANTS

"A GLORY TO THE GRANDEUR OF SPACE"

The Ghetto Pastoral Mode and the Politics of Place

> Like fixed massed sentinels guarding the approaches to the great metropolis, again the pyramids of New York in their Egyptian majesty dazzled my sight like a miracle of might and took my breath like the banging music of Wagner assaulting one's spirit and rushing it skyward with the pride and power of an eagle. . . . The feeling of the dirty steerage passage across the Atlantic was swept away in the immense wonder of clean, vertical heaven-challenging lines, *a glory to the grandeur of space*.
> —CLAUDE MCKAY, *A LONG WAY FROM HOME* (1937)[1]

> They did what human beings looking for freedom, throughout history, have often done. They left.
> —ISABEL WILKERSON, *THE WARMTH OF OTHER SUNS* (2010)[2]

I was not unaccustomed to hearing the word used before. It was common vernacular for a young generation of Black folk who may have even heard it from their parents in passing, whose parents no doubt may have heard it from *others* with different intentions to say the least. So, when I heard the word "n---a" ring out from the stands at a South Side tennis tournament in Chicago, the occurrence was not met with any particular anger or surprise. My eventual, albeit passive, response was in part the result of the immediate place and circumstance of this otherwise profane utterance. The speaker of

3

the notorious and capacious term was a Black man in his late twenties or early thirties who spoke with relative assurance about the outcome of each match. He punctuated every phrase with the historically freighted word, offering observations like "that n---a' can't serve and volley," or "that n---a better attack the backhand if he wants to win." None of these expressions were particularly offensive in *this* particular space of upwardly mobile Black middle-class professionals, but something about it (perhaps it was his cavalier usage of the word to accentuate everyone and everything) that struck me as unseemly. Eventually, when the speaker refused to "keep it down," as I reluctantly asked him, what had been a fairly minor occurrence quickly became something of an incident. Of course, he refused my request. Still feigning polite conversation, I informed him that I was from Mississippi, that I thought it ironic I had not heard *that* word used in the Deep South nearly as much as I had heard it used here in Chicago. As if he were experiencing a sudden epiphany, the young African American man offered the quick rebuttal, "Well, you're not in Mississippi anymore." Nearly defeated, I craned my neck to spot a sponsor's advertisement I had read earlier. More confident upon finding the pertinent statement, I issued a retort of my own. Triumphantly pointing to a sign that read, "Eat at the *Mississippi Café*," I told him, "We are *always* in Mississippi."

As a Black migrant of a much different sort, a graduate student from Mississippi attending that "University on the Midway" as Richard Wright once described it in *Native Son*, I experienced *that* word with equal parts revulsion and fascination. It offered a glimpse into the decades-long peregrination of a concept that was now a coarse reminder of the history of racism and violence it once engendered. That word had migrated to Chicago along with the scores of Black migrants decades earlier from places like my hometown of Jackson, Mississippi. And like those denizens of the Great Migration, it too had come to the city to be transformed beneath the long shadows of skyscrapers and stacked tenements. However, just as those migrants struggled to "hurdle several generations of experience at a leap," that word had fallen short of slipping the yoke that forever linked it to the very worst of Black lived experience in the South.³ And so the tension I felt (that we both felt) in that brief moment at the South Side tennis tournament was not unlike the tension that had defined a generation of Black migrants whose stories were also equal parts fascination and revulsion.

Reflecting this tension, the African American Great Migration novel emerged as popular mode of fiction in the decade of the 1920s. Not surprisingly, the decade that saw both the Harlem Renaissance as well as the thunderous onset of the roaring Jazz Age also provided the backdrop for Black migrant stories of personal triumph and transformation set in the potent symbolic urban landscape of America's iconic cityscapes. However, while these novels represented the powerful symbol of the Northern city as a proverbial promised land, they also reflected the urban pastoral conflict that defined Black migrant experience. Indeed, these novels are best understood as employing a variant of the urban pastoral mode that historian Michael Denning has termed the "ghetto pastoral."[4] In this book, I marshal Denning's concept of the ghetto pastoral to examine the ideological tension between rural and urban modes of experience in these novels. I argue that the ghetto pastoral mode as a variant of urban pastoralism functions in Black migration novels as a dialectical trope that (re)frames as it (re)presents concepts of race and cultural identity.

My close readings of these novels build on the work of Michael Denning, whose book *The Cultural Front* defines my operational term, the "ghetto pastoral," as a "yoking of naturalism and the pastoral," stories that dialectically represent urban experience as an "allegorical cityscape composed in a pidgin of American slang and ghetto dialect, with traces of old country tongues."[5] To read Black migration novels through the lens of the ghetto pastoral mode reveals the thematic tension produced by cultural displacement and racial deracination. What my reading of these novels as ghetto pastoral stories of Black migration also demonstrates is the way in which these texts destabilize concepts of race and identity even as they attempt to locate Blackness in the transformative spaces and places of the Northern city. I argue that it is precisely this conflict at the center of Black migration novels that produces the major figure of the New Negro movement—that is, the liminal Black migrant standing at the proverbial crossroads of rural/ Southern and urban/Northern experience. This figure of the Black migrant does the important symbolic work of embodying at once the ideals of the Black Renaissance with its thematic focus on the powerful valorization of Black vernacular culture and the attenuating racial tension that defined the genre of Black migration fiction.[6] As figures defined by their liminal status as both rural and urban, as both Black people and "New Negroes," as both the product of rural vernacular expressions and expressive of a more urban experience in the promised land, the Black migrant is a trope that comes to define not only a generation of Black artistic expression but also stands as the culmination of the African American literary tradition.

I apply the ghetto pastoral to this body of literary texts as both a descriptive term expressive of the historical content and context of these stories about Black migration at the turn of the century and as a rhetorical trope revealing how Black migration stories function as an ideological basis for a radical new conception of Black identity. The ghetto pastoral is for Denning a process of acculturation in which (im)migrants reconcile their "old world" identities with the urban landscape and cultural exigencies of US cities. Therefore, the first challenge for these newcomers was to shed their ethnic identities. Indeed, to become white was the tacit goal of these European immigrants and, in so doing, to privilege an identity that would dissolve the boundaries of nationality.[7] Perhaps most instructive in Denning's account is the tension always present in this process of negotiating an identity for oneself in the city. It is one always fraught with the ambiguity of their new identities—identities that are always already capacious signifiers of race, nationality and social class. However, unlike Black migrants, whose identities are always fractured in the last instance by the powerful narrative of white supremacy, Denning's white immigrants can aspire to the social legitimacy that whiteness confers upon them.

In contrast to Denning's white immigrants, the characters of Black migration novels are always attempting to (re)define their identities as first-class citizens, as Black people hoping to escape the dehumanizing practices of Southern racism and violence. In other words, they are necessarily preoccupied with the fundamental goal of becoming human in a culture where most already assume their humanity as an essential birthright. For this reason, the authors of Black migration novels eschewed the traditional narrative of social ascent wherein European immigrants only had to shuffle off the coil of Old-World cultures to embrace a new American identity. Nevertheless, despite the differences between the experiences of Black and white (im)migrants, Denning's ghetto pastoral concept offers critical insight into the ways in which stories of Black migration reveal the dialectical terms of Black lived experience. These stories of Black migration were a literary appropriation of W. E. B. Du Bois's concept of double consciousness in that they represented the competing forces that shaped the lives of Black people, that forced them to acknowledge at once the promise of America (embodied as it where in the image of the North as a proverbial promised land) and the material reality of racial segregation, a legal and ideological statement of Black inferiority and second class citizenship.[8] This sort of dialecticism is at the center of the Black migrant experience. It reflects the ways in which stories of Black migration where simultaneously representative of the ideals that defined the American Dream with its emphasis on individual success and upward mobility in contrast to their representation of the material realities that attended the egalitarian myth of the North particularly and American society generally.

The emergence of Black migration novels at the turn of the century reflects an important historical and critical linkage between the racial uplift novels of the late nineteenth century and the Black modernist novels of the mid-twentieth century.[9] The works of post-Reconstruction era Black authors like Frances E. W. Harper and Charles W. Chesnutt sought to (re)imagine African American lived experience as denoting endless possibility despite the failures of Reconstruction. The Black migration novels of the early twentieth century imagined the realization of this vision in Northern cities. Through my close readings of several important Black migration novels, I will shed light on one of the most important literary tropes of African American modernity: namely, the Black migrant standing at the proverbial gates of the Northern city—standing as it were betwixt and between Southern folk culture and the transformative cultural spaces of the Northern city. I read Black migration novels as making an important critical intervention in how we understand the relationship between place and identity. Like Erin Battat in her luminous study of white and Black migration narratives, *Ain't Got No Home: America's Great Migrations and the Making of an Interracial Left*, I discuss Black migration literature as part of an emerging tradition of radical writing in the 1920s and 1930s that challenged racial assumptions.[10] However, in addition to the political themes motivating this literature, my book examines the important role of Southern Black culture in shaping the portrayal of urban spaces in these novels—urban spaces such as Harlem that gave rise to a distinctive portrait of Black lived experience in Northern cities.

My book also aims to intervene in recent debates about the social and political factors that led to the massive exodus of African Americans from the traditional South in the early part of the twentieth century. While some commentators understand the migration as solely a direct response to the economic and social conditions besetting Black people in the South, others have painted a more nuanced portrait of that history that emphasizes the cultural meanings that also provided the impetus for the movement. For example, in her book *Leaving the South*, Mary Weaks-Baxter describes the ways in which stories of northward migration "challenged concepts of Southern nationhood" as these narratives "remade and reconfigured how Southern identity was and still is interpreted and represented."[11] For Weaks-Baxter, these literary accounts of "border crossings" are more than simply stories of leaving the South. They are stories of cultural transformation in which "Southernness was redefined by the experiences and representations of Southerners who were leaving the region."[12] As my book demonstrates, the complex interplay of both economic and cultural factors in the decision to leave the South is at the center of Black migration narratives. Northern cities were not only places where one could "get ahead," they were places where one could become whole as an individual. As Weaks-Baxter further describes, the prevailing "image" of Northern cities was a powerful draw for Black migrants: "Many Southerners were motivated to leave the South because of a push and pull. African Americans tended to leave the South for Northern cities such as New York, Chicago, and Philadelphia not only because of racism and poor economic conditions in the South but because of the deeply rooted image in African American history of the North as a promised land. And city life also had its draw."[13] The image of the North as a proverbial promised land and the draw of Northern cities were both part of the lore surrounding the Great Migration. This idealism associated with migration alongside the material forces motivating this movement were two sides of the same coin.

The *ideal* and the *real* converge in Black narratives in ways that challenged both racial identity and the so-called promise of Northern cities. The promise of the North would have been a popular narrative for Black migrants at the turn of the century. However, in these novels, the story of Northern cities as the proverbial promised land is often juxtaposed with the material realities of city life. One of those realities was the racial segregation that had come to define American cities in the early twentieth century. This reality often meant that Black and brown communities in Northern cities were racial and economically demarcated as nonplaces where hope and opportunity presumably did not exist. In *Urban Underworlds: A Geography of Twentieth Century American Literature and Culture*, Thomas Heise argues that the racial stigmatization of Black and brown communities has created what he describes as "urban underworlds" in major cities.[14] According to Heise, these are racially quarantined spaces, designated as it were as sites of the other, marked off within the urban cityscape as veritable no-man's-lands.[15] What I hope to contribute to this discussion of racial marginalized spaces is an examination of the way in which Black migration authors sought to create a counter-hegemonic narrative that would reclaim Black urban communities as transformative cultural spaces.

No other social movement besides the civil rights movement of the 1960s has been more important in shaping the cultural identity of African Americans than the Great Migration. In addition to the economic necessities that motivated Black people to leave the South in droves, there was also a prevailing social narrative of Northern cities as places where Black people could find greater recognition if not untapped freedoms previously denied to them. Thus, the history of the Great Migration includes examinations of the social factors that motivated African American to leave the South (the so-called push factors) as well as the social factors that incentivized them to head for the North (the "pull" factors). This traditional framing of the period illustrates the oppressive conditions of the South while extolling the economic benefits of the North, citing both as reasons for the massive exodus of Black migrants. However, this perspective can often obscure the cultural narratives that informed the decisions of Black Southerners to leave the South. These personal stories of migration took on many forms, from the published accounts in newspapers like the *Chicago Defender* and journals like W. E. B. Du Bois's *New Masses*, to the numerous pamphlets that extolled the benefits of life in Northern cities. Echoing Alain Locke's famous proclamation in *The New Negro*, in which he describes the Great Migration as a cultural shift from "Medieval to modern America," these accounts sought to frame the migration as an important moment of cultural advancement for African Americans in the South. A common thread running through these stories of Black migration is a desire to make a new life for oneself in places conducive to personal growth and transformation.

The subject matter of this book is timely as we rethink the meaning of Southern culture, a term seemingly mired in the amber of tradition. Indeed, there is now a renewed emphasis on Southern culture that paints a more nuanced portrait of the region as far more varied and diverse than previously imagined. In this era of strategic rebranding, the American South is witnessing a renaissance of sorts as many of its commentators actively seek to distance the region from its previous investment in "lost cause" narratives rooted in racism and white supremacy. The retiring of Confederate flag emblems that once flew above Southern states and the removal of monuments that celebrate (not merely record) a bygone era of racial segregation are signs of a region that is increasingly (re)defining itself in modern terms. In the wake of these social changes, the mobilizing concept of the Global South has (re)emerged as a term denoting the collective interests and informal solidarity of marginalized regions and nations. To view the American South as part of this informal bloc is to understand the ways in which the history and the character of the South are represented in myriad perspectives each told from different vantage points in their relationship to power. One of the goals of this book, then, is to locate what Zandria F. Robinson calls "the Black South," an ideal she describes as existing in the interstices between "the idea of the place (as country, backwards, rural, for instance)" and "the lived reality of a place."[16] Robinson describes this project as a "Sisyphean exercise," for it requires an interrogation of multiple voices and perspectives each one contradicting the other while offering a different version of the South.[17] However, one way to understand a place like the South, as the structure of

William Faulkner's novels reveals, is to give credence to a multiplicity of voices and perspectives despite their seemingly disparate and contradictory nature. It is precisely the confluence of these competing perspectives in Black migration novels that make them potent signifiers of Black cultural identity, an identity formed at the intersection of Southern culture and modernity.

The Black Migration Novel

While Black migration narratives include works ranging from poetry to short stories, this book will focus on the Black migration novel. The novel is an especially important form within the broader range of Black migration narratives. The novel as a form (re)produces as it represents social relations, thereby making it an important cultural agent in ascribing meaning to the places and spaces where people reside. Therefore, the tacit goal of the Black migration novel is to establish a sense of belonging for Black migrant characters within a fragmented symbolic landscape of disparate human relations. Raymond Williams illuminates the function of the novel form in this regard. He writes, "Most novels are in some sense knowable communities. It is part of a traditional method—an underlying stance and approach—that the novelist offers to show people and their relationships in essentially knowable and communicable ways."[18] Similarly, and as my specific readings will show, the Black migration novel as a form is invested in revealing the ways in which Black migrants establish a sense of place and belonging in the city. This ideal of community is always contested in Black migration novels by the rural and urban conflict that defines the experiences of Black migrant characters. These novels of transition reflect the displacement that Black migrants experienced in Northern cities during the Great Migration. Thus, the characters of these novels are represented as having to negotiate a sense of place that lies tenuously between "the country and the city."

The emergence of the Black migration novel at the turn of the century brought to bear a new urban perspective in the representation of Black lived experience. [19] Prior to the Great Migration, Black cultural expression was geographically rooted in the South, where over 80 percent of Black people resided before 1910.[20] A symbolic economy of sharecropping influenced Black cultural expression in the South, as Black cultural forms had to define themselves against the social backdrop of an oppressive regime of white supremacy. Houston Baker's metaphor of the "Blues performer" is an apt way of describing the mode of cultural production that was operative in the South after Reconstruction and before the massive exodus of Black migrants to Northern cities.[21] Baker's blues performer is representative of the Black artist who had to negotiate his marginal social status in order to produce a bivocal or coded form of cultural expression. Baker's "blues matrix" allows for the possibility of Black cultural expression in the rural South, within what he terms "blues geographies," or spaces where Black expression can flourish and find meaning. Such expression must necessarily take as its source the "race ideology" of the South, where the Black artist [read blues performer] must wear the "minstrel mask" in hopes of inverting its racist meanings. The salient point that Baker makes is that Black cultural production in the South necessarily involved a recognition of marginality, so that Black artists had to attend constantly to an "economics of slavery" (which after 1865 became an "economics of sharecropping") as the "social ground" providing the content for their expressions.[22]

In figuring "the city" as a dominant trope in African American literature, Black migration novelists effectively shifted representations of race beyond the aesthetic and conceptual boundaries of a Southern, romantic tradition, which had narrowly defined race and folk culture.[23] Whereas the South evoked static notions of Black lived experience and proscriptive ideologies of race, the urban setting of Northern cities challenged the normative meanings that defined rural Black experience. The conception of an authentic rural Black experience was dislodged by the modernist themes of alienation and urban displacement, problematic concerns that defined the experience of Black migrants in the Northern city. The characters of Black migration novels are often represented as marginal figures tenuously positioned between two competing geographical conceptions; on the one hand, they are the immediate products of a Southern rural experience; on the other hand, they aspire to the urbane promise of (re)imagining themselves as "New Negroes."[24] This sort of characterization figures Black migrant experience and identity as a source of racial and cultural conflict. Thus, the migration novels addressed in this study frame rural and urban conflict as a defining element of Black migration, thereby (re)presenting the city as a staging ground for urban struggles, where concepts of race and collective identity encounter the ideological landscape of industrial capitalism, mass cultural production, and racial segregation.

To anticipate my critical readings, I will assess the representation of urban spaces in Black migration novels, arguing that these spaces foreground the complex and often conflicting relationship between rural folk identity and urban consciousness. For the Black migrant characters of these novels, attending to this urban conflict requires a (re)envisioning of folk identity that calls into question static notions of race and cultural authenticity. In part, my emphasis on the dialectical nature of urban space as such is a response to Hazel Carby's call for a critical perspective that affirms the "transformative power of both historical and urban consciousness."[25] As Carby accurately points out, interpretations of Black vernacular forms have often centered on rural folk tradition instead of attending to the historical and cultural conflicts produced by social displacement and Black migration. Because of this critical emphasis on rural folk tradition, "the fact that imaginative re-creations of the 'folk,' including the ex-slave, are themselves produced and distributed primarily within the urban environment and for urban consumption is not critically examined."[26] Rather than reassert the cultural primacy of Black vernacular forms, my readings will reveal the ways in which Black migration novels question the relationship between rural folk identity and urban consciousness. Thus, my goal is to assess the kinds of conflict that stem from the appropriation of rural forms and practices (e.g., blues, religion, values) within the various urban spaces (e.g., kitchenette apartments, storefront churches, nightclubs) that form the cityscapes of Black migration novels. This confluence of rural and urban modalities, which Carby identifies as a defining feature of Black culture, produces both a source of meaning and conflict in Black migration novels.

The past few decades have seen the publication of several major studies of Black migration writing.[27] Much of this interest has grown out of discussions of multiculturalism and, more recently, discussions of postracialism. These ongoing critical discussions presume that race in general and Blackness in particular have undergone some rather significant shifts in meaning over the last century. The tradition of Black migration writing, including works of nonfiction and autobiography, offer a glimpse into the history of an important cultural shift that changed how Black people understood themselves as American citizens. This shift has occurred in stages with Black people attempting to define themselves in the era of slavery as simply human beings, in the era of Reconstruction as marginalized citizens aspiring to the goal of full integration, and in the era of Black migration as "New Negroes" seeking to revise the very terms of racial identity. The Black migration novel then reveals the ways in which Black authors saw themselves as part of a racial peregrination that saw negros and colored folk become Afro-Americans by the early 1900s. The Black migration novel reveals a crucial moment in this history at which the shift in Black racial identity and consciousness is beginning to occur. Viewed in this way, the Harlem Renaissance was more than simply a flourishing of Black artistic expression. Indeed, it may best be characterized as a reimagining of what it means to view oneself as a racial subject. The Black migration novel was a central artistic expression of the Harlem Renaissance, one that (re)imagined what it meant to be Black and how Black lived experience could be situated in transformative cultural spaces.

Denning's conception of the ghetto pastoral effectively describes the artistic efforts of Black migration authors. Works such as James Weldon Johnson's *Autobiography of an Ex-Colored Man* and Nella Larsen's *Quicksand* disrupted the standard narratives of Black culture and lived experience. More than merely stories of Black migration, these are stories of historic and geographic transition in which racial normativity runs up against the disruptive force of history. While several major studies of Black migration novels have attended to this history, most tend to obscure the ghetto pastoral conflict of rural and urban experience as the thematic and rhetorical basis for these novels. Many instead privilege the centrality of Black Southern folk culture as thematic basis for these novels. The overwhelming presumption of this critical discourse is that Black migrants must access a Black ancestral past as a necessary condition for establishing their place in the city. This presumes that the terms of that ancestral past are already stable concepts in Black migration narratives. I argue instead that the ghetto pastoral conflict represented in these novels necessarily complicates the centrality of Southern Black culture as basis for Black identity. Indeed, rather than valorizing Black Southern folk culture, many of these novels foreground the conflict between rural and urban Black experience. This conflict is borne out of the dialectical urban spaces of lived experience that comprise the figure of the city in Black migration literature—prominent Black cultural spaces such as the "nightclub" and the "storefront church," among others. Urban locales such as Seventh Street in Washington, DC, signify at once the valorized character of the "low down folk"—as Langston Hughes describes it in his autobiographical account—as well as the image of "bootleggers in silken shirts," as Jean Toomer writes in his experimental migration novel *Cane*. As sites of ghetto pastoral conflict, urban spaces such as these are emblematic of the Black migrant's struggle to overcome her displacement in the city. Moreover, these urban spaces are contested sites of cultural recognition where Black migrant characters must struggle to understand if not reconcile the terms of their social displacement.

Farah Griffin's important study of Black migration narratives, *"Who Set You Flowin'?,"* examines the rural and urban conflict that Black migrant characters experience in the northern city. Griffin's interpretation rightly reveals the ways in which these fictions imagined how Black migrants (re) constructed the ideal of home and belonging in Northern cities. According to Griffin, migrants accomplish this by establishing "safe spaces" in the Northern city. Griffin's description of these "safe spaces" is instructive in gauging how Black migrants marshal cultural and collective experience in order to establish a sense of place in the city. Griffin writes that "narrative safe spaces are often resistant to traditional narrative form. They appear in song, food, elements of oral culture, the silences around ritual, and in dream sequences."[28] These narrative forms provide a basis for conceptualizing ideals of home and place for the displaced and deracinated Black migrant. As Griffin points out, these narrative forms, and the urban spaces where they are observed and practiced, invoke a sense of shared experience that provides an initial foothold for Black migrants in the unchartered terrain of the city. Furthermore, these "safe spaces" are sites where migrant characters may seemingly transcend the urban conflicts surrounding them by evoking the proverbial spirit of the ancestor. Griffin writes, "In the context of the migration narrative, urban spaces—kitchenettes, workplaces, street corners, prisons, and theaters—are some of the sites where migrants, white power holders, and Northern Black middle class vie for control."[29]

Although her reading identifies an important feature of these texts, her interpretation mitigates the ghetto pastoral conflict at the center of these novels. Griffin believes that migrant characters are engaged in a power struggle to overcome class conflict. In her reading, these "safe spaces" become "pockets of resistance" where migrants may reassert cultural values and practices otherwise suppressed by white power structures. In turn, these sites of rebellion become in Griffin's folk-centric reading "sites of the ancestor," mythical spaces where an idealistic authentic Black experience is symbolically evoked. Presumably, the cultural forms of the *ancestor* can be observed and practiced within the context of these semi-autonomous spaces that somehow function as fixed and determinate sites of cultural meaning. However, Griffin's folk-centric reading assumes that there is already an established notion of the *Folk* in these settings that need only be accessed as a mode of urban resistance. If these sites of the ancestor allow Black migrants to access a usable past, it is almost certainly a past fraught with ambiguity and conflict. The past then is often a source of trauma as many of these stories are about Black folk leaving the South to escape the imminent threat of racial violence.

To be sure, the Black migrant characters of these novels are portrayed as resilient in the face of cultural displacement. Their urban ascent in Northern cities is facilitated by an ability to create viable spaces of belonging. The spaces they create for themselves are informed by a collective memory of Southern culture and an urban consciousness of life in the Northern city. However, these "safe spaces" appear more complicated in the novels themselves than in Griffin's reading. Indeed, what remains unclear in Griffin's assessment is the extent to which urban ascent in Black migrant fiction is ordered merely by a simple acknowledgment of the past. My own sense of how these "safe spaces" function centers on the inevitable *slippage* that occurs within them. While Black migrants do "invoke the ancestor" in the urban spaces of the city, they can never (re)claim the past in a way that would make it entirely meaningful or coherent in the context of the city. When the past is invoked in these novels, it immediately becomes a source of conflict and ambiguity. This becomes the central complication in establishing a sense of place and belonging for the Black migrant characters of these novels: the cultural practices, narrative forms, and (most importantly) racial terms that once "counted as" the symbolic basis for constructions of place are shot through with indeterminacy in the urban spaces of the city.

Lawrence Rodgers's study of Black migration novels, *Canaan Bound*, centers on the complications that Black migrant characters face in ordering their postmigration, urban identities. Rodgers argues that the immediate goal of migrant characters is to re-establish a sense of folk culture in the North as a way of ordering their urban, postmigration selves. What distinguishes this from Griffin's reading is that Rodgers readily acknowledges the overwhelming influence of urban spaces and the city itself in (re)shaping the ideals of *folk* culture that Black migrants bring with them. As Rodgers points out, this adaptation/appropriation of folk meanings is crucial to the success of Black migrants in the city: "Migration liberates migrants from the constraints of the South only if it can lead, in the North, to an authentic reattachment to an urbanized version of African-American community life that recognizes and draws from its undeniable connection to Folk culture."[30] Without "models of behavior" that take as their source recognizable forms of Black culture, Black migration is doomed to failure. Thus, for Rodgers, the success of the migrant entails her immersion into the urban life of the city that will necessarily take the form of a "communal ascent." The possibility of urban ascent will then depend on the migrant's ability to develop and maintain a conscious awareness of her history and culture, thereby enabling her to recover a sense of communal identity in the alienating context of city life.

Rodgers's reading of migration narratives is instructive in gauging how these fictions posit ideals of communal ascent in response to the cultural displacement that migrant characters experience. However, similarly to Griffin's argument, what remains unclear in Rodgers's assessment of these novels is the extent to which communal ascent can be ordered merely by a simple acknowledgment of the past. His claim that these novels portray an urbanized version of Southern Black culture mitigates the uncertainty with which migrant characters approach the immediate circumstances of their displacement in the northern city as well as the previous circumstances of their past in the rural South. Indeed, it appears that communal ascent in these narratives is complicated for Black migrant characters by the thematic tension the Southern past necessarily produces in the text. Therefore, the past is always already an immediate source of conflict rather than a means of simple resolution in these migration novels. Such conflict is immediately reflected in the various kinds of urban spaces that comprise the Northern settings in Black migration novels. The image of city in these novels is almost never that of a "promised land," but more often reflects a site of internecine conflict and cultural displacement. In short, the ideal of community and place is not immediately available to the Black migrants of these novels. Instead, the establishment of communal spaces is always an elusive if not impossible ideal that signals both the promise and the failure of Black migration to create viable spaces of lived experience.

In response to nostalgic, folk-centric readings of Black migration narratives, I argue that these novels expose the ideological fissures of Southern culture, race and Black identity. I demonstrate in my readings that race and identity are necessarily complicated in Black migration novels by the ghetto pastoral conflict that frames the experience of migrant characters within the various urban spaces of Northern cities. Therefore, the Southern past is always already an immediate source of conflict (rather than a source of identity) in these novels. Such conflict is grounded in the various kinds of urban spaces that comprise the Northern settings in Black migration novels. Thus, the figuration of the cityscape in these novels reflects a dynamic space marked by internecine conflict and displacement. For this reason, the task of place making in these novels becomes a thematic imperative for Black migrant characters. The Black migrant characters of these novels often encounter the landscape of the city as detached spectators unable to immediately identify with the urban forms and practices that define the city. Their sense of self is immediately suspended between the country and city; the liminal position these characters occupy becomes both a source of conflict as well as a "symbolic space" of identity formation. In other words, the conflict that attends the act of migration in these novels also becomes the basis upon which the Black migrant must order his postmigration urban identity.

The characters of these novels must then establish a sense of place that can both attend to their tenuous position in the city and mediate the competing terms of rural and urban experience. Black migrants are displaced characters, cut off from an "authentic" cultural experience in the South, so the meanings they ascribe to places in the city necessarily reflects a tension of rural and urban experience. Therefore, the sense of place they establish is formed at the interstices of a recognizable (albeit also traumatic) way of life in the

South and a transformative (albeit disruptive) way of life in the North. This ambiguous formation of place and identity for the Black migrant characters of these novels reflects also the tumultuous history of Black migration at the turn of the century and the tenuous social position they occupied in the segregated spaces (and places) of the urban North.

Indeed, when Southern Black migrants began pouring into Northern cities in the early twentieth century, Black sharecroppers were not the only ones who had reason to celebrate the passing of an era. Alain Locke proclaimed the 1920s as the decade of the "New Negro," and described the rural-to-urban migration of Black people as a "deliberate flight not only from countryside to city, but from medieval America to modern."[31] Locke was responding to several decades of Black migration, which he saw as paving the way for the establishment of Black cultural centers in the North, while also providing the social conditions for the formation of a modern Black aesthetic. It was in this context of social and cultural transition that the Black migration novel emerged as distinct genre of fiction. Not only did these novels represent Black migration as a social ideal, but they also attended to what Locke called the "problems of adjustment," his description of the inevitable conflicts that Black migrants would encounter in the urban spaces and places in the North.[32]

As a distinct genre of fiction, the Black migration novel emerged as a glowing testament to social change and as a cautionary response to the rising tide of Black migration at the turn of the century. Despite the optimistic discourse surrounding Black migration during this period, most of these early migration narratives portray the dangers of city life, and nearly all emphasize the belief that Black migrants would necessarily have to endure social displacement in the North. The latter concern would come to define the migration politics of these early novels, particularly those written before the height of the Harlem Renaissance. This period before the New Negro movement of the 1920s is significant in the development of the Black migration novel. Before Northern cities emerged as the "cultural centers" of Black expression, the politics of Black migration was primarily defined by economic (rather than cultural) concerns. The issue of Black migration rested almost solely on the so-called push-pull factors, as Southern forms of economic and racial exploitation (e.g., lynchings, race riots, Black sharecropping, the system of prison labor) "pushed" Black farmers and laborers from the South, while the job opportunities of Northern industry and commerce "pulled" them to the North.[33] But coming to the North presented its own unique challenges, as many Black migrants were forced to break important cultural and kinship ties, often leaving family members behind as they sought better lives in Northern cities.

For this reason, the early Black migration novels written in the first decade of the twentieth century figured the problem of social displacement as a defining feature of Black migration to the North. These novels reveal the various difficulties (e.g., the search for adequate housing, the issue of cultural adaptation, etc.) that complicate the ideal of urban ascent for Black migrants in the city. The ideal of the "promised land" is always undercut by the problem of displacement in these novels. The resolution of this problem is the formation of place(s) that mitigate (if not reconcile) the competing terms of Black lived experience in the city. In other words, the Black migrant characters of these fictions must establish a sense of place in an urban setting that has not evolved an adequate space for them, and they must do so without being able to (and perhaps not wanting to) recreate the practices and institutions that had previously shaped their lives in the South.

The Northern city is always fraught with contradictions in these novels because of the ever-present problem of displacement. Although the city is represented as a powerful symbol of redemption in the early Black migration novel and a symbol of self-recognition in later novels such as *Invisible Man*, the material promise of the city is never immediately available to the migrant characters of these novels. While the act of migration itself creates the possibility of urban ascent, the realization of this for the Black migrant is always deferred and depends on her ability to establish a viable and enduring place of belonging in the city. Early Black migration novels, such as Paul Laurence Dunbar's *Sport of the Gods* (1903) and James Weldon Johnson's *Autobiography of an Ex-Colored Man* (1912), figure the problem of displacement as the central complication migrant characters must overcome if they are to make a viable place for themselves in the city.

Journalistic accounts of Black life in Northern cities during the 1920s often conveyed a similar point of view. Mary McLeod Bethune describes the confluence of hope and despair that characterizes the experience of Black people living in Northern cities in her article, "The Problems of the City Dweller:"

It is ever the problem of living a rational, healthy life in the midst of an environment which for the masses is for the most part, unfavorable. It is the problem of fresh air, wholesome food, sunshine and freedom within limits as pitilessly circumscribed as prison walls. It is the problem of making an increased wage, a better school, an easily accessible and cheap means of transportation, electric light, motion pictures, parades and band concerts, a policeman on the corner and propinquitous neighbors, compensate for the sweep of the hill, the greenness of expansive meadows, and the lure of the endless road. It is the problem of getting a chance to live the abundant life, the door to which in our urban centers yields only to the touch of a golden key.[34]

Despite these challenges the economic draw of urban cities was the "golden key," as Bethune puts it, that gave Black migrants reasons to brave the perils of urban displacement.

Echoing these observations, the Black migration novel reflected both the promise and failure of Black migration and urbanization. For example, Dunbar's *Sport of the Gods* was a cautionary tale expressing the allure and danger of the urban North. The Black migrant characters in the novel are displaced in the urban spaces of the North from the outset. Thus, the principal imperative of Black migration novels like *Sport* is the (re)establishment of place and belonging for deracinated Black migrant characters. These characters are represented as having to marshal the cultural forms and practices of Southern folk culture as a symbolic basis for establishing a sense of home in the city. However, the appropriation of these cultural forms and practices (e.g., blues, gospels, jazz) is also a point of inflection for rural and urban conflict. As the characters of these fictions marshal these forms in the city, the cultural materials themselves become a profound and sometimes traumatic reminder of the past experiences and the place(s) they left behind in the South. The representation of urban spaces in these novels, therefore, reveals the tenuous position of the Black migrant who find themselves positioned betwixt and between the country and city.

The problem of displacement in these novels was a political issue as well. The Great Migration as a social movement pitted Washingtonian advocates of Black racial uplift in the South against proponents of Black self-determination in the North.[35] The question of Black migration was as much a political concern for Black people as it was an economic one. Indeed, the act of migration is almost always represented in these novels as constituting a social and political awakening for the Black migrant. In this sense, these novels reflect the political bildungsroman fictions of authors such as Upton Sinclair, Theodore Dreiser, and John Steinbeck, among others.[36] But while that tradition of proletarian literature emphasized class struggle as a central complication for their white characters, Black migration novels revealed the intersection of race and class as a central complication for Black migrants who were attempting to escape both the economic and racial structures of oppression in the South.

The Great Migration as Social Movement

The Black migration novels addressed in this study are informed by a history of Black cultural engagement and social struggle. In this sense, the story of Black migration is represented in these novels as part and parcel of the cultural desires of Black people to establish a sense of place in American society; that is, a place that is culturally situated in the American mainstream. The historical fact of Black migration, its economically motivating factors and concerns, is bound to these political concerns as well. The task of establishing places of belonging in the city for the Black migrants of these fictions is represented as a cultural act affecting concepts of race and identity. A brief overview of the history of Black migration in this country will reveal the cultural and racial concerns that energize these novels.

Before 1920, almost 90 percent of the Black population in this country lived in the South.[37] Over half of those people, about seven million, resided in rural areas where farming was the main industry and cotton was still "King."[38] Although some owned their own land, the vast majority of Black farmers worked as sharecroppers. Tenant farming emerged as one of the largest labor occupations in the South, though gradually the system began to resemble a modern form of slavery. Black sharecroppers were provided with small tracts of land, ranging in size from fifteen to forty acres, on which they cultivated and harvested cash crops, especially cotton. The planter in turn provided a monthly stipend of about fifty dollars, a "furnish" to cover all living expenses until the crop was harvested in the fall, as well as "seed money" for cottonseed and cultivation tools. The sharecropper would pay for the cost of fertilizer (the costliest item in crop cultivation), and when harvest came in the fall, he would assume a share of the "profit." However, a profit rarely materialized for sharecroppers, who were often the victims of unscrupulous accounting practices and exorbitant material costs in which farmers were assessed imaginary costs for services or repairs that were never provided by the landlord. After the harvest was in, the sharecropper was called to the plantation office to "settle up" for the year. Inevitably, the accounting figures usually revealed (or were made to reveal) that the sharecropper had (at best) broken even or (typically worse) fallen into debt. The revolving debt that sharecroppers experienced kept them perpetually bound to the land in a kind of contractual form of slavery or serfdom.

For Black Southerners who fled the corrupt sharecropping system, the Northern city represented a place where one could at least conceive of "getting ahead." As James Grossman points out, even among the vast majority of Southern Black people who did not migrate to the North, many opted for "less exotic destinations within the South" that could provide them with a better (and more urban) way of life.[39] Although Black people who migrated to Northern cities could be seen as giving up one form of "slavery" for another, the "wage slavery" of the North at least offered the possibility of upward social mobility. Whereas Black people had known a cycle of poverty in the South, they foresaw life in the North as a break from the status quo. The more optimistic race relations in the North were a concern for Southern white planters and businessmen who acted quickly to head off the flood of Black labor pouring into Northern cities, in some cases offering Black laborers "incentives" to remain in the South, including higher wages and improved work conditions. Nevertheless, the cumulative offensives against Black people in the South, along with the promise of "full citizenship" in the North, were enough to convince many Black people to leave their "natural home" in the South. Some migrants saw themselves as darker-skinned versions of "Ragged Dick," Horatio Alger's fictional embodiment of the American Dream. Those who dreamed of a better life envisioned themselves then as "New Negroes," upwardly mobile, Black aspirants to the middle-class.[40]

This general explanation of Black migration, as a direct response to social economic exploitation, understands it in terms of the push and pull factors that correlate with economic oppression in the South and economic mobility in the North respectively.[41] According to this point of view, Black people were primarily responding to the economic reality of their present circumstances. Yet, there is some evidence to suggest that other social factors also contributed to (and provided some of the impetus for) the migration of Southern Black people into Northern cities. For instance, William Cohen views the intellectual movements rooted in the emerging field of Black studies as a corollary to the Great Migration. Cohen writes that "the Great Migration occurred just as the movement for the study of Black history was taking root and the two become intertwined with one another."[42] The implication is that the Great Migration gained fuel from the various kinds of social and political movements that it also encompassed. Another historical glance at the period also reveals that migration patterns coincided with increasing educational opportunities for Black people in the North. Even before the migration began in roughly 1910, a small cadre of educated Black people had already relocated to urban centers in the North.[43] These first early migrants were drawn to the educational systems of the North, which they believed would open a world of possibility for them.[44]

Reflecting the optimism of the 1900s, the call for Black people to migrate North was as pervasive in this period as the call for westward expansion had been for white frontiersmen almost a century earlier. Just as the frontier movement rested on ideals of social ascent, so too did the Great Migration of Black people depend on their investment in ideals of urban ascent in Northern cities. Southern Black people received news reports from Northern publications such as the *Chicago Defender*, which promoted migration and lauded the social advantages of Northern city life. These publications encouraged potential migrants to shake off the vestiges of rural life, and to develop a *race consciousness* that would allow them to move beyond the peonage and violence of their Southern existence.[45] Black migrants were frequently admonished to adhere to certain standards of respectability. As Isabel Wilkerson notes, publications like the *Defender* often printed lists of "do's and don'ts:"

> Don't Hang Out The Windows.
> Don't Sit Around In The Yard And On The Porch Barefoot And Unkempt.
> Don't Wear Handkerchiefs On Your Head.
> Don't Use Vile Language In Public Places
> Don't Allow Children To Beg On The Streets.
> Don't Appear On The Street With Old Dust Caps, Dirty Aprons And Ragged Clothes.
> Don't Throw Garbage In The Backyard Or Alley Or Keep Dirty Front Yards.[46]

The popular rhetoric of Black migration thus extolled both the economic and social opportunities available in the North. This optimistic discourse of personal growth and self-determination provided further impetus for Black Southerners to leave the South, a move that would presumably also transform their character in the process.

Although the overwhelming majority of Black people did remain in the South, a significant number of them decided to leave. Spurred by glowing accounts of city life, Black migrants steadily came to Northern cities in search of that elusive ideal of social (and economic) prosperity. In fact, the population of Black people in Northern cities increased by almost half a million during the decades of 1910 and 1920.[47] The net Black migrants from the South to the North steadily increased in the 1920s, and peaked before the depression to roughly 750,000 new migrants.[48] When that migration peaked in the 1940s, "urban had become a euphemism for black."[49] The Northern city came to symbolize for Black people a sense of optimism and possibility. It also signified a place where racial differences may not be as pronounced. Indeed, the perceived "negro problem" that Black migration was seen as producing was mitigated for many white Northerners by the labor force these Black migrants represented. As one white observer of Black migration writes, "The Negro is here. It does no good today to point a fault-finding finger. He is part of our national life whether we like it or not. He requires food, he requires shelter, he requires clothes, he has other human needs. On the other hand, he has earning power."[50]

Although some saw the North as a viable social and economic alternative to the South, most also realized the problems posed by city life. Nicholas Lemann, describing the changes brought about by the Great Migration, writes, "The move is from race to demography, from isolated community to urban sprawl. Since the city both offers and restricts possibility, the difference between the races may be of degree rather than kind."[51] In the North, race still mattered, as Black migrants were often subject to discrimination at the hands of slumlords and corrupt business owners. The built structures of the city also contributed to an increasing sense of spatial displacement, as Lemann's observations reveal. Black people were routinely corralled into racial enclaves in the city such as Chicago's "Black Belt" district. Black migrants were certainly accustomed to racially segregated space, having already endured it in the South. However, they were not accustomed to the segregated slum areas in Northern cities that delimited both their physical and social mobility. Thus, for Black migrants, the challenge of migration was the formation of a viable way of life and place in an otherwise hostile urban environment.

From the perspective of this history, the Great Migration cannot merely be understood as a reaction to economic conditions but must also be viewed as a social movement motivated by an increasing sense of race consciousness among Black people in the South. The Great Migration as a social movement enabled them to redefine themselves as a socially mobile people whose geographical and cultural associations did not preclude the possibility of making a new life and a new place elsewhere. In other words, the conscious decision to migrate was for Southern Black people based on a fundamental recognition that the South was not necessarily their "natural home." Lawrence Rodgers echoes this in part, writing, "The Great Migration designates much more than simply a geographic movement; it signals the need for a change of internal consciousness and an entirely new apprehension of external reality."[52] This kind of recognition, according to Rodgers, was a precondition for Black migration. In order to make their place in the city, however, Rodgers asserts that Black migrants needed to "maintain a consciousness of their history and culture."[53] Yet, it can also be argued that the Great Migration as social movement transformed Black consciousness, thereby redefining the culture and (his)story of Black people. If the Great Migration opened a new era in Black history, it also provided the cultural and artistic capital for reconsidering the past as well. In this way, the migration did more than merely provide cheap labor—as a social movement, it established a new staging ground for the redefinition of Blackness itself.

The Great Migration as Aesthetic Movement

As Black migrants searched for their cultural identity in Northern cities, they had clearly not heeded Booker T. Washington's call to "drop your buckets where you are," as evidenced by their exodus from the South. But neither had they entirely accepted W. E. B. Du Bois's argument for political self-empowerment through liberal education. Access to institutions of higher learning was limited to only a small Black middle class, many of whom had already migrated north before 1900.[54] Lynched, politically disenfranchised, economically exploited, and generally disillusioned—they saw migration as a necessary step in achieving both cultural and material advancement in the race. In this sense, the prevailing view of Black migration, which saw Northern cities as providing both a cultural and material basis for Black self-determination, displaced the cultural/material dichotomy that had characterized the Washington/Du Bois debate. The political rhetoric of migration seemed to suggest that if Black people wanted to become first-class citizens, they would need to break away from the social and economic constraints of their Southern existence and attend to both the cultural and material aspects of their lives. Because the North was largely perceived as a cultural and material land of possibility, Black artists and intellectuals saw rural-to-urban migration as a necessary condition for the formation of a modern Black aesthetic.

Alain Locke's anthology of Black fiction and essays, entitled *The New Negro* (1925), sought to reflect the themes of urbanism and modernity that characterized the experience of rural-to-urban, Black migration. Alain Locke's conception of the "New Negro," which he defines in an opening essay of the anthology, was at once an amalgam of the cultural and material forces that were shaping the postmigration identities of Black migrants in the city. The "New Negro" can be read as expressing the modern condition of Black people after migration, at a time when they found themselves at the crossroads of rural and urban life. What Locke found "new" about this condition was that Black people were now able to conceive of themselves as complex and multifaceted individuals. While the South had reduced all Black people to one class of people residing at the bottom rungs of society, the North provided a differentiated context of human relations that brought into view gender, social, and above all, class differences. The fact that Black doctors and lawyers could be found in 1920s Harlem provided a counterpoint to the popular stereotypes of Black people as "lazy," "watermelon-eating" rural types. But what is most salient here is that Locke did not view these stereotypical images as mere farce in themselves—rather he saw them as misrepresentative precisely because they did not acknowledge the full range of human possibilities with respect to Negro life and culture. For this reason, Locke announces, "The Negro to-day wishes to be known for what he is, even in his faults and shortcomings, and scorns a craven and precarious survival at the price of seeming to be what he is not."[55] This mode of Black realism amounted to a rejection of racial homogeneity as a conceptual framework for Black expression and Black culture generally. Thus, the racialist discourse of the "New Negro" aesthetic attempted to shift the focus away from Black culture's relation to mainstream white society, by instead emphasizing the intraracial distinctions that existed among Black people themselves.

Locke believed that the migration of Black people into Northern cities would provide an urban/material basis for the expression of a modern race consciousness. Black migrants could take their social outlook from the multiplicity of urban life, where they would be surrounded by various examples of Black self-determination and social empowerment. In this sense, life in the city would ideally give the masses of Black migrants some bearing on who they really were or could be. Locke points out that this "spiritual coming of age" would necessarily extend to Black artists and writers—"The migrant masses, shifting from country side to city, hurdle several generations of experience at a leap, but more important, the same thing happens spiritually in the life-attitudes and self-expression of the Young Negro, in his poetry, his art, his education and his *new outlook*, with the additional advantage, of course, of the poise and greater certainty of knowing what it is all about" [emphasis mine].[56]

The "new outlook" that Locke envisioned for Black writers and intellectuals would actually entail a reassessment of old materials and themes. The multiple perspectives that the city offered would give Black cultural producers a rich tableau against which they could represent the complexities of both rural and urban identities. They could presumably translate across the divide of rural and urban life as the cultural arbiters of a modern race consciousness. As Locke writes "the immediate hope rests in the revaluation by white and black alike of the Negro in terms of his artistic endowments and cultural contributions, past and prospective."[57] The rural-to-urban migration of Black people would provide the social and material conditions for a revaluation of rural/folk forms in the urban spaces of cultural production and inscription. Locke's belief that Black migration offered the occasion for this sort of cultural revaluation turned on his assumptions about the historical meaning of migration itself. The urbanization of Black culture meant that the expressive materials of a rural Black folk culture could now be invested with a dignity that had been denied to them in the South. Although Locke saw these cultural materials as the unrefined, raw materials of Black experience, he believed that their expression would constitute a kind of modernist form of historical revision. In short, Locke believed that the New Negro writers of the present would necessarily reinvent the "Old Negro" materials of the past in the urban context of the city.

Locke viewed the urban spaces and places in the North as the staging ground for Black expression and self-determination. His notion of an urban Black aesthetic centered on the ideal of the New Negro as representing a synthesis of rural and urban—past and present—Black experience. Appropriating the urban landscape of the North as its setting, Locke's New Negro functioned as both a racial and spatial ideal that sought to mitigate the cultural displacement of Southern-transplanted Black folk who leaped from "medieval America to modern." In this sense, the move from blackface minstrels, mammies and Jim Crow was a spatial, as well as conceptual, shift in representation. The city offered a kind of countercultural space not available to them in the South. To invoke Bakhtin, the trope of the city in urban narratives brought together a heteroglossia of modern discourses. To invoke Gramsci, the urban provided the content and form for counterhegemonic cultural expressions that undermined static concepts of race and cultural identity.

Locke's racial ideal, however, is complicated in the Black migration novels of the period that do not figure an easy synthesis of rural and urban meanings for Black migrant characters. Instead, these novels portray characters whose urban personae as New Negroes is always contested by the competing terms of their postmigration, urban identities. So, rather than provide for the formation of an urban consciousness based on the ideals of the New Negro, the Black migration novels addressed in this study represent Black migrants as having to live and struggle within contested spaces in the city, wherein the discourses of rural and urban experience produce a dialectical construction of Black migrant place and identity. Urban spaces such as clubs, ballrooms, kitchenette apartments, middle-class homes, street corners, and pool halls are often represented in migration fiction as the staging grounds for interpretive struggles, as migrant characters wrestle to order their postmigration, subjective selves. Therefore, migrant characters encounter these spaces as sites of rural and urban conflict, in other words, spaces that signify a dialectical conception of place that exists betwixt and between the folk-rural ideals of the South and the cosmopolitan-urban ideals of the North.

Another source of conflict these migrants encountered were the demonizing narratives marshaled against Black migrant communities. Despite the growing optimism of the New Negro movement, spurred on by vibrant Black cultural spaces in New York City and Chicago, the anti–Black migrant rhetoric stood as a stark reminder of the challenges posed by institutional racism in the North. Davarian Baldwin describes these challenges in his book *Chicago's New Negroes: Modernity, The Great Migration and Black Urban Life.*[58] In mapping the contours of "New Negro" culture in Chicago, Baldwin describes both the material and ideological meanings associated with Black migrant spaces in Chicago. Baldwin writes, "in newspapers, legislative investigations, and academic studies, Black Chicago, among other ethnic enclaves, was represented as the antithesis of Progressive Era industriousness and productivity. [. . .] Migrants were demonized as helpless peasant refugees ignorant of urban life with a culture that needed adjustment, containment, and discipline."[59] Despite these instances of institutional bias, Baldwin notes, "there was still a mix of fascination and fear of the 'foreign' culture these migrants carried with them from the South that was simply reinforced by the physical concentration of more black bodies in a confined space."[60] This mixture of "fear" and "fascination" reveals one of the thematic problems of the Black migration novel. These stories figured the problem of Black migrant cultural expression within spaces where it was both privileged and contested.

Ghetto Pastoral Spaces

For turn-of-the-century Black migrants, the immediate challenge of migration was the task of establishing viable cultural spaces in the city. The symbolic possibility that migrants could appropriate/adapt rural forms of cultural expression was also a central thematic concern of Black migrant fiction. These symbolic spaces are often figured in these narratives as communal sites of cultural recognition, where Black migrants can order their postmigration identities in relation to a Southern past and to an urban present. But as sites also shaped by the internal struggles of displaced migrant characters, these spaces also foreground the competing values of rural and urban experience. These urban spaces, although generic in themselves, can be read in these fictions as ghetto pastoral spaces that reflect both the symbolic struggles of identity formation and the concrete struggles of urban life. In other words, they reveal the day-to-day struggles of migrants to order their postmigration selves in the city.

The Black migration novels addressed in this study foreground rural and urban conflict in their construction of urban spaces. The symbolic shift from rural community to urban displacement in these texts establishes a tension between the old folk values of the country and the newly adopted urban values of the city. In these stories, the urban émigré must negotiate a place (or space) of belonging for himself orherself in the Northern urban cityscape. However, the complication that arises in these transitional narratives involves the dialectical nature of urban space itself. The loss of communal structures and the displacement of rural values force the migrant character to create urban spaces that can attend to the cultural and material demands of identity formation in the city. Thus, the urban is portrayed in the Black migration narrative as a ghetto pastoral space connoting both endless possibilities and perpetual struggle. Denning's conception of the ghetto pastoral is instructive in that it foregrounds the tension between "old country tongues" and new ways of speaking and thinking in postmigration, urban spaces. For Black folk, these ghetto pastoral spaces were transformative, not only in the way of life they ushered but also in the ways of speaking and thinking they made possible. After all, to think of oneself as a New Negro necessitates not only a change of perspective but also a change of locale.

The ghetto pastoral is best understood as a spatial trope signifying at once a sense of place and identity even as its geographical and conceptual boundaries delimit the cultural practices that operate inside its distinctive spaces. These are not "safe spaces" but rather locales marked by the inexorable tension of the culture within these spaces moving against the contours of the dominant culture without. As Michael Denning describes, "the geographical boundaries of the community are reinforced by historical boundaries; the ghetto pastoral continually *runs up against* a historical block" [emphasis mine].[61] Inside these privileged yet contentious cultural spaces are the everyday cultural expressions of Black folk, many of them first generation migrants hoping to cast aside the social limitations of Southern plantocracy even as they encountered the oppressive economic and social forces of the industrial city. "What is the history of these relatively recent communities," writes Denning, "cut off from any past that inhabits the streets, buildings, and even words?"[62] The common answer conveyed by the Black migration novels considered here is a history fraught with the collective trauma of the past, a theme vividly portrayed in novels like Paul Laurence Dunbar's *The Sport of the Gods* and James Baldwin's *Go Tell It on the Mountain*. The "fugitive migrants" in these stories escape a tumultuous Southern past only to find pivotal moments of reckoning in

Northern "promised lands." These inevitable moments involve encounters with the material realities of the city (e.g., economic scarcity, corruption, urban violence), which in turn become charged moments of introspection where Black migrants must attempt to reconcile their Southern past while coming to terms with life in the big city. Dunbar's migrants must come to grips with their displacement from a relatively comfortable Southern existence as they become victims of the "alluring witch" that is New York City. Baldwin's "praying saints" must reconcile the perceived sins of a Southern past while hoping to find redemption in a storefront church in the heart of the morally corrupt Northern city. This ironic conflation of salvation and destruction, hope and despair, rugged individualism and oppressive conformity, constitute the binary terms that define urban spaces and the figure of the promised land in these novels of Black migration.

The representation of ghetto pastoral spaces in these novels thus reveals the collective struggle of Black migrants to establish a place of belonging in the Northern cityscape despite the social forces there that conspire against them. These ghetto pastoral spaces in turn become contested sites of identity formation for Black migrants in the Northern city. The symbolic cultural forms and practices therein establish, on the one hand, recognizable modes of expression and experience. On the other hand, these Black cultural expressions are marshaled against the stultifying and displacing aspects of urban life in the city. The symbolically potent space of the Harlem nightclub, for instance, represented a locus of Black cultural expression and lived experience in the city. Urban forms such as jazz and ragtime were spatial expressions that ordered the identity formation of Black migrants in the city. They offered a sense of place(ness), and so they constituted the substantive elements of cultural expression that Black migrants utilized in constructing their urban identities. As the cultural constituents of spaces such as the nightclub, Black migrants could imagine themselves as an integral part of the urban landscape around them. However, many notable venues like the famous Cotton Club in Harlem, New York, were racially segregated spaces. These were also spaces in which the most unflattering representation of Black people could be found, the most notorious of which was Black face minstrelsy.[63] James Weldon Johnson's *The Autobiography of an Ex-Colored Man* is a literary testament to the often-pejorative racial meanings that segregated venues like the Cotton Club engendered. A ghetto pastoral reading of these spaces, therefore, accounts for the broad range of possibilities that exists there for Black people. From these symbolically charged spaces emerge the progressive trope of the New Negro and the cultural self-determination that would define this period of "Black Renaissance." However, just as well, the limitations of Black expression are also woven into the cultural tapestry of these oft segregated spaces, circumscribed by the oppressive structures of Jim Crow cities and the exigencies of race.

Despite the conflict and struggle that often marked these ghetto pastoral spaces, Black migrants assigned meaning to these places in the city to validate their racial and social identity. This process of cultural adaptation was a way of designating certain spaces in Northern city as "Black spaces" even (or especially) when Black people found themselves marginalized in those spaces. As Stephen Haymes argues, "place making is tied to the idea that places are significant because we assign meaning to them in relation to our specific projects."[64] Applying Haymes's concept of "place making," Black migration novels can be read as constructing new identities and new places for Black folk in the city. The representation of urban spaces such as the nightclub can be read as positing specific cultural meanings that reflect a shared past experience rooted in the South, as well as a unique lived experience in the city. As Haymes points out, Black migrants defined urban spaces in relation to their rural and folk culture, but also in relation to the particular demands of urban society.[65] Their primary goal was to make places in the city that would facilitate the processes of social adjustment and cultural assimilation without entirely disavowing the beliefs and practices that defined Southern Black culture. This dual function of Black migrant spaces, Haymes notes, was based on the presumption that Black people, unlike other marginalized groups and white immigrants, were defined solely and irrevocably by their "oppositional identities."[66] In other words, Black migrants could not hope to make places that would one day be subsumed into the larger public sphere of American society. The best they could hope for were places that necessarily reflected both the particular interests of Black folk and the general interests of white society.[67]

Black migrant settlements, Haymes observes, were also assigned negative value by a racist ideology that figured Black people as "intruders" into the urban spaces that had been historically marked "white only." Haymes is worth quoting at length on this point:

> Preceding the "Great black Migration" to northern and midwestern cities, urban areas were mainly white. After the formation of large black urban settlements resulting from the migration, the urban was described metaphorically as a jungle, as being dominated by bestial, predatory values. With the mass migration of southern blacks to cities in the north, the "city as a jungle" began to operate as a racist metaphor to describe inner-city blacks.... The metaphorical construction

of the urban around "race" is of particular significance given that in a white supremacist culture that identifies race with being black and not being white the urban becomes another way to signify the "evils" of blackness and black people.[68]

The pejorative meanings often assigned to Black settlement spaces were part of the dual character of urban spaces in cities like Chicago and New York. In Northern cities, Black people were excluded from certain parts of the city while being corralled into racially segregated neighborhoods through restrictive housing covenants. These segregated spaces such as Chicago's "Black Belt" and New York's Harlem neighborhood signified at once the opportunities that city life afforded Black people and the limitations placed on them in an urban landscaped demarcated by race.

Even as Black migrants tried to establish a sense of belonging in response to the racism and discrimination they faced, they were often met with resistance from their white neighbors. As Brian McCammack notes in *Landscapes of Hope: Nature and the Great Migration in Chicago*, Black migrants who retreated to "public pastoral spaces" in Chicago "to counter unhealthy and discriminatory conditions at home and on the job" often found themselves "confronted [by] race violence at the city's parks and beaches."[69] Chicago urban planners had meticulously built pastoral spaces in the city to feature both natural landscapes and the iconic lake front that ran along the downtown and South Shore areas. One such natural landscape was Washington Park in Chicago's South Side neighborhood. Washington Park became a mainstay for Black migrants seeking refuge in a green space reminiscent of their Southern homes. However, as McCammack notes, when the number of Black visitors to the park increased in the 1910s, reaching its height in the 1920s, tensions between white and Black patrons also increased there and throughout the city, extending to other public pastoral spaces.[70] Describing the wide spread nature of this violence, McCammack writes "Washington Park was but one of many of Chicago's public landscapes of hope where African Americans were the targets of white violence during the Great Migration years."[71] However, owing to a desire to access these vital "landscapes of hope" in the city, Black migrants continued to make use of these public pastoral spaces despite the racial violence that threatened to exclude them, prompting one white property owner to comment "the park ought to be rechristened 'Booker T. Washington.'"[72] As McCammack notes, the response to this encroachment on public pastoral spaces designated as white only was swift, as white residents living near the park "draft[ed] restrictive covenants that prevented African Americans from renting or buying homes there."[73]

The history of Washington Park that documents its transformation from a "landscape of hope" for Black migrants into a site of internecine racial conflict reveals the central complication for Black migrants tasked with making a viable place for themselves in Northern cities. These migrants sought places in the city that could serve as both reminders of the Southern homes they left behind and as communal spaces where they could find respite from the demands of city life. However, as the history of Washington Park reveals, the desire of Black migrants to make viable spaces of belonging in the city was constantly frustrated by the built structures of the city itself that demarcated places along racial and economic lines. These lines of demarcation were not always clearly drawn on a map, but they were, nevertheless, well known to anyone living in the city. As Richard Wright famously wrote, these lines were not only manifestations of a material system of segregation but also constituted the "Ethics of Jim Crow," its underlying ideology of separation based on white supremacy. When Bigger Thomas, the protagonist of Richard Wright's literary masterpiece *Native Son*, asks his friend Gus "where the white folks live?" Gus's literal response ("over there across *the line*; over there on Cottage Grove Avenue") is rejoined by Bigger's expression of frustration:

> "Naw; they don't, Bigger said,
>   "What you mean?" Gus asked, puzzled. "Then, where do they live?"
>   "Right down here in my stomach," he said.
>   Gus looked at Bigger searchingly, then away, as though ashamed.[74]

Wright understood the challenge faced by Black boys given the impossible task of establishing a place of belonging and identity in a city that had not evolved adequate spaces for them but rather had defined them as perpetual outsiders. Ironically, when the resident head of my dormitory at the University of Chicago warned me to "never venture alone beyond Cottage Grove," I began to suspect that this fact had not entirely changed.

Like Wright's *Native Son* (which I will discuss later in the book) Black migration novels foreground the central complication of places like Chicago, New York City, and Washington, DC, places that represented at once the ideal of the "promised land" and the problem of urban displacement. By marshaling the concept of the ghetto pastoral in my reading of the Black migration novels considered here, I want to clarify how the representation of urban spaces in these novels enables the Black migrant characters in these stories to forge a sense of place and belonging in response to the central problem of urban displacement in these stories. The chapters that follow will then examine the various conceptions of place that Black migrant characters marshal in attending to their displacement in the city. These conceptions of place constitute the symbolic forms with which the Black migrant could (re) establish a sense of place and identity. In other words, the material reality of places in the city is juxtaposed in these novels with the symbolic meaning(s) that Black migrants ascribe to those places. Therefore, each chapter will analyze a particular conception of place that functions as a locus of Black migrant experience in city. It is my goal to produce a conceptual mapping of the urban settings of Black lived experience that comprise the setting of the Northern city in these novels.

Chapter 1 begins with a discussion of the mock pastoral mode in Paul Laurence Dunbar's *The Sport of the Gods* and James Weldon Johnson's *Autobiography of an Ex-Colored Man*. I describe the function of the mock pastoral in these novels as satire that critiques the underlying terms of Southern pastoral idealism. I interpret Dunbar's and Johnson's works as establishing the critical foundation for dismantling the racist plantation tradition with its symbolic investment in the "Lost Cause" narrative that imagined an idyllic Southern society prior to the emancipation of enslaved Black people. In so doing, both novels provide a critical basis for (re)imagining Southern society as both a place of racial oppression and as a source of collective memory for Black people. These two inaugural Black migration novels published prior to the Harlem Renaissance of the 1920s then establish the central themes that would shape the genre in the next several decades to come. Through their marshaling of a mock pastoral perspective, both novels also distinguish the genre of Black migration fiction, with its investment in the ghetto pastoral mode, from traditional urban pastoral stories. Whereas traditional urban pastoral stories figured the possibility of reconciling rural and urban conflict in the lives of their (im)migrant characters, Black migration novels would foreground such conflict as a necessary condition for their Black migrant characters.

In chapter 2, I discuss Jean Toomer's seminal literary masterpiece *Cane* as an early example of the ghetto pastoral mode and as a kind of literary epilogue to romanticized portrayals of the "Old South."[75] Toomer's elegiac invocation of the ghetto pastoral mode laments the symbolic passing of Southern Black culture and announces its figurative (re)birth as urban Black cultural experience in Northern cities like Washington, DC, and New York. Indeed, Toomer's personal experience as an educator in the South inspired him to write the novel. He moved to Sparta, Georgia, to work as an elementary school principal. It was there that he felt both the alluring quality of Southern Black folk culture as well as the stultifying racism and inequality that characterized the Deep South. Toomer's ghetto pastoral novel marshals this tension in its portrayal of Southern Black culture and lived experience, an experience he believed was receding into "song" and memory, and its urban transformation as Black migrant lived experience in Northern cities.

In chapter 3, I discuss two Black migration novels of the Harlem Renaissance, Nella Larsen's *Quicksand* and Walter White's *Flight*. These novels reveal one of the central problems that Black migrants faced in Northern cities: namely, the struggle to (re)establish an ideal of homeplace in the concrete jungles of Northern cities. As ghetto pastorals, both novels also reveal the tension inherent to the project of making domestic spaces of belonging for their Black migrant characters. The potent symbolic space of Harlem, New York, for which the cultural and literary movement is named, was also a racially fraught place in which the progressive symbolism of the New Negro movement ran up against the material realties of racial segregation and exploitation. For this reason, both Larsen's and White's novels reveal the high cost of realizing an ideal of domestic belonging for their Black female protagonists. Both protagonists must ultimately reject this ideal outright because of the facile quality of life attached to it. In the end, these novels deprive their Black migrant female protagonists of a comfortable middle-class home in the city, even returning one of them (White's protagonist Helga Crane) back to the South.

In chapter 4, I discuss Ralph Ellison's singular masterpiece, his novel *Invisible Man*, as the critical and aesthetic culmination of the Black migration novel and the ghetto pastoral form. Ellison's protagonist is a modern expression of the figure of the Black migrant who straddles the conflict that defined earlier Black migration fictions. Ellison's invisible man stands at the proverbial crossroads of Black lived experience betwixt and between rural and urban, North and South, Black and white. Although he is not a "passing figure," his decision to affirm a liminal identity as an invisible man indicates his willingness to complicate racial norms and standards. In his fictional metanarrative, (we find him writing the story we are subsequently told), he marshals the musical tradition of the blues, what he also refers to as the "music of invisibility," to articulate and to make sense of his condition of invisibility. Therefore, I read Ellison's novel through the blues perspective offered by his protagonist, a perspective that gives meaning to his liminal subject position even as it reveals the tension inherent to his existence as an alienated figure relegated to the margins of society, living beneath the streets of Harlem in a cramped coal cellar.

My conclusion discusses the legacy of the Black migration novel as it relates to the perceived failures of Black migration. I argue that while Black migration failed to deliver the material conditions that Black migrants sought in the proverbial promised lands of Northern cities, it did fundamentally alter how we understand African American culture and lived experience. The South was no longer an exclusive signifier of Black cultural experience. This cultural shift would shape how a subsequent generation of Black authors such as Richard Wright and James Baldwin represented Black culture and lived experience in their fictional works. I conclude with a discussion of James Baldwin's first novel *Go Tell It on the Mountain*. Baldwin's novel revises the trajectory of the traditional Black migration novel in that his Black migrants recount their Southern experience as collective memory while already living in New York City. It is not the act of migration itself that is a source of rural and urban conflict in the novel. Rather the act of remembering becomes the source of conflict for Baldwin's Black migrant characters. Baldwin's "threshing floor," the sacred alter space inside the primary setting of a storefront church, functions as a ghetto pastoral space par excellence, as his "praying saints" seek redemption for the perceived sins and collective trauma of their Southern past.

Chapter One

THE MOCK PASTORAL MODE AND THE EMERGENCE OF THE BLACK MIGRATION NOVEL

Paul Laurence Dunbar's *The Sport of the Gods* (1901) and James Weldon Johnson's *Autobiography of an Ex-Colored Man* (1914) were literary precursors to the ghetto pastoral narratives of Black migration that would become popular in the decades to follow. Published in the decade prior to the Great Black Migration, Dunbar's novel struck an early cautious tone in its depiction of Black migration by portraying the North over and against the South as the lesser of two evils. Dunbar, who had spent much of his career as a Black vernacular poet, wrote *Sport* near the end of his life at a time when his career was nearly in shambles. While his Black dialect verse had gained him notoriety, it had also largely alienated him from an increasingly influential Black intelligentsia who saw his poetry as part of a racist plantation tradition.[1] *Sport*'s send up of Southern pastoral idealism can be read in this context as Dunbar's attempt to project a valorized image of Southern Black culture over and against the caricatured images of Black folk made popular by the plantation tradition. Johnson's anonymously published novel appeared more than a decade later when the Great Migration was in full swing.[2] While *Autobiography* would strike a more optimistic tone than *Sport* in its appraisal of Northern Black migration, the thematic point of emphasis in the former novel remains Black Southern culture. Johnson's nameless protagonist endeavors to construct a viable representation of Black Southern culture despite the social inequalities and racial violence that proscribe Black culture and lived experience in the South. Both novels then marshal what is best understood as a mock pastoral perspective that challenges the prevailing "lost cause" Southern narrative while (re)inscribing Black Southern folk culture as positive value to counter the prevailing racial caricatures of the day.

The mock pastoral emerges in both novels as satire sending up romanticized ideals of Black Southern folk culture while also conveying a cautionary tone in their appraisal of Black migration to Northern cities. Ironically, James Weldon Johnson and Paul Laurence Dunbar were both at various points in their careers guilty of marshaling stereotypical representations of Black people to advance their artistic careers. Dunbar made his career on writing and performing Black dialect poetry, much of which portrayed Black people through the lens of racial and cultural stereotypes. In this role, he was much sought after, his readings often drawing prominent white literati and potential benefactors, most of whom gathered to hear Dunbar perform the Black dialectic of his popular poetry. He rarely disappointed in his jocular renditions of poems written from the unlettered perspective of his Black rustic personas. Johnson similarly traded on the stereotypical images of Black folk on the vaudeville musical stage. The very same man who penned the words to "Lift Every Voice and Sing," a song often described as the Black national anthem, also wrote musical scores centered in the dubious tradition of Black face minstrelsy.[3] Like Dunbar, who believed his popularity as a Black dialectic poet was the proverbial price of the ticket, Johnson sold his musical fare to a mainstream white audience enamored by "darkie ditties."

Both novels are linked historically, as they were published just over a decade apart from each other before the largest waves of Black migrants began pouring into Northern cities after World War I.[4] The cautionary tone of Black novels owes in large part to the uncertainty associated with migration to the North. As Leah Platt Boustan observes, "few blacks moved North before 1915, despite the higher wages and greater social equality available in the region."[5] Boustan points to "the role of migrant networks in facilitating migrant flows to new destinations" as one explanation for the slow trickle of Black migrants before World War I.[6] She further argues that the absence of sustained Black migrant communities during this initial period of migration made it difficult for these new arrivals to find well-paying jobs or decent living arrangements without the assistance of social networks.[7] Therefore, it stands to reason that especially Dunbar writing in 1901 and Johnson writing over a decade later would strike a decidedly cautionary tone in their novels regarding the promise of Northern cities for Black migrants. Their migrant characters are portrayed as fish-out-of-water as they attempt to fit into urban environments that had not yet evolved an adequate place for them. Dunbar's

Black migrants find it difficult to find a place of belonging. Their inability to "fit in" ultimately leads to material and moral ruination as they encounter one misfortune after the other. Johnson's nameless protagonist similarly encounters an urban landscape replete with dangers that test his resolve. These representations of the North as a promised land in name only begs the question of cultural legitimacy for Northern cities where Black migrant populations had not yet achieved a critical mass.

Also linking both authors were their unequivocal literary responses to the mainstream cultural demand for Black stereotypes. Both novels can be read as polemical statements that effectively cast aspersions on the racial stereotypes that delimited Black artistic production at the turn of the twentieth century. Dunbar's *Sport of the Gods* was his first novel that centered on the portrayal of Black characters.[8] Dunbar sought to dispel the racist caricatures and stereotypes that traditionally defined representations of Black people in his portrayal of the Hamiltons, a Black middle-class family residing in the South. The Hamiltons are a symbol of Black respectability as they have established good social standing in the Black community. However, they are forced to leave the South after Berry, the family patriarch, is wrongfully accused of stealing money from a white man and sentenced to prison. His wife and children must then migrate to New York City, where the family experiences even greater hardships in the proverbial promised land of the North. Although Berry is later exonerated of his crime, Dunbar's naturalistic tale cannot afford the Hamiltons a happy ending, a fact underscored by the novel's title and its mock pastoral framework. Berry is reunited with his wife only after her marriage to another man comes to an end when he is murdered for unpaid gambling debts. To further compound this macabre tragedy, Joe Hamilton, Berry's son, is convicted of murder, while his sister Kit is morally corrupted by the vaudeville stage.

The success of the novel belied the overwhelming popularity of his dialect poetry, which William Dean Howells once described as his "real contribution."[9] As though a direct response to the American "father of realism," Dunbar wrote *Sport* as a decidedly bitter novel that exposed the human tragedy at the center of Southern plantocracy. His story of Black migration does more to excoriate white Southern culture and society than it does to celebrate the Black folk culture rooted there. Rejecting his mantle as "Negro poet laureate," a somewhat dubious distinction that Booker T. Washington bestowed on the young poet, Dunbar assumes the position of a literary satirist writing a scathing critique of Southern pastoral idealism. Dunbar's popularity as a Black vernacular poet was for him both a blessing and a curse. While Black vernacular poetry secured commercial success for Dunbar, it was a style of writing that imposed artistic limitations on the young poet who increasingly wanted to avail himself as simply a poet rather than merely a "dialect poet." Dunbar then marshals the mock pastoral mode in his novel as both a disavowal of Southern pastoral idealism and as a critique of the racist symbolism that delimited his own artistic endeavors.

So, too, does James Weldon Johnson marshal a mock pastoral framework to critique Southern pastoral idealism in *The Autobiography of an Ex-Colored Man*. Bearing elements of his own life, Johnson's aptly titled novel marshals the figure of the tragic mulatto, the ex-colored man, whose story recounts the events that led him to disavow his Blackness and "pass" for white. Johnson's iconic portrayal of Black racial liminality centers on a character whose name is never revealed. The novel's protagonist believes he is white until his school's headmaster reveals to him that he is indeed biracial. After this pivotal moment, he resolves to enter into the "freemasonry" of the race by learning everything he can about Black culture. For much of the novel, he pursues this cultural self-awareness. However, submerged within that main plot is the protagonist's struggle to define himself within a Southern society that commits violence against Black people with "absolute impunity." His response to pass for white is at once an attempt to escape such violence and a tacit acknowledgment that the cultural contributions of Black people cannot mitigate their violent subjugation in a Jim Crow society. As disturbing as *Autobiography* is for readers who experience its violence in visceral detail, the more disturbing truth is the ex-colored man's admission of "shame" after witnessing the gory lynching of a Black man. In this climactic moment, he not only rejects the Blackness he has so sought to cultivate but also rejects its cultural source in the South. His final act of defiance is the decision to live the remainder of his life as a white man.

The Autobiography of an Ex-Colored Man is comparable to *Sport of the Gods* in that Johnson's impetus for writing the novel of racial passing was also borne out of his own pursuit of artistic legitimacy. Indeed, just as Dunbar hoped to escape the dubious mantle of "Negro poet laureate," Johnson similarly sought to avail himself of a position as a Black writer without the limiting qualifiers of race. That is certainly not to say that Johnson did not want to be regarded as a Black writer. Rather, he wanted to expose the facile representations of Black life popular at the time that traded on racist caricatures and demeaning stereotypes. In his autobiography *Along This Way*, Johnson wrote of the efforts of writers, both Black and white, to portray the "dramatic values" of Harlem. He writes, "writers of fiction, white and black, have limited their stories to Harlem as a playground, and have ignored or not recognized the fundamental, relentless forces at work and the efforts to cope with them." Johnson's realization of this artistic vision in his only novel paints a more vibrant and realistic portrait of Harlem. Ironically, the promised land in *Autobiography*, the "Black mecca" that was Harlem, is often portrayed in less-than-ideal terms.

Indeed, both authors reveal the complex relationship between Black Southern culture and the urban spaces in Northern cities. Thus, the mock pastoral mode that gives shape to both of these migration novels provides an immediate source of thematic conflict. While traditional ghetto pastoral narratives privilege the dialectical urban spaces of the Northern city, the novels considered here privilege the rural landscape as both a symbolic repository of cultural meaning and racial identity for Black migrants, as well as an oppressive place from which their Black migrant characters must escape. The promise of the Northern city is registered here as a hopeful respite to the material realities of Southern life, but the cultural practices of the city itself are seen as poor substitutes for what is presumably a more authentic Black Southern culture and lived experience. Indeed, both Dunbar and Johnson privilege a Black vernacular tradition that runs the gamut between music, folktales and the everyday lived experience of Southern Black people. These early migration novels then at once portray the South as a source of African American cultural identity and as a site of individual struggle to define Black humanity. The Black migrant characters of these novels must then locate themselves within a complex cultural matrix of signifiers that both affirm and subvert their fraught racial identities. Indeed, the conflict that defines these early Black migration novels would provide the thematic basis for the ghetto pastoral, Black migration novels of the 1920s set in Harlem, New York. Both novels, therefore, anticipate the major themes that would drive ghetto pastoral narratives of Black migration and racial formation. They also anticipate the major figures of those novels, the liminal Black migrant positioned at the interstices of rural and urban experience.

The Oak and the Ivy

Perhaps the most celebrated poet of Black vernacular verse, Paul Laurence Dunbar was but an elevator operator in Dayton, Ohio, in the spring of 1893. He sold his modest volume of standard and dialect verse poems *Oak and Ivy* between work shifts to supplement the meager $4.00 per week wage he received.[10] Despite this inauspicious start to his writing career, the young poet slowly gained notoriety, and in April of that year Dunbar traveled to Detroit to read from his growing catalog of standard and dialect verse poems.[11] On his return trip to Dayton, he stopped in Toledo at the request of a friend to read some of his poems for the distinguished men of the exclusive West End Club.[12] On the evening of his recital, another featured speaker, Dr. W. C. Chapman of Toledo, presented a paper entitled "The Negro in the South," a work that severely criticized the majority of Black Southerners as lazy and idle while making the rare allowance for exceptional Black men such as Dunbar.[13] Incensed by these racist statements, Dunbar made an abrupt departure from his scheduled recital.[14] Instead, he read from his standard verse poem, "An Ode to Ethiopia," a poem that begins with the stanza "O Mother Race! To thee I bring / This pledge of faith unwavering, / This tribute to thy glory. / I know the pangs which thou didst feel, / With thy dear blood all gory."[15] Those in attendance that night undoubtedly expecting to hear Dunbar read from his popular dialect poems were instead treated to a Pan-African statement of Black racial solidarity.

Much like his West End Club rebellion, Dunbar's final novel, *Sport of the Gods*, was also an abrupt departure for the popular dialect poet. Published near the end of his life, Dunbar's novel portrays the Hamiltons, a middle-class Black family forced to leave the South after the family patriarch is falsely accused and convicted of theft. Upon leaving the South and their meager prosperity for what is presumably a fresh start in New York City, the Hamiltons eventually succumb to the worldly trappings of Northern city life. In contrast to the optimistic discourse of Black migration prominent in the literature of this period, Dunbar's novel offers an alternative message that figures Black lived experience in the South (although circumscribed in the novel) as more authentic than its cultural counterpart in the North. On its face, this cautionary tale of Black migration presents a Southern pastoral alternative to the urban squalor and immorality of New York City. However, Dunbar's novel also exposes the racial and ideological structures that proscribe Southern Black culture and lived experience. In this way, the novel reflects the author's own personal and artistic predicament. Indeed, Dunbar would struggle his entire career to break free from the artistic limitations imposed on him by a reading public enamored with images of Black mammies and shuffling slaves, racial caricatures that were the thematic mainstays of Southern pastoralism and plantation fiction.

His artistic sacrifice at the altar of white public opinion had failed to open an artistic causeway into the literary mainstream for the writer, whose decision to write in dialect verse in order "to gain a hearing" strained toward obligation near the end of his life. The timing of *Sport*'s publication (four years prior to Dunbar's death) coupled with Dunbar's growing disillusionment with his role as a regional dialect poet is suggestive of the novel's subversive meaning. His tacit critique in the novel of the romanticized Old South challenges the facile quality of Southern pastoral idealism. Dunbar's novel may be read in part as a literary and political response to his tenuous position as a Black dialect poet forced to couch much of his poetry in Southern pastoral stereotypes. The novel does so through an explicit mockery of the underlying terms of Southern pastoralism. Dunbar's novel functions then as a mock pastoral at once portraying the value of Black folk culture and lived experience while also revealing the material conditions that suppressed it in the South.

Indeed, Dunbar's novel is an important variation of the ghetto pastoral mode, as it establishes the broader thematic framework for the Black migration novel as an influential genre within the African American literary tradition. Dunbar problematizes the terms of Southern pastoralism by portraying the South as a privileged, if also tragically flawed, cultural space for Black folk. *Sport of the Gods* is, therefore, a transitional text within the tradition of African American letters. Dunbar's "fugitive migrant" tale bridges the gap between Black pastoral fictions of the nineteenth century and the ghetto pastoral stories of the early twentieth century.[16] An earlier Black pastoral tradition, borne out of the trauma of slavery in the South, consisted of stories rooted in the imaginative folklore of Southern Black culture. Charles W. Chesnutt, a contemporary of Dunbar and a more accomplished novelist, reclaimed that tradition of Black folklore from a plantation tradition of writing that exploited and mocked Black culture and lived experience. Chesnutt's *The Conjure Woman*, a collection of Black folktales told from the perspective of a former slave, provided a counterpoint to the racist caricatures that filled the pages of Southern romance books such as Thomas Nelson's Page's *In Ole Virginia*. Dunbar subsequently reimagines that earlier tradition by effectively critiquing the underlying terms of Southern pastoralism, thereby both anticipating the themes of the Harlem Renaissance and establishing the critical basis upon which the ideal of the "New Negro" would be founded by a later generation of Black authors and poets.

When *Sport of the Gods* was published in 1902, Dunbar was foremost a Black dialect poet. For this reason, early criticism of the novel dismissed it as a literary aside for the man Booker T. Washington had anointed "the Negro poet laureate." Benjamin Brawley, Dunbar's early biographer, dismisses the novel almost entirely, describing it only as "the fourth novel . . . in which the chief characters are Negroes."[17] For Dunbar, however, the novel was more than a mere aberration in his otherwise successful poetic career. Indeed, Dunbar's novel challenged prevailing racial norms and attitudes, expressing a distinctively more radical tone than can be found in any of his former poetry or fiction. The novel's engagement of the plantation tradition as a racial construct is a rejection of the mainstream standards under which Dunbar wrote and published. Thus, Dunbar's achievement in *Sport of the Gods* reflected a movement away from the stock racial characterizations of plantation fiction and toward a critical (re)assessment of the cultural material that inspired much of his poetry.

Although recent criticism has sought to understand the novel as an integral part of Dunbar's literary corpus, these critical appraisals do not view the novel in relation to Dunbar's celebrated and controversial work as a Black dialect poet. In his study of early Black migration fiction, Laurence Rodgers describes *Sport* as a key part of Dunbar's literary corpus for what it reveals about the poet's approach to and understanding of Black Southern culture. Rodgers writes, "It is significant that Dunbar, a northern-born plantation poet with tenuous personal connections to southern folk culture, wrote a novel about the high cost of repudiating southern black experience—and conversely the centrality of that experience as a necessity for formulating a northern identity—during a particularly hostile era of U.S. racial history."[18] Rodgers asserts that Dunbar's novel initiates a thematic approach in which "black southern culture provides the key that unlocks the possibilities of northern life."[19] However, to this I would add that Dunbar's mock pastoral thesis in the novel also provides the key to understanding much of his work as a poet writing *within* the plantation tradition. Dunbar's view of the South in the novel is decidedly more ambivalent and ultimately more critical than Rodger's comments would seem to indicate. Indeed, while Dunbar's novel reveals the "high cost of repudiating southern black experience," it also reveals the equally harsh cost of romanticizing Southern Black experience in a way that fails to acknowledge the material reality of Black lived experience in the South. This was the irony of Dunbar's dialect poetry—its penchant for celebrating Black vernacular culture while also revealing the structures of inequality out of which it emerged. Thus, Dunbar's critique of Southern pastoralism from his position as a Northern-born plantation poet turned novelist signals an effort to qualify and contextualize a Black Southern cultural tradition that was the singular source of his poetry. His mock pastoral depiction of the South in the novel exposes both the oppressive structures of rural Black Southern life as well as the idealistic promises of the urban North. In this regard, the novel can be read as both a personal and literary metanarrative. The subversion of plantation ideals and motifs in the novel may then be best understood as Dunbar's tacit attempt to qualify his efforts as a poet and author writing in and influenced by the plantation tradition.

Criticism is divided over the extent to which Dunbar privileges South-ern Black culture in the novel. On the one hand, Laurence Rodgers reads *Sport* as signaling the importance of Southern Black culture, while on the other, Thomas L. Morgan reads the novel as a direct critique of Southern pastoralism. In contrast to Rodgers's Southern thesis, which privileges the importance of Black vernacular culture in the South, Morgan argues that Dunbar constructs a countervailing "urban blackness" in the novel through his portrayal of Black life in New York City.[20] He writes, "while Dunbar was not the first to use the city in African American fiction, he was the first to use both the novel and the space of the city to rhetorically reveal the limitations created by inherently linking African Americans with the pastoral South."[21] Morgan's reading demonstrates how the novel figures the Northern city as a transformative space where Black urban consciousness can take shape. However, as my reading of the novel will show, the space of the city is also represented in the novel as a site of rural and urban conflict. Although the urban North in the novel holds the promise of social mobility for Black migrants, it is also a scene of cultural displacement for Black Southerners who leave home to venture into the unknown city. And while the rural South represents home and place for Dunbar's Black migrant characters, it is also the source of the racial oppression that forces their leaving in the first place. Dunbar marshals the mock pastoral as a way of adjudicating both perspec-tives by revealing the possibilities and limitations that attended Black lived experience in either the rural South or the urban North.

Perhaps the best study of Dunbar's novel as it relates to his marginalized position as a dialect poet is Gregory L. Candela's 1976 article "We Wear the Mask: Irony in Dunbar's *Sport of the Gods.*" Candela's article responds to the overwhelming scholarly consensus that Dunbar was beholden to the literary and social conventions of the plantation tradition. Candela describes this view as "an unfortunate pattern" in the critical discourse surrounding Dun-bar's work as a poet and author.[22] According to Candela, the major flaw of this criticism is its "[focus] on the elements of plantation tradition in [Dunbar's] dialect pieces and, later, his fiction, disregarding serious literary technique or racial protest in his work."[23] Through the subversive function of irony in the novel, Candela argues, "Dunbar tried to reach an American audience that he knew was more interested in 'coon shows.'"[24] Candela is right to read *Sport* as satire meant to disarm the contrived Southern idealism of the plantation tradition. But to this I would add that Dunbar accomplishes a great deal more in the novel than subverting the racist assumptions of plantation fiction. As my readings will show, Dunbar also (re)defines Southern Black culture and lived experience by exposing the conditions that delimited it in the South. In doing so, he portrays Southern Black culture and lived experience as tragi-cally blighted in the face of Southern oppression. And yet, his final portrayal of the Hamiliton family, irrevocably destroyed by Southern racism, neverthe-less reveals the ways in which Black people "lived as they must" despite the stultifying conditions they faced. It is this dialectical view of Southern Black lived experience in the novel that reflects Dunbar's own liminal position as a Northern-born Black author writing within the limitations of Southern pastoralism while also writing against it as a protest novelist.

Recent criticism complicates the view of Dunbar as merely a tortured artist who believed his career was a failure because of the constraints placed on him. In his oft cited poem "Sympathy," the poignant image of a caged bird does more than just symbolize the constraints placed on Black artistic expression. It is also suggestive of the rhetorical strategies Black artists marshaled as a means of overcoming those constraints. Gene Andrew Jarrett's outstanding biography, *Paul Laurence Dunbar: The Life and Times of a Caged Bird*, figures the "biographical metaphor" of Dunbar's caged bird as signifying the "societal constraints on his life and literature."[25] However, as Jarrett makes clear, the potent image of the caged bird does not entirely encapsulate Dunbar's story. "One must tell the full story," writes Jarrett, "of an African American who privately wrestled with the constraints of America in the Gilded Age, but who also sought to express or mitigate this strife through the written and spoken word."[26] My examination of *Sport of the Gods* also understands the novel as Dunbar's attempt to mitigate the considerable strife of his personal and professional life, albeit through his prose fiction. I describe Dunbar's literary critique of Southern pastoralism and urban idealism in *Sport* as a tacit commentary on the social limitations placed on him as a Black writer. Donna Campbell offers a similar reading of *Sport of the Gods,* drawing paral-lels between Dunbar's literary project in the novel and the Black Lives Matter movement. Campbell argues that Dunbar's critique of systemic forms of racism such as the criminal judicial system emphasizes "what many today call mass incarceration or the prison industrial complex, wherein the slavery of the plantation system is replicated by the disproportionate incarceration of Black men in the often for-profit prisons that have emerged over the past several decades."[27] For Campbell, Dunbar's novel gives voice to not only the "literary or rhetorical" means of achieving social change, but also to "physi-cal" and "primal" responses to social injustice.[28]

Dunbar's mock pastoral perspective in the novel deconstructs the con-trived idealism of Southern pastoralism by exposing the material realities that suppressed Southern Black culture and lived experience. Describing the mock pastoral tradition in the context of late-eighteenth-century poetic satire, Cameron Nickels defines the mock pastoral as a literary vehicle that "juxtapose[s] idealized rural life and the ostensibly 'real' peculiarities of rustic character, manners, and language."[29] Nickels locates the satirical figure of the "rustic New England Yankee" in a series of political poems written in response to "Jeffersonian Republicanism" with its emphasis on the common man whose self-worth was measured by his spiritual communion with the land.[30] In contrast to this pastoral ideal, the mock pastoral revealed the dual (and often competing) image of America as signifying both rural expanse and urban industry. Moreover, in response to Jefferson's ironic vision of America as an expanding nation driven by the vision of yeomen farmers, the mock pastoral acknowledges this dual trajectory as an ideological contradiction in the service of racial and class interests.

Dunbar's use of the mock pastoral in the novel similarly reveals the tension that was at the core of the African American Great Migration narrative. While Southern pastoral ideals necessarily formed the basis for Black folk culture, they also provided the ideological cover for unscrupulous economic practices such as sharecropping as well as the disarming romantic vision of plantation fiction. In response, Dunbar evokes the mock pastoral mode in the novel as a way of juxtaposing Black folk culture and lived experience over and against the social conditions that systematically opposed it in the South. Thus, the mock pastoral vision in the novel provides a means of (re)presenting Black folk culture as positive value while simultaneously dismantling the facade of Southern pastoralism that obscured the structures of racial oppression.

One of the ways in which the novel evokes this mock pastoral vision is through its naturalistic framework. Dunbar marshals the tradition of naturalism with its emphasis on social determinacy as a counterpoint to an ideology of rugged individualism throughout the novel. His most obvious expression of naturalistic themes is the title of the novel itself, which references the pessimistic words spoken by Shakespeare's Gloucester in *King Lear*: "As flies to wanton boys, are we to th' gods, / They kill us for their sport."[31] The blinded Gloucester, expressing his despair at the irresistible dictates of fate, clearly resonated with the poet novelist whose artistic career was proscribed by the racial standards of his day. Dunbar's characters share in his fate as they too are circumscribed by the material force of history. William Andrews describes the ambivalence with which Dunbar and other African American novelists appropriated naturalism's themes: "Naturalism's honest portrayal of the human condition as one of struggle against an indifferent or hostile environment had an appeal to African-American writers of Dunbar's era, but the tendency of naturalism to minimize or dismiss individual will and human reason as effective means of changing one's environment or fate has always made naturalism problematic for writers and readers of African-American fiction."[32] Just as naturalism sought to reject pastoral ideals of transcendence that envisioned an idyllic green landscape, Dunbar's mock pastoral vision in *The Sport of the Gods* rejects the dream of Southern transcendence in the form of an idyllic plantation society. However, perhaps also reflecting Dunbar's own ambivalence regarding the naturalism that frames the novel, he stops short of rejecting altogether the symbolic potency of Southern Black culture and lived experience. Instead, Dunbar posits agency in the symbolic forms and practices of Black Southern culture while also revealing the material conditions that oppressed Black people in the South. Therefore, his mock pastoral vision reveals the incongruities of Black cultural life in the South, a place where Black people were simultaneously at home and under siege.

The mock pastoral vision in the novel is also suggestive of the growing distance between the dialect poet best known for humorous sketches of Black life and the increasingly disillusioned man whose career had become a source of personal anxiety and artistic disappointment. Reportedly penned in the span of thirty days, Dunbar's final effort at novel writing occurred at a time when his health and marriage were quickly deteriorating.[33] During this time the poet began to seriously reflect on his legacy as a Black artist and as an individual. Dunbar expressed regret for the limitations placed upon him as a Black dialect poet, a sentiment that became increasingly evident in his volumes of poetry and in poems like "Sympathy."[34] It may well have been this overwhelming sense of regret and guilt that motivated his feverish effort to get *Sport* out.

Ironically, were it not for his fraught achievements as a Black dialect poet, critics may not have even taken notice of the novel. Dunbar rose to fame upon the release of his second volume of poetry *Majors and Minors* in 1896. The most resounding admiration for the volume came from William Dean Howells, who wrote an encouraging review of it in *Harper's Weekly* magazine, a review that was published on Dunbar's birthday. In his review, Howells praises Dunbar as "one of the most refined and modest men I had ever met," and writes that his poetry makes a "realistic portrayal" of Black characters.[35] Howells's review instantly established Dunbar as a serious poet and a competent writer. However, the review also made a negative impression on the young poet as it lauded his dialect poems as the real strength of the volume but made only passing references to his standard verse pieces. Dunbar received this endorsement with a great deal of ambivalence, recoiling at the suggestion that he "write more dialect pieces," for in Howells's words, "they're your contribution to American letters."[36] The review epitomized the

artistic and personal struggle of Dunbar's life. He always believed himself
to be a poet of standard English verse and saw dialect poetry merely as a
means to gain a hearing from a white audience captivated by stereotypical
plantation images of Black folks.

For this reason, Dunbar grew increasingly frustrated by the artistic con-
cessions he was forced to make as a Black dialect poet and came to view his
fame as deeply problematic, coming as it did at the expense of his literary and
perhaps even his personal integrity. In his standard verse poem "Sympathy,"
Dunbar evokes the symbolism of a caged songbird incessantly beating its
wings against the "cruel bars." An apt symbol of Dunbar's proscribed artistic career, the poem's central image signifies the epistemological dilemma
inherent to African American literary production.[37] As a poet forced to write
in dialect verse despite his desire to establish himself as a poet of standard
English verse, Dunbar's career reveals both the accomplishments and the
limitations of a nineteenth-century Black poet and novelist attempting to
gain a hearing from a predominantly white audience. Undoubtedly sensing
the double bind of his success as a dialect poet, Dunbar pens the lines to
the stanza that would prove prophetic in anticipating his legacy as an artist:

> Mere human strength may stand ill-fortune's frown,
> So I prevailed, for human strength was mine:
> But from the killing strength of great renown
> Naught may protect me save a strength divine.
> Help me, O Lord, in this my trembling cause,
> I scorn men's curses, but I dread applause![38]

Reflecting this dilemma, much of Dunbar's early poetry attempts to negotiate a symbolic field that stretched between nostalgic depictions of the "Ole
South" and stereotypical representations of Black people. He does so in his
first two volumes of poetry, *Majors and Minors* and *Oak and Ivy*, by coun-
terbalancing his dialect pieces with poems written in standard English verse.
Apparent in the titles of these volumes is Dunbar's intention to create a formal
and ideological separation between his dialect and standard verse poems.
Although some scholars have suggested that Dunbar's use of terms like
"minors" and "ivy" in his titles reflects the subordinated status of his dialect
poems, it is possible that Dunbar chose to make these kinds of distinctions
because they suggested a binary relationship between his standard and dialect
verse. While his dialect poems served to gain the interest of white readers,
these poems were also substantive expressions of Southern Black culture and
lived experience even when viewed alongside his more refined standard verse

poems. Indeed, Dunbar's standard verse poems were an extension of his Black dialect poems in that the former gave the latter both context and meaning. In his biography of Dunbar, Benjamin Brawley writes, "When Dunbar began his work there was not only general emphasis on the sentimental in American literature, but also special emphasis on what were supposed to be the good times in the South before the war. It was natural for him to be affected by what seemed to make strong appeal, and so he was; but he soon realized the shortcomings of his models and struck a more distinctive note."[39] This "more distinctive note" can be heard in standard verse poems like "Sympathy" and "The Crisis," both of which challenge the racial proscriptions placed on Black artistic expression in a racialized society.

Sport of the Gods would strike perhaps the most distinctive note in revealing the social conditions that suppressed Southern Black life and expression. These were social conditions that plantation authors glossed over in their fictions. The novel's mock pastoral framework provides a critical framework for qualifying Dunbar's efforts as a dialect poet writing in the plantation tradition. As a work of protest fiction, the novel also refutes the often-levied charge that Dunbar was complicit in the racism of the South because of his regional dialect poetry. Indeed, Dunbar's novel tacitly (re)appropriates Southern Black culture by wresting it away from the racist framework of the plantation tradition. The novel accomplishes this by exposing both the systemic ways in which Black people were oppressed in the South as well as their resilience in the face of such racial oppression. Ironically, Dunbar's migration novel reverses the symbolic trajectory of Black migration by evoking the central importance of Black folk culture and lived experience despite the failures of Southern society to provide an adequate place for Black people at the turn of the twentieth century. Sport of the Gods thus reflects an effort to (re)envision the Southern Black cultural experience from which he drew inspiration as a Black dialect poet.

(Re)envisioning the South

Anticipating the ambivalence of New Negro authors and intellectuals, many of whom regarded the Southern pastoral narrative with suspicion if not outright scorn, Dunbar marshaled Southern pastoralism in his poetry and literature as an ideal fraught with racial degradation, intermittent violence, and social proscription.[40] It is no wonder that even his most comical, lighthearted works bear within them an undercurrent of cynicism and bitterness. For Dunbar, the Southern pastoral mode was a powerful but mostly unattainable ideal for Black writers who regarded the South as both a source of cultural inspiration and a site of historical trauma. His poetry in particular revealed this tension between a Southern pastoral ideal, on the one hand, which imagined a Southern landscape of infinite possibilities untrammeled by the racial sins of a not too distant past, and a South of historical fact, on the other hand, whose brutal past was always visible, even celebrated, in a postbellum landscape of Corinthian columns, "deserted plantations," and "lost cause" narratives.

"The Deserted Plantation," Dunbar's haunting poem told from the perspective of an ex-slave turned plantation caretaker, evokes sentimental images of plantation life that would have been popular fare for his readers. The speaker of the poem pines for the days of "de da'kies . . . dat used to be a dacin' evry night befo' de ole cabin do,'" as he laments the passing away of "all dat loved me an'dat I loved in de pas."[41] While Dunbar's ex-slave repeatedly asks why everyone has left the place to its gradual decay, his question is merely rhetorical. He answers the question definitively in the stanza that follows: "Gone! not one o'dem is lef' to tell de story; / Dey have lef' de deah ole place to fall away. / Couldn't one o' dem dat seed it in its glory / Stay to watch it in de hour of decay?"[42] The real question that motivates his elegiac response is who will remain to tell the story. That the speaker has taken this burden on himself indicates his personal stake in the past and the necessity of retelling the story. But while his fidelity to this memory is admirable, it is also tragic. The speaker is incapable of imagining a life beyond the "deserted plantation," indeed, can only imagine a life-after-death that bears a striking resemblance to life on the plantation: "So I'll stay an' watch de deah ole place an' tend it / Ez I used to in de happy days gone by. / 'Twell de othah Mastah thinks it's time to end it, / An' calls me to my qua'ters in the sky."[43] The irony of this final image may have been lost on Dunbar's readers, but it becomes clear when understood in the context of his life and career.

Artistically, Dunbar also stayed behind on the old plantation as a Black dialect poet writing in the plantation tradition. While a younger generation of poets, most notably Countee Cullen and Langston Hughes, would years later forge progressive themes of Black self-determination, Dunbar remained true to a plantation tradition based largely on themes of racial subservience. Yet, like the venerable speaker of "The Deserted Plantation," Dunbar's fidelity to the past is also tinged with irony. Dunbar built his career on celebrating in verse Black culture in the South. His (re)memory of "happy darkies" and "shuffling slaves" in his dialect poetry was problematic on its face, but these images often functioned as ironic caricatures in his dialect poetry. In other words, they were exaggerated figures within a tradition that sanctioned (indeed, privileged) such representations of Black culture and lived experience. Although indefensible as "accurate" representations of Black lived experience, they were nevertheless willful misrepresentations meant to elicit humor if not also evoke subtle irony. As Dunbar's dual poetic vision attests, he understood the past as a constructed narrative that functioned as both history and parody.

The Sport of the Gods opens with a similar regard for the past. Dunbar begins by lamenting the literary aspersions that have been cast on an era of "masters and slaves," an ironic statement to be sure that sets the tone for the entire novel. He writes, "Fiction has said so much in regret of the old days when there were plantations and overseers and masters and slaves, that it was good to come upon such a household as Berry Hamilton's, if for no other reason than that it afforded a relief from the monotony of tiresome iteration" (1).[44] In portraying the Hamilton's story as an alternative to the "monotony of tiresome iteration," Dunbar tacitly critiques the nostalgia of this bygone plantation era. Like the speaker of Dunbar's dialect poem, Berry Hamilton has stayed on the "ole plantation," remained faithful to his former master, and has managed to secure for himself and his family some measure of prosperity. Unlike the speaker of the poem, however, Berry is subject to forces beyond his control, and following the titular implications of the novel, is made to suffer the irresistible fate that is figuratively the "sport of the gods." The "gods" in this sense may refer to Dunbar's white characters in whose hands Berry's fate resides. But it may just as well refer to the authors of the racist archetypes that portrayed the Old South as a veritable paradise lost. Where those plantation authors had evoked images of benevolent white masters, Dunbar instead exposes the inherent contradictions of that romanticized fiction. From the outset then Dunbar's novel functions as a metatextual commentary on the plantation tradition by revealing it to be both a source of inspiration and circumscription.

Following this initial portrayal, the novel subverts the plantation tradition by altering the terms of that fiction. Where Dunbar's poetry was suggestive in its tacit critique of plantation fiction, the novel is much more explicit. Berry is the quintessential Black servant who demonstrates his loyalty through years of faithful service to Maurice Oakley. Oakley, for his part, is the benevolent white master-turned-employer who retains his former slave as the house butler. However, these roles are subverted when the thin veneer of Southern gentility is torn away by the overwhelming influence of racial difference. Although Berry has upheld his obligation to his master-turned-employer, his loyalty ultimately counts for nothing in the face of racial ideology. When Oakley's younger half brother concocts a story that his travel money has been stolen, Oakley's suspicions are immediately drawn to his longtime servant, Berry Hamilton, despite his brother's assertion that "Hamilton is beyond suspicion." Oakley's response that "no servant is beyond suspicion" tacitly asserts class distinctions as a basis for his recriminations. However, his explanation quickly turns to race when he describes the moral regression of Black people since the abolition of slavery:

> This spirit of trust does you credit, Frank, and I very much hope that you may be right. But as soon as a negro like Hamilton learns the value of money and begins to earn it, at the same time he begins to covet some easy and rapid way of securing it. The old negro knew nothing of the value of money. When he stole, he stole hams and bacon and chickens. These were his immediate necessities and the things he valued. The present laughs at this tendency without knowing the cause. The present negro resents the laugh, and he has learned to value other things than those which satisfy his belly. (15)

By characterizing Black people who have recently learned the "value of money" as inherently unethical, Oakley mobilizes an ideological point of view that seeks to uphold an old racial status quo. The very idea of Black achievement in this social context challenges the prevailing racial order. Thus, "a negro like Hamilton" is faced with the transcendent dilemma of aspiring to a social mobility available only to white people. This fact further chips away at the facade of Southern pastoral idealism that envisioned the new South as an egalitarian society where Black people could presumably get ahead.

Dunbar's initial portrayal of Southern society also exposes the ethical contradictions inherent to Southern pastoralism. Although the plantation tradition portrayed the South as a pastoral landscape signifying the high ideals of civilized society, it relegated Black people to a servile and marginalized position on the arbitrary basis of racial difference. As one of Dunbar's white characters remarks, "[Black people] are unacquainted with the ways of our higher civilization, and it'll take them a long time to learn" (30). A fellow in conversation with him offers a more definitive, if not also ironic, account of the Negro's innate sense of moral depravity. Relating the story of his Negro servant who used his prized hound to hunt opossum, the man offers a view of Black people as unredeemable social outcasts in Southern society. His rationale for describing the actions of his Black servant as "total depravity" rest on the assumption that Black people cannot belong in any meaningful way to this idealized Southern pastoral society (31). Ironically, the Black servant is already an active and meaningful participant in the pastoral scene of the South. In contrast to the "training" the dog received in the daytime from his white master, it is the surreptitious nighttime hunting of opossums that links both dog and man to a genuinely Southern pastoral ideal. What denies the Black servant a meaningful place in this pastoral landscape has nothing to do with his ability to uphold the standards of the ideal, but rather the arbitrary racial distinctions that necessarily exclude him.

The Southern section of the novel ultimately reveals a pastoral scene where the plantation myth has given way to social reality. The Hamiltons are displaced from the outset in the Southern pastoral scene because of their race and class. The former seals Berry's fate as a Black servant who is easily framed for a crime he did not commit. The latter seals his family's fate as they are summarily ostracized following Berry's conviction by Black people who already perceive them as overreaching snobs. Just as Southern pastoral conventions preclude the possibility of Berry defending himself against the false accusations of a white man, so too does it prevent the Hamiltons from being viewed by their racial peers as anything more than uppity Negroes. Appropriately, the passage that describes their Southern exodus is reminiscent of the Old Testament description of Lot's departure from the corrupt city of Sodom and Gomorrah: "[Joe] attended to all the details of their getting away with a promptness that made it seem untrue he had never been more than thirty miles from his native town. He was eager and excited. As the train drew out of the station, he did not look back upon the place which he hated, but Fannie and her daughter let their eyes linger upon it until the last house, the last chimney, and the last spire faded from their sight, and their tears fell and mingled as they were whirled away toward the unknown" (45). The Hamilton women look back on the sordid scene as Lot's wife does in the biblical story, but their regret of having lost their home does not transform them into pillars of salt. Rather, their salt-tears signal the subversion of a Southern pastoral ideal. The passage initiates the thematic arch of the novel that traces the symbolic trajectory of Black migration. The Hamiltons leave the known world of Southern contrivance for the unknown world of the Northern city.

Mock Pastoral and the Urban Cityscape

Dunbar's mock pastoral perspective in *Sport of the Gods* reveals the complex and often contradictory relationship between rural folk identity and urban consciousness. Dunbar represents the Northern cityscape in the novel as consisting of dialectical spaces in which Southern Black culture runs up against the urban practices of northern black communities. In this way,

Dunbar's novel anticipates much of the fiction of the Harlem Renaissance or New Negro movement that emphasized the racially transformative power of the city, particularly the urban Black community residing in New York's Harlem neighborhood. Although Dunbar's representation of New York City strikes a more cautionary tone than many of the novelists of the Renaissance, his novel does capture the dialectical quality of Northern Black communities as places tenuously situated between a residual folk culture and a nascent urban consciousness. The mock pastoral vision that Dunbar mobilizes in his portrayal of these urban spaces reflects an ironic view of Black migrant communities in the North. While the Black migrants of these communities saw themselves as fugitives escaping Southern oppression, the symbolic practices that shaped their Northern communities attested to the lasting influence of Black folk culture. In other words, the South, the very place they sought to escape, is constantly reinvoked as a symbolic presence in the so-called promised land of the Northern city. Dunbar marshals the mock pastoral to reveal the limitations of Southern pastoralism in light of the material realities of the Northern city.

In contrast to the moral and cultural ideals of Southern pastoralism, Dunbar's cityscape is structured by places that are figuratively nowhere, places otherwise marked as inauthentic in that they do not provide an adequate place of belonging for the displaced Southern Black migrant. This naturalistic portrayal of the urban landscape in *Sport* is the immediate source of alienation for Dunbar's Black migrants. Jillmarie Murphy's reading of *Sport* reveals the ways in which Dunbar's style of naturalism in the novel "destabilize[s] the already narrow boundaries that traditionally exist between race and environment."[45] Murphy describes the displacement of Dunbar's Black migrants in the city as "the putative inverse of place," a definition that highlights their attachment to a Southern home fraught with exploitation and their experience of a Northern urban environment that offers no real alternative.[46] Indeed, Dunbar's archetypal description of the individual upon first arrival in the city reads here as a cautionary tale for Black migrants looking for viable places of belonging in the city's urban spaces: "He will stay and stay on until the town becomes all in all to him; until the very streets are his chums and certain buildings and corners are his best friends. Then he is hopeless, and to live elsewhere would be death. The Bowery will be his romance. Broadway his lyric, and the Park his pastoral, the river and the glory of it all his epic, and he will look down pityingly on all the rest of humanity" (47).

Following the thematic implications of its title (*Sport of the Gods*), the city in the novel emerges as a powerful force that giveth and taketh away in a conflation of salvation and destruction. The false idols of urban life are represented as inadequate substitutes for rural-Southern modes of experi-ence, thereby becoming a potential source of cultural corruption for newly arrived Black migrants. The novel in turn laments the steady flow of Black migrants into the city, thereby offering a literary counterpoint to the opti-mistic discourse of Black migration that defined the period. However, while Dunbar presents the South as a repository of moral values presumably absent in the North, he does not valorize the South in turn. Instead, the mock pasto-ral perspective in the Northern section of the novel extols the values of Black folk culture while decrying the oppressive conditions Black migrants left behind in the rural South only to find in varying degrees in the urban North.

Dunbar thus celebrates the symbolic potency of Southern Black culture while lamenting its inevitable erosion under the constant pressure of Northern white mainstream society. His description of the "coon ditties" that dominated the musical stage at the turn of the century reflects the same social pressures that circumscribed his own poetry. When Dunbar describes Kit's decision to participate in this musical farce, he may as well be describing his own artistic dilemma as a Black poet writing in the plantation tradition: "The quick poison of the unreal life about her had already begun to affect her character. She had grown secretive and sly. The innocent longing which in a burst of enthusiasm she had expressed that first night at the theatre was growing into a real ambi-tion with her, and she dropped the simple old songs she knew to practice the detestable coon ditties which the stage demanded" (74). Kit's moral dilemma reflects the artistic dilemma that framed Dunbar's entire poetic career. Indeed, the "simple old songs" of Black folk culture and the "coon ditties" of the stage were part of a cultural continuum—the former representative of Black lived experience and the latter an expression of its degradation. Dunbar, however, frames both in dichotomous terms, investing the former with cultural authen-ticity while disparaging the latter as mere farce. In other words, he celebrates the "simple songs" of Black folk and mocks those that the "stage demanded."

While Dunbar's mock pastoral framework in the novel reveals the farce present in the myth of the Old South and in the "coon" songs of the North, it in turn posits a countervailing authenticity rooted in Southern Black folk culture. Dunbar's mock pastoral perspective figures Southern Black folk culture as tenuously situated between Southern oppression and Northern displacement. After Joe Hamilton is arrested for murder, his Banner Club companions lament the steady flow of migrants into the city while extolling the virtues of a rural lifestyle: "Oh, is there no way to keep these people from rushing away from the small villages and country districts of the South up to the cities, where they cannot battle with the terrible force of a strange and unusual environment?" (122). Dunbar amplifies this voice of reason in his own narrative voice: "They wanted to preach to these people that good agriculture is better than bad art—that it was better and nobler for them to sing to God across the Southern fields than to dance for rowdies in the Northern halls" (122). Their collective reasoning that "wollen-shirted, brown-jeaned simplicity is infinitely better than broad-clothed degradation," valorizes Black folk culture as an alternative to either the plantation myth of the South as pastoral panacea or to the urban myth of the North as the promised land (122). In other words, Dunbar's mock pastoral imagines an idealized Black Southern experience that can be mobilized as an ideological counterargument to the racist plantation mythology of the South and to the idealistic urban mythology of the North.

Dunbar's novel functions then as a metanarrative that comments on the very terms of its own fiction. Indeed, Dunbar's own career reveals the ideological constraints placed on Black authors forced to limit their works to simple pastoral narratives.[47] For the dialect poet turned novelist, however, the meanings that informed Black artistic expression were much more complex, as they emanated from both rural and urban settings and reflected the contested nature of both. Although the South is central in Dunbar's fiction and poetry, it is at once an object of devotion and derision. Put another way, within Dunbar's artistic vision, the South evokes both inspiration and deprivation. It is precisely this mock pastoral perspective in the novel that indirectly comments on his work as a poet of Black vernacular and dialect verse. Perhaps the most revealing passage in the novel as it relates to Dunbar's poetic career is one that makes explicit reference to Black dialect poetry. In response to the yellow journalist Skaggs's observation that "dancing is the poetry of motion," Sadness adds, "and dancing in rag-time is the dialect poetry" (116). Dunbar relates to the reader Skaggs's unspoken thoughts on the matter: "The reporter did not like this. It savoured of flippancy and he was about entering upon a discussion to prove that Sadness had no soul" (116). This exchange is suggestive of Dunbar's own ambivalence as a dialect poet. For the reluctant poet of Black vernacular verse, the "flippancy" of his dialect verse had certainly robbed his subject matter (and perhaps himself) of its proverbial "soul."

Appropriately then, it is the yellow journalist Skaggs, Dunbar's ironic voice of reason, who discovers the truth behind Berry Hamilton's conviction. Skaggs learns of the story from a drunken Joe Hamilton, who believes his father was falsely convicted. Skaggs travels to the South ostensibly in the name of justice, although his real motivation is his own professional advancement and the pursuit of a "big sensation for [his] paper" (117). He ultimately succeeds in wresting (quite literally) from Maurice Oakley's breast pocket the truth in the form of a damning letter in which his brother admits to spending the money to pay off gambling debts, then forcing Berry to take the blame. Berry is subsequently pardoned after the truth behind the sordid affair is made public news. The novel then speeds to its naturalistic conclusion, with Berry's freedom restored but his life otherwise in shambles. His wife remarried, his daughter ruined by the stage, and worst of all, his son convicted of murder, Berry returns to a bleak existence. Dunbar conveys in this unhappiest of endings an enduring cliché that would define his entire career: the truth that Skaggs uncovers is indeed stranger than the fiction that had once obscured it.

The final chapter of the novel exposes the strangeness of this truth by returning Berry and his wife to a veritable Southern Gothic existence. The Hamilton's marriage union is restored when Mary's husband, a "race track man," is conveniently killed in a dispute over his unpaid gambling debts. Berry and his wife then return to their Southern cottage where Oakley's guilt-ridden wife has prepared a place for them. Although their home and marriage are restored, the Southern Gothic imagery that frames their existence finally dispels the pastoral idealism that once colored this Southern scene. Unable to bear the truth of his brother's deceit, Maurice Oakley goes insane with shame and grief. The reunited couple is then forced to live out their days "listening to the shrieks of the madman across the yard and thinking of what he had brought to them and to himself" (148). As Dunbar lastly informs us, "it was not a happy life, but it was all that was left to them" (148). The only solace his characters possess comes from the inescapable reality that this was their fate as though "they were powerless against some Will infinitely stronger than their own" (148).

That Dunbar consigns his main characters to a living hell says a great deal about the embittered poet near the end of his life. Dunbar clearly strikes a somber tone in the novel's conclusion in the midst of this Southern Gothic bleakness. In her reading of the novel's ending, Bridget Harris Tsemo argues "the end of the text could suggest that the Hamiltons are returning to slavery, but read closely and in conjunction with some of Dunbar's other writings, the ending can be read as the Hamiltons facing insurmountable adversity with dignity and strength."[48] Indeed, the ending may be read as an allegorical commentary on Dunbar's own personal and artistic struggle to avail himself as more than simply a Black dialect poet. Dunbar had assailed the literary heights of stardom only to conform to the racist standards of plantation fiction. He was also forced to listen to the "shrieks of madm[e]n" that he write more dialect poetry, for this was his only acceptable contribution to the world of letters. He also believed himself to be "powerless against some

Will infinitely stronger than [his] own," a will that delimited the scope of his artistic expression. However, much like the resilient Hamiltons, Dunbar returned always to the South in his poetry, thereby hoping to capture the authentic character of a Black vernacular tradition that was for him both a blessing and a curse.

New Negroes and Ex-Colored Men

James Weldon Johnson's singular literary masterpiece *The Autobiography of an Ex-Colored Man* anticipates the prominent themes of the Harlem Renaissance through its literary ethnographic descriptions of Black culture. In his preface to the anonymously published 1912 version of the novel, Carl Van Vechten referred to the book as a "human document," a description that fueled speculation about whether the book was based on a true account of the author's life.[49] The uncertainty surrounding the novel's initial publication obscured its status as a literary text. It was not until the republication of the novel in 1927 as a work of fiction with Johnson's name attached that *Autobiography* received renewed scrutiny from literary critics and scholars. This fact may explain why *Autobiography* is most often associated with the themes arising from the Harlem Renaissance, although the novel is more closely linked to an earlier period of Black literary production. Indeed, *Autobiography* anticipated the major themes of the Harlem Renaissance as well as the burgeoning genre of Black migration fiction. These themes focused on the integral relationship between Black folk culture in the South and modern representations of Black lived experience centered in places like Harlem. *Autobiography* can be read as a text that conceptually bridges the gap between rural and urban, old and new, Black and white, folk and modern. It is a transitional work of African American fiction that foregrounds the thematic and social tensions that would inform the works of Harlem Renaissance authors in the 1920s.

The novel's initial publication in 1912 came at time when the Great Migration of Black Southerners into Northern cities had just begun.[50] The geographical movement of Black people into Northern cities was a response to decades of social and political unrest in the South. Jim Crow segregation had received federal backing after the *Plessy v. Ferguson* decision of 1896 established the mandate of "separate but equal." Much of the African American literature of the Reconstruction era had focused their fictions on the theme of racial uplift for Black people after the systematic failures of Reconstruction.[51] *Autobiography* is the culmination of the "race novels" of the late nineteenth century that problematized racial difference through the portrayal of tragic mulatto characters.[52] In addition, the novel is also a precursor to the Black middle-class fictions of the Harlem Renaissance that marshaled the ideal of the "New Negro." Johnson's wide-ranging social commentary in the novel responds to an earlier tradition of Black cultural expression while also anticipating the works of a later generation of novelists, most notably, Ralph Ellison's literary masterpiece, *Invisible Man.* The social commentary that frames the novel, particularly on the controversial subject of "racial passing," situates the novel within a critical discourse on race that would provide the thematic focus for much of the literature of the Harlem Renaissance.

The publication history of the novel provides insight on how the text functions as both literature and social commentary. The initial publication of the novel in 1912 raised speculation about its authorship since Johnson did not attach his name to the original manuscript. It would be another fifteen years until *Autobiography* was republished as a definitive work of fiction. Upon its initial publication, many believed that the work of fiction was an actual autobiographical account. When the novel was reprinted in 1927, and its authorship rightly attributed to Johnson, it was regarded by many commentators as a fictional account based on Johnson's life. Johnson later wrote of the ambiguity surrounding the novel's publication in his 1933 autobiography *Along This Way.* Johnson notes, "when the book was published most of the reviewers, though there were some doubters, accepted it as a human document."[53] He admits that he "had done the book with the intention of its being so taken," while also expressing regret he did not publish the novel as a "frank piece of fiction" from the very outset.[54] Although the 1927 edition clearly stated that the novel was not an accurate recounting of his life, Johnson recalls the countless letters he received "inquiring about this or that phase of my life as told in it."[55] Johnson attributes this as "one of the reasons" he set out to write his official autobiography.[56]

That Johnson would set out to distinguish his own life apart from his fictional work is suggestive of the novel's purpose as a work of fiction. There are certainly parallels in the novel to Johnson's actual experiences. For example, his ex-colored man resolves to gather up the "raw materials" of Black vernacular culture in an effort to elevate and refine them. Similarly, Johnson wrote in his personal autobiography of the "Harlem of story and song," what he believed to be the facile image of Harlem made popular during the period of the 1920s but which necessarily belied the quotidian beauty of the New York City neighborhood.[57] He admits that there is a continued fascination of the "Harlem of story and song" that writers of the day had seized upon for both for artistic and commercial gain. However, to quote Johnson at length, there is another untapped source of beauty in the cityscapes of Harlem as well: "But there is the other *real* and *overshadowing* Harlem. The commonplace, work-a-day Harlem. The Harlem of doubly handicapped black masses engaged in the grim, daily struggle for existence in the midst of this whirlpool of white civilization. There are dramatic values in that Harlem, too; but they have hardly been touched. Writers of fiction, white and black have limited their stories to Harlem as a playground, and have ignored or not recognized the fundamental, relentless forces at work and the efforts to cope with them."[58] This "sterner aspect" of Harlem, as Johnson goes on to write, is for any writer willing and able to portray it an opportunity to capture the "real" Harlem. Indeed, the Harlem that Johnson portrays in *Autobiography* is distinct from its portrayal in other popular novels of the period. It is a portrayal of Harlem that would have necessarily belied the assumptions of readers who had come to expect merely the primitive and exotic. Instead, Johnson paints a complex portrait of the Harlem, revealing what W. E. B. Du Bois would later describe as the "curious cross-currents" that comprise the cultural landscape of the city.

One way to understand *Autobiography*, then, is to read it as a literary example of the standard of realism that Johnson describes in his own auto-biography. The experiences of the novel's protagonist bear some similarities to Johnson's own life. However, these instances in the text do not function primarily as autobiographical descriptions but rather as a means of under-standing the material circumstances of his life. Much like his own protago-nist, Johnson found himself betwixt and between his Southern birthplace of Jacksonville, Florida, and his adoptive home of New York City. When Johnson declares, "I was born to be a New Yorker," it is a declaration borne out of an acceptance of his alienation in the world (indeed, an embracing of it), for as Johnson writes, "if, among other requirements for happiness, one needs neighbors; that is, feels that he must be on friendly terms with the people who live next door . . . he is not born for a New Yorker."[59] Rather than the bucolic sense of place that extols the virtues of intimate connection and community, Johnson privileges a sense of liminality as a basis for self-identity. Even before he travels to New York for the first time, he describes the "dual sense of home" that characterized his sense of place and identity, having heard his parents talk about New York City as a veritable "homeland" from which they were seemingly exiled.[60] For this reason, he develops a dual sense of place and identity that positions him between Jacksonville and New York, between the intimate sense of belonging that defined his Southern existence and the individualistic cosmopolitanism that defined the urban spaces of the great Northern metropolis.

Autobiography is then an expression of the contradictions that framed Johnson's life. Rather than an autobiographical account of his actual experiences, the novel instead represents the paradox of his existence as a Black artist in a society that has not evolved an adequate place for him. Johnson himself embodies the contradictions that defines the experience of his protagonist, as he too lives betwixt and between the racist ideology of the color line that celebrated Black culture but subjugated Black people.[61] Johnson expresses this duality not only in terms of his marginalized place in American society, but also as it relates to the constraints placed on his work as an artist. Johnson poignantly describes this artistic circumspection in "The Dilemma of the Negro Author," writing, "if the Negro author selects white America as his audience he is bound to run up against many long-standing artistic conceptions about the Negro; against numerous conventions and traditions which through age have become binding; in a word, against a whole row of hard-set stereotypes which are not easily broken up."[62] This "dilemma" for Johnson was simply how to write *for* an audience expecting nothing more of him than a facile portrait of Black humanity. For Johnson, the "numerous conventions and traditions" that informed the popular white sentiment viewed Black people "in the brighter light" as a "simple, indolent, docile, improvident peasant."[63] However, "in a darker light," Black people were viewed in the most dehumanizing terms as "impulsive, irrational, passionate savage, reluctantly wearing a thin coat of culture."[64] Johnson's response to his dilemma is to envision a "fusion" of artistic perspectives that would necessarily appeal to both white and Black audiences—a paradoxical approach that acknowledges the fact that anything appealing to one side would invariably alienate the other.[65]

Johnson's paradoxical approach comes to fruition in *Autobiography*, making its republication in 1927 (two years after the publication of Alain Locke's seminal "New Negro" essay) especially timely. Indeed, Johnson's novel foregrounds the paradoxical terms (e.g., old/new; rural/urban; simple/complex) that underwrote the ideal of the New Negro, an ideal that reflected for many Black artists of the Harlem Renaissance the modern condition of Black folk in America. *Autobiography* does so by evoking a mock pastoral framework in a way that is similar to *Sport of the Gods*. However, Johnson advances Dunbar's critique of Southern pastoralism through his portrayal of a Black mulatto turned ex-colored man whose acute critical perspective tacitly challenges the normative structures of meaning that moor Southern culture and society. Unlike Dunbar's cautionary tale, *Autobiography* does not figure the act of migration as an immediate source of conflict or tension in novel. Rather, the culture of the South itself produces much of the conflict in the novel as its nameless protagonist struggles to enter into the "free-masonry" of his race. For this reason, the struggle for identity initiated by the act of migration occurs much earlier in *Autobiography*—well before its protagonist travels to New York City for the first time. Johnson's protagonist is already displaced by the accident of his birth, as he is born to a white man and his mulatto mistress. When he later struggles with questions of his own racial identity, he sets out on picaresque journey to discover the essential quality of his being as a person of color. The social contradictions he encounters in the course of his migrations (i.e., white supremacy, racial segregation, the presumption of Black inferiority) thereby create the internal conflict that will shade his narrative perspective, finally leading him to disavow his racial identity as a Black man. As my readings will show, his perspective reveals a mock pastoral sensibility that constantly ruminates on Southern culture and the unrealizable pastoral ideal it represents.

Black Migration as Identity Formation

Autobiography is the story of a nameless protagonist who is able to "pass" as white. Johnson's protagonist is born to a "mulatto" mother and white father; as a result, he appears white, although as a child he is unaware of his "racial mixture." He believes that he is white until it is revealed to him that he is Black by the principal of his school. After this realization, the protagonist flounders about until a dramatic oration by one of his Black classmates inspires him to take up the causes of his race: "I felt leap within me pride that I was coloured; and I began to form wild dreams of bringing glory and honour to the Negro race. For days I could talk of nothing else with my mother except my ambitions to be a great man, a great coloured man, to reflect credit on the race and gain fame for myself" (46).[66] Rather than extol the inherent virtues of rural Black folk culture, he constantly attempts to appropriate and refine these otherwise "raw materials," a pattern that produces a constant source of internal conflict throughout the novel.

The liminal status of its nameless and displaced protagonist is precisely what makes *Autobiography* a valuable text in understanding Black migration and the identity politics of the period. The dual perspective of the ex-colored man (who ultimately announces himself as neither Black nor white) produces what Henry Louis Gates Jr. calls a "freeze frame" narrative of African American cultural practice.[67] Gates argues that this narrative device "sto[ps] the novel's action so that white readers, uninitiated into the world of black culture behind the veil of race in America, would be forced to encounter, consider, and possibly admire the *complexity* of a culture which they prob-ably did not know existed."[68] I would add to Gates's assessment that the complexity of these scenes is registered by his radical subjectivity that places him perpetually outside the Black experience he is attempting to discern. Instead of describing Black cultural experience as an active participant, he more often assumes a liminal position that places him on the margins of that experience. It is precisely his unwillingness to embrace Black cultural experience that anticipates his radical departure from a racialized identity by the end of the novel.

Criticism of *Autobiography* has often focused on the unreliability of the ex-colored man whose liminal status places him on the margins of a Black cultural experience he ostensibly celebrates. M. Giulia Fabi, in describing the "ironic tone" of *Autobiography*, writes, "[the novel's] unreliable first-person narrator is indicative of a new interest in portraying how reality is filtered, recreated, and mystified by individual consciousness."[69] For Fabi, this "mystification" is more a result of the protagonist's "blindness" and "self-deception" than any conscious effort to problematize or understand his own experience. Kenneth Mostern, however, finds a greater sense of agency and self-recognition in the ex-colored man's account. In examining the ex-colored man's decision to forfeit his racial commitments and pass as white, Mostern writes, "If [his] narrative leads to a life of material success (coded white) rather than cultural creativity (coded colored), it is not that the racial conditions which could have provided the alternative possibility were unavailable to him."[70] The implication of Mostern's reading is that, while the fact of the narrator's "passing" complicates race, "it in no way calls into question [its] existence."[71] Mostern's reading emphasizes the subjective quality of the ex-colored man's experience but stops short of describing that experience as racially or culturally transformative.

Both readings are useful in that that they locate meaning in the novel as a product of the protagonist's subjective, "filtered reality," though they differ on the extent to which Johnson's protagonist truly apprehends the reality of his lived experience. My reading of the novel as a mock pastoral emphasizes how the ex-colored man's perspective attempts to interpret his experience while also constructing a version of that reality in the service of his satirical ends. He states at the beginning his desire "to gather up all the little tragedies of my life, and turn them into a practical joke on society" (3). Given this blatant admission by the narrator of his desire to subvert meaning in his story (to make it serviceable to his own satirical ends), it is important to recognize the discursive relationship between the narrator's initial descriptions of his experiences and his subsequent rational explanations of what it means. One way of reading the novel then is to emphasize how the protagonist defines these spaces of everyday lived experience as a liminal figure, whose mock pastoral sensibility precludes the possibility of embracing an ideal of the South as a source of Black cultural experience or an ideal of the North as a veritable promised land.

In describing his fictional account as a "cruel joke," Johnson's nameless protagonist embodies a mock pastoral perspective from the outset. Indeed, the satirical framework he establishes at the outset foreshadows the novel's ending, when he will disavow his identity as a Black man, but it also establishes the critical basis upon which he will navigate social spaces as a displaced migrant throughout the novel. This narrative perspective enables him to interpret the meaning of those spaces in response to his cultural displacement within them. As an arbiter of meaning in these spaces, he effectively changes his character, (literally as a passing figure) to adapt to the particular demands of the people and places he encounters throughout the course of his travels. In fact, Johnson initially toyed with the idea of calling the novel *The Chameleon*, though his publishers (thankfully) nixed the idea. The first instance of the protagonist's adaptability comes after his racial outing at school, when he learns that he is Black. His conscious decision to enter into the "freemasonry of the race" is followed by an attempt to read the requisite texts in order to facilitate his racial initiation: "I read with studious interest everything I could find relating to coloured men who had gained prominence. My heroes had been King David, Robert the Bruce; now Frederick Douglass was enshrined in the place of honour. When I learned that Alexandre Dumas was a coloured man, I re-read *Monte Cristo* and *The Three Guardsmen* with magnified pleasure" (24). That the protagonist "re-read . . . with magnified pleasure" the classical works of authors with whom he now shares a racial affinity suggests the self-reflexive mode of perception that will frequently color his reality. His interest in ragtime—a frenetic and modulating form of music—can be traced back to the kinetic sense of self the protagonist develops early in his life story. This racial and cultural adaptability allows the ex-colored man to walk on both sides of the color line in the rural and urban places he visits, thereby enabling him to pose as both a racial insider and as a detached spectator.

The protagonist's fluid autobiographical account attests to the double quality of his character, as indicated by his racially disavowed status as an "ex" person of color. In reality, he is neither Black nor white, but rather effectively betwixt and between the veil of racial difference as a both a negative and divided embodiment of the self. In his discussion of "ethnic autobiography," John Lowe points out that "immigrant American and African American

Life stories usually do include, but are virtually always read as containing, a bifurcated self."[72] Similarly, Johnson's ex-colored man exhibits a "bifurcated self" in that his affinities are divided between his "mother's people" (read Black folk) and the values of white society. This bifurcation represents two distinct images of the self that emerge from the contested aspects of his everyday lived experience—the rural versus the urban; folk versus cosmopolitan; white versus Black. In other words, Johnson's novel does not push toward a definition of essential Black experience so much as it attempts to posit in the figure of the ex-colored man a sense of racial and cultural fluidity.

The protagonist's detached perspective, along with his ability to "pass," thereby allows him to occupy both sides of the color line through the course of his travels. This becomes another way in which the ex-colored man subjectively frames his own reality. His divided self is the literal embodiment of Du Bois's concept of double consciousness, which the narrator provides his own account of after reading *The Souls of Black Folk*. Yet, the protagonist's racial identity also complicates Du Bois's concept of psychological duality. Because of his ability to "pass," the protagonist constantly shifts his racial identity within the "veil of racial difference." His racialized self is fluid throughout the novel, flitting back and forth between an acknowledgment of his father's influence and his "mother's people." And yet, as Lawrence Rodgers observes, the protagonist is constantly attempting to establish a "better and truer self" that will "bridge the gap between the folk sources of his most cherished musical forms [ragtime]" and the "mainstream values" of white society.[73]

The protagonist's desire to migrate to the North and later to Europe is motivated by the promise of self-identity that the transformative space of the city offers. In contrast, however, to the transformation the city promises, his accounts of Southern life reveal the static discourses of race and culture that operate there. He sarcastically points to the "generally accepted literary ideal" of Southern Black folk as comical buffoons. This ironic perspective can be read as a mock pastoral that extols Southern Black culture while tacitly critiquing its underlying terms:

This was my first real experience among rural coloured people, and all that I saw was interesting to me; but there was a great deal which does not require description at my hands; for log-cabins and plantations and dialect-speaking "darkies" are perhaps better known in American literature than any other single picture of our national life. Indeed, they form an ideal and exclusive literary concept of the American Negro to such an extent that *it is almost impossible to get the reading public to recognize him in any other setting*. [emphasis mine] (187)

On the other hand, the protagonist's description of life in the city reveals that life's complexity in comparison to his static description of Black rural life. The narrator's description of the "Club" is especially revealing of the differentiated quality of Black lived experience in the urban spaces of the city. As the narrator points out, "a great deal of money was spent there," a fact that owes to the class of Black people that came to the bar, a class that included "great prize-fighters," "famous jockeys" and "noted minstrels." In this regard, the "Club" becomes a symbol of Black achievement and social mobility, albeit circumscribed to the arenas of sport and entertainment. As the narrator points out, "the walls were literally covered with photographs or lithographs of every coloured man in America who had ever 'done anything.'" (104). The ex-colored man's description of the "Club" also reveals the diverging concepts of race and Blackness that operate there as well. Blackness can be valued or parodied in the "Club," where Black performance is shaped by the demands of a white audience who come there "slumming." The narrator describes a Black minstrel who "whenever he responded to a request to 'do something,' never essayed anything below a reading from Shakespeare" (106). This artistic rebellion of sorts is nevertheless met with racist condescension, as the same man "made people laugh at the size of his mouth, while he carried in his heart a burning ambition to be a tragedian" (106). The contested status of the Black performer's basic humanity is not lost on the narrator, who laments that "after all he did play a part in a tragedy" (106).

The protagonist's description of the "Club" also reveals the complex ways in which race relations exist there. The Harlem nightclub of the 1920s was frequently a segregated space. But it was also a space where Black people and white people could socially interact. Rudolph Fisher describes this social aspect of the Harlem nightclub in "The Caucasian Storms Harlem." There he writes, "They're not like theatres and concert halls. You don't just go to a cabaret and sit back and wait to be entertained. You get out on the floor and join the pow-wow and help entertain yourself. Granted that white people have long enjoyed the Negro entertainment as a diversion, is it not something different, something more, when they bodily throw themselves into Negro entertainment in cabarets?"[74] Fisher gestures toward an optimistic reading of this cultural phenomenon, the practice of "slumming" when white folks cross the color line into Black cultural spaces. For Fisher, Black and white people could find a kind of common ground with each other in the culturally dynamic space of the Harlem nightclub. Therefore, where whites had preceded them, "Now Negroes go to their own cabarets to see how white people act."[75] This level of interaction between Black and white people in the Harlem nightclub gives Fisher reason to believe that one day it may "extend far beyond cabarets."[76] He concludes that, if nothing else, "maybe they are at last learning to speak our language."[77]

The ex-colored man's account similarly attempts to bridge the gap between the everyday experience of Black folks and the normative values of white society. His extended account of the "Club" focuses on the quality of interaction between Black and white people in that space. Just as he has attempted to do throughout his narrative, he tries to forge a link between the cultural practices of Black folk (e.g., ragtime and language) and the social expectations and standards of white folk. Indeed, the protagonist reproduces a cultural integrationist model that resembles one of his boyhood idols, W. E. B. Du Bois.[78] The logic of his position assumes that, in order for Black people to make a place for themselves in society, they would need to establish a legitimate cultural basis for their integration into white society. The ex-colored man is compelled to become a classical ragtime musician because he believes that the "raw materials" of Black folk culture can and ought to be *refined*, thereby serving as a bridge between the races. Therefore, his initial desire to enter into the "freemasonry of the race" is replaced by a desire to integrate Black folk culture (and himself) into white society.

However, the protagonist's goal of establishing a viable sense of place and identity in the urban North is frustrated when he witnesses the lynching and burning of a Black man in the rural setting of Georgia. This brutal scene of violence spurs the narrator to a disavowal of his musical and cultural aspirations and forces him toward a conscious realization of his contested racial self: "It was over before I realized that time had elapsed. Before I could make myself believe that what I saw was really happening, I was looking at a scorched post, a smouldering fire, blackened bones, charred fragments sifting down through coils of chain; and the smell of burnt flesh—human flesh—was in my nostrils" (187).

As the narrator cloaks himself in a veil of protective "whiteness," he takes in the circus-like atmosphere once again as a detached observer. The spectacle of the lynched Black man, however, forces him into the uncomfortable position of having to identify with the victim of this brutal scene. The immutable fact of what has occurred is registered for the narrator through the visceral experience of smelling "burnt flesh" and viewing "blackened bones." These images cannot be rationalized away, nor can the narrator simply avert his gaze as he has done throughout the novel. Instead, his eyes are transfixed by this scene of violence as though it reflects the only moment of certainty in his entire account. Indeed, the scene of lynching constitutes a fixed site of meaning, where "every sign of degeneracy" is stamped onto the body of the victim. For the narrator, this inscription of the lynched body

also extends to an entire race of people "who could be so dealt with" puni-
tively. This tragic generalization is both a final realization and a negation of
the narrator's identity as a Black man. He then resolves in this moment to
"neither disclaim the black race nor claim the white race" (190). This last
suspension of racial subjectivity places him in a permanent liminal position
betwixt and between rural and urban, Black and white, real and constructed.

The novel's horrifying image of a lynched and burned Black man registers the failure of the ex-colored man's ideal of cultural ascent. This scene
of violence also represents the logical outcome of Johnson's mock pastoral perspective. The South is finally revealed here as a space incapable of
sustaining Black self-determination. Anticipating a similar scene in Jean
Toomer's novel *Cane*, the pastoral imagery and symbolism of the Southern
section is completely undone by the gratuitous violence Johnson's protagonist witnesses.[79] His subsequent attempt to rationalize this racial violence
by making Black people the direct object of his criticism further underscores the failure of his cultural vision. Not only does he resolve to quit his
dream of elevating the raw materials of Black culture, but he also decides to
renounce his claim to Blackness altogether. In this final disavowal of racial
and cultural identity, Johnson's ex-colored man becomes the embodiment
of the mock pastoral mode, a mock figure himself symbolizing the erasure
of Blackness in a Southern society where Black people can be summarily
executed with absolute impunity.

Anticipating Ralph Ellison's observations, the ex-colored man is both
literally and figuratively "no-where" by the end of his narrative.[80] Although
he finds a comfortable place for himself as a real estate agent, his permanent
disavowal of racial identity leaves him perpetually displaced in the promised
land of the Northern city. As a Black migrant who can "pass for white," he has
access to a world in which he can live without the stigma of race. However,
his deferred dream of becoming a classical musician, symbolized vividly by
the "yellow pages" of his sheet music, marks a symbolic landscape and place
of belonging that is no longer available to him. The protagonist, in the hope
that he can establish a "safe" existence as a white man, also casts the most
progressive aspects of Black culture and everyday experience aside. Thus,
he relegates himself to a position of racial and cultural anonymity, thereby
denying himself access to his "birthright," which he has in turn traded for
a "mess of pottage." This final inscription of his account offers an implicit
warning to those seeking to cast off the albatross of racial identity for the
spoils of mainstream society.

The ex-colored man's equivocal perspective on race and culture, his subsequent suspension of racial identity, and his permanent status as a displaced

migrant are expressions of the mock pastoral. Johnson's mock pastoral reveals the failures of Southern society and the social limitations of Northern cities. Like Dunbar's *Sport of the Gods,* Johnson's novel anticipates the prominent themes that would define the genre of the Black migration novel for decades. *Autobiography* thus stands as a precursor to the Black migration novels of the 1920s set in New York's Harlem neighborhood. Indeed, Johnson's novel framed what was perhaps the most significant problem facing Black writers of the Harlem Renaissance: that is, the problem of representing Black Southern culture without mythologizing it or minimize its importance. These authors would seek to establish a narrative of place in the city that reflected the unique challenges faced by displaced and deracinated Southern Black folk in the heart of the city. The Black Harlem of the 1920s that James Weldon Johnson once feigned as the "climax of the incongruous" was in fact a place waiting to be inscribed with the meaning of its own history.

Chapter Two

"WHEN THE SUN GOES DOWN"

The Ghetto Pastoral Mode in Jean Toomer's *Cane*

The 1920s ushered in a period of optimism for Northern Black urban populations. Harlem emerged as the epicenter of Black cultural production. Vibrant Black communities were formed in other Northern cities as well, notably in places such as Chicago, Pittsburgh, and Washington, DC. The debate over Black migration seemed resolved by the human tide of Black migrants pouring across the Mason–Dixon line—a tide whose numbers would easily exceed one million between 1917 and 1920.[1] Just as the Great Migration itself had given rise to Black migration fiction more than a decade earlier, the present demographic changes would have a profound influence on both the nascent genre of Black migration literature as well as the literary flourishing of the coming Harlem Renaissance. In addition, the migration would alter the topographical and symbolic motifs associated with urban spaces in the North, giving rise to a conception of the city as a place that could provide viable spaces for Black culture and expression. Indeed, the symbolic task of envisioning a place of belonging in the city for Black migrant populations was for these Harlem authors the impetus of their writing about the Black urban experience.

Jean Toomer's *Cane*, a work comprised of lyrical pastiche, short vignettes, and poetical pieces, is widely considered the inaugural literary masterpiece of the Harlem Renaissance.[2] When *Cane* was published in 1923, the migration of Black Southerners to Northern cities had already peaked to its highest levels in almost two decades.[3] The novel was at once a harbinger of the literary experimentalism that would characterize the modern New Negro movement, and a forbearer of the new thematic and social concerns that migration novelists would adopt during the Renaissance.[4] Prior to the novel's publication, the bloody race riots that occurred during the Red Summer of 1919 had already made apparent the social divisions that would demarcate the racial boundaries of Jim Crow Northern cities, thereby establishing both the material and symbolic contours of Black urban life in the North. These instances of racial violence further galvanized the resolve of Black migrants to establish their "place" in the urban North, through direct means if neces-sary.[5] *Cane*'s appearance during this period of social and demographic change marks a pivotal moment in the emerging genre of Black migration literature, as it reflects both the cautionary tone of earlier migration novels as well as the growing urban optimism of the period. Unlike the previous migration novels considered, *Cane* goes beyond the artistic boundaries of urban real-ism in its representation of Black urban life. The symbolic presence of folk culture in the urban spaces depicted in *Cane*'s Northern section attests to the dialectical relationship between rural and urban modes of experience in the novel. In this sense, the Northern section of the novel casts an elegiac image of Southern Black experience that is both a source of conflict as well as continuity for its migrant characters.

The formal division between Northern and Southern settings in the text establishes the cultural displacement of migration as an explicit problem. More specifically, these separate sections, when viewed together, reveal the cultural rift that emerged between the rural folk traditions of Southern Black culture and the postmigration, urban experience of Northern Black popu-lations. In this regard, *Cane* comes close to the thematic form of earlier migration novels in that it figures this cultural rift as the result of the social displacement that Black people experienced in Northern cities after the Great Migration. Unlike those novels, however, *Cane* produces an alternative mapping of Black urban experience that does not foreclose the possibility of social ascent in the city. In other words, the novel complicates the tradi-tional rural-urban dichotomy that defined previous works of Black migra-tion literature—instead revealing an alternative cityscape that incorporates into its constitutive spaces a reconfiguration of both ideals. The result is a "ghetto pastoral" representation of Black cultural experience in both rural and urban settings in the novel.[6]

Michael Denning's description of the ghetto pastoral is again useful in reading Black migration novels like *Cane*. Denning points out that ghetto pastoral stories were both aspirational and realistic in their account of immi-grant life in the big city.[7] According to Denning, these stories sought to provide a more accurate portrayal of ethnic working-class experience in contrast to traditional pastoral narratives, which privileged a transcendent pastoral ideal in response to the alienating aspects of modern society. The ghetto pastoral narrative instead revealed the ways in which ethnic and racial categories "mapped" the experience of working-class immigrants in the city. These were stories of displaced immigrants in the city attempting to reimagine themselves in relation to a pastoral landscape "back home." However, they were also stories about how race and ethnicity complicated that transformative ideal. As Denning writes, "Ethnicity and race had become the modality through which working class peoples experienced their lives and mapped their communities."[8]

Denning offers as examples of the ghetto pastoral mode the work of authors such as Mike Gold, Claude McKay, and Anzia Yezierska, novelists whose works arose out of the proletarian moment of the 1920s and 1930s. Ghetto pastoral novels such as McKay's *Home to Harlem* and Gold's *Jews Without Money* revealed the ways in which race and ethnicity challenged the transcendent ideal of a green landscape that was at the core of conventional pastoral narratives. Indeed, these ghetto pastoral narratives portrayed a contested urban landscape composed of the old and the new, past and present—at once bringing together the symbolic elements of ethnic folk culture and the harsh material realities of urban life. Rather than the boundless potential expressed in traditional pastoral narratives, ghetto pastorals were stories that revealed how racial and ethnic boundaries delimited the lives of displaced (im)migrants. At the same time, these stories expressed the ways in which migrants pushed against these boundaries to create liminal spaces of existence, spaces formed at the interstices between the pastoral dream of transcendence and the urban realities of "working class tenements, sweatshop and factory labor, and cheap mass entertainments."[9]

Cane's version of the ghetto pastoral represents an inaugural representation of the form in the Black migration novel. The novel revises the traditional pastoral form made popular in the nineteenth century. Whereas the traditional pastoral was a symbolic testament of the individual's relationship to the natural world, Toomer's ghetto pastoral work acknowledges the permanent displacement of Black folk in either the rural South or the urban North. Rather than romanticize Black Southern culture, Toomer figures the Southern pastoral as a faded dream, and ideal that reflects the failure of the South to provide a viable space for Black, folk culture and expression. More pessimistic in its outlook than traditional pastorals, *Cane* dramatizes the disconnection between the old materials of Black Southern folk culture and the modern expression of Black urban experience in Northern cities after the Great Migration. It is precisely an inability to reconcile rural and urban modes of experience in that text that suspends the possibility of an "authentic reattachment"[10] to a folk past, an explicit problem that had shaped earlier migration narratives, most notably Paul Laurence Dunbar's *The Sport of the Gods*. As my specific reading will show, Toomer's novel marshals a ghetto pastoral ideal as a way of attending to the problem of displacement that had figured earlier Black migration novels. Thus, Toomer marshals the ghetto pastoral mode a means of expressing the liminal status of Black migrants.

Criticism of *Cane* has often focused on its contested status as novel. Darwin Turner once wrote of Jean Toomer's literary masterpiece that "[*Cane*] inspires critical rhapsodies rather than analysis."[11] Turner's observation is suggestive of the critical challenges that *Cane* poses. While there is no consensus regarding *Cane*'s formal structure, critics have often described it in thematic terms as a pastoral work. Bernard Bell's reading of *Cane* as "a pastoral work, contrasting the values of uninhibited, unlettered black rustics with those of the educated, class consciousness black bourgeoisie," privileges the lyrical elements of the novel and its indebtedness to an "Afro American tradition of music as a major structural device."[12] Yet his analysis here only extends to the poetic pieces that intersperse the novel without comparing them to the prose narratives that provide a thematic and structural counterpoint to them. Lucinda MacKethan also offers a reading of the novel as a pastoral narrative, arguing that Toomer "mold[ed] [*Cane*] into a version of Southern pastoral perceived with the black man's double vision of deep belonging and forced alienation"[13] Although instructive, MacKethan's description of Toomer's "ironic pastoral vision" in *Cane* does not adequately attend to the rural and urban conflict that frames the novel's portrayal of culturally displaced Black people in the North. If, indeed, Toomer's Black migrant characters possess a "double vision," it is one that is necessarily complicated and always obscured by their liminal subject position betwixt and between rural and urban modes of experience.

One way to adjudicate these divergent appraisals of the novel is to read *Cane* as a ghetto pastoral, a variant of the complex pastoral form that foregrounds the conflict necessarily inscribed within stories of deracinated (im)migrant peoples. Leo Marx defined complex pastoralism as the veritable "machine in the Garden," his classical metaphor describing the dual trajectory of American society in the industrial age. Marx's interpretation clarifies the dialectic that forms the basis for the ghetto pastoral mode as he describes the work of American authors whose work acknowledged both the symbolic potency of the green landscape and the progressive potential of the urban cityscape: "The work of Faulkner, Frost, Hemingway, and West comes to mind. Again and again, they invoke the image of the green landscape—a terrain either wild or, if cultivated, rural—as a symbolic repository of meaning and value. But at the same time, they acknowledge the power of a counterforce, a machine or some other symbol of the forces that have stripped the old ideal of most, if not all, or its meaning. Complex pastoralism, to put it another way, acknowledges the reality of history."[14] Marx's last point is revealing, as it suggests historical materialism as the conceptual basis for the complex pastoral mode. The "reality of history" is, as Karl Marx put it, a product of class conflict. This is precisely the distinguishing feature of complex pastoralism—its acknowledgment of the contradictions inherent in modern capitalist societies. That is to say, while the complex pastoral mode posits the ideal of transcendence in the form of a symbolic green landscape, it simultaneously acknowledges the intractably built structures of modern society.

As a variant of complex pastoralism, ghetto pastoral narratives reveal the ways in which racial and ethnic conflict reflect the realities of history. The ghetto pastoral narrative figures the ethnic- or working-class neighborhood as a communal space where displaced (im)migrants can acquire a sense of place and identity. However, although these communal spaces are represented as sites of identity formation, they are also places where racial and ethnic demarcation occur. Denning describes the force of history in reinforcing the racial and ethnic boundaries of the ethnic working-class neighborhood: "The geographical boundaries of the community are reinforced by historical boundaries; the ghetto pastoral continuity runs up against a historical block. What is the history of these relatively recent communities, formed by migrations, cut off from any past *that inhabits the streets, buildings, and even words?*"[15] Ironically, then, even as the ghetto pastoral mode privileges race and ethnicity as communal ideals, it also reveals the way in which social structures formed on the basis of race and ethnicity delimit the experience of the immigrant characters of these stories.

Cane's version of the ghetto pastoral similarly reveals the force of history in shaping the lives of displaced Black migrants. The formal division of the novel between the rural Georgia landscape and various urban locales in the North establishes a tacit rural-urban dichotomy. However, *Cane's* ghetto pastoral mode complicates the traditional rural-urban, Southern-Northern dichotomy that formed the thematic basis for the Black migration novels of the 1920s. These novels portrayed the South as a point of departure (both physically and culturally) while portraying the North as a veritable (although imperfect) promised land. Rather than a place of no return, Toomer's South is a symbolic repository of meaning. It is a place that represents the life blood of Black culture and lived experience. But it is also a place in which such experience exists only in memory. Although this aspect of the novel is frequently read as expressing Toomer's "swan song" for Black folk culture in the South, it is perhaps better understood as expressing an elegiac pastoral vision. Toomer commemorates the potency of Black folk culture as a symbolic form even (or especially) as Black migration was radically altering the cultural landscape in the North. Ironically then, Toomer constructs Southern culture as a potent signifier of Black identity in a historical period that saw the massive exodus of Black Southerners into Northern cities. It is precisely this elegiac pastoral vision that forms the basis for the ghetto pastoral mode in the novel. The ghetto pastoral mode in the novel thus reverses the symbolic trajectory of Black migration by evoking elements of Black Southern culture in the places and spaces of the North. Toomer's characters must then struggle to imagine a place for themselves in the symbolic nexus between Southern and Northern cultural spaces.

A novel widely considered to be the inaugural literary masterpiece of the Harlem Renaissance, *Cane* anticipates the problem of urban displacement that would shape the literature of this period.[16] The Northern section of the novel figures the city through the artificial glow of "arc-lights" and the symmetrical shapes of tree-lined boulevards. But it is also a city that is deeply divided along racial lines. Unlike in the pastoral South, however, these racial lines are reinforced by the built structures of the city—structures that both contain and separate different races. The contrived order of the Northern city contrasts with the symbolic, but eroding, order of the Southern landscape depicted in the novel's opening section. Yet, in the midst of this built city, Toomer's Black characters struggle to reconcile their racially proscribed place in this social order with the potent ideal of Southern pastoralism. Like the young trees described in the story "Avey" that will inevitably outgrow their boxes, the Black characters of the Northern section of the novel push toward the margins of their enclosed urban spaces and the lost cultural forms of their Southern pastoral roots. The convergence of this Southern pastoral vision with the limitations of Northern urban spaces produces in these narratives and vignettes both a sense of unresolved conflict, as well as a prevailing sense of liminality, wherein characters struggle to exist as if between two kinds of reality—two modes of perception—neither affirming nor denying the primacy of the other. As David Nicholls observes, the spectral presence of Black folk culture in the novel attests to the potency of the pastoral vision of transcendence.[17] But as the novel's Northern section reveals, this pastoral vision runs up against the racially demarcated spaces of the Northern city. The novel's thematic structure as a ghetto pastoral thus diverges into two themes: that of Black culture, on the one hand, and lived experience, on the other. In short, it is an experience that exists at the convergence of rural and urban modalities. Moreover, it is an experience divided between narrow conceptions of race and transcendent forms of self-expression.

Criticism of *Cane* similarly describes this dialectical representation of Black experience in the novel. William M. Ramsey argues that "Toomer's authorial stance actually was both in and outside the South, and this bivalent rhetorical perspective made possible *Cane*'s unique creative vision."[18] For Ramsey, this means the figuration of "two Souths" in the novel. He explains that "one is a temporal South of disturbing historical oppression and despairing lack of progress. The other is what could be called Toomer's transcendent or 'eternal South,' existing above time and social particulars."[19] While Ramsey admits that this unique rhetorical perspective "makes *Cane* so hard to define and so unique to encounter," viewing the novel as representative of the ghetto pastoral mode also works to clarify the novel's rhetoric.[20] The force of history or what Denning refers to as the "historical bloc" is the central source of complication in the ghetto pastoral mode as it reveals the ways in which race, class and gender systematically shape the lives of culturally displaced Black folk in the city. Toomer's migration narrative similarly reflects the historical reality of Black migrants forced to leave the South—a place that simultaneously provides the cultural foundation of their collective identity even as it also represents the oppressive conditions that force their leaving.

Other critics have echoed the view that *Cane* is a novel deeply influenced by the historical realities of Black migration and cultural displacement. David Nicholls's description of *Cane*'s formal structure as pastiche seeks to "read history back into [the novel]."[21] Responding to the common reading of *Cane* as a dialectical text "progressing toward wholeness," Nicholls offers an alternative interpretation that views the novel as a manifold work reflecting multiple settings and perspectives: "Rather than seeking Toomer's incorporation of rural and urban settings into *Cane* as productive of a synthetic dialectic striving toward wholeness, we might instead see the book as presenting multiple settings though which to interpret the changes affecting 1920s America. *Cane* understands that the widespread effects of this historic change occurred in different sites and that they could be interpreted through different forms of representation."[22] For Nicholls, reading the novel as pastiche does not mean viewing it as "a benign plurality of points of view," however. Instead, he sees "pattern of interests" emerge in the novel.[23] I would argue that it is precisely this simultaneous trajectory of the novel toward literary pastiche and organic unity that marks it as a ghetto pastoral narrative. Nicholls is right to assert that the novel's manifold form produces a necessary tension in the narrative that reflects the historical movement(s) of Black people during the Great Migration. One way of understanding how the novel registers meaning within or makes sense of its own complex form is to examine its aesthetic investment in the ghetto pastoral mode. As my readings will demonstrate, Toomer's ghetto pastoral vision in the novel gestures toward a cultural dialecticism in which neither rural nor urban is privileged as a signifier of Black culture and lived experience. In short, *Cane*'s ghetto pastoral narrative posits Black culture as a liminal experience—an experience displaced as it were both between and within rural and urban settings.

(Re)imagining the South

Cane was published at a time when the migration of Black Southerners into Northern cities was fundamentally altering both the geographical and conceptual boundaries of Black experience. The conflict of rural and urban modes of being it depicts is at once a general reflection of this history as well as the personal history of its author. Toomer's experience as a "person of color" reveals some of the underlying conflicts that shaped both the novel and the period in which it was written. Indeed, part of the creative impetus for writing *Cane* stemmed from Toomer's belief that "Negro Folk culture" was gradually disappearing in its physical form, even as he and other Renaissance authors sought to reproduce this material in their literature. In a letter to Waldo Frank, a close friend of Toomer and a financial contributor to his artistic efforts, Toomer conveys his concern that the Negro folk culture he revealed in *Cane* was more myth than reality. A section of the letter is worth quoting at length here,

> As an entity, the race [of Black people] is loosing [*sic*] its body, and its soul is approaching a common soul. If one holds his eyes to individuals and sections, race is starkly evident, and racial continuity seems assured. One is even led to believe that the thing we call Negro beauty will always be attributable to a clearly defined physical source. But the fact is, that if anything comes up now, pure Negro, it will be a *swan-song*. Dont [*sic*] let us fool ourselves, brother: the Negro of the folk-song has all but passed away: the Negro of the emotional church is fading. A hundred years from now these Negroes, if they exist at all will live in art. And I believe that a vague sense of this fact is the driving force behind the art movements directed toward them today.[24]

Toomer's belief in the essential literariness of Black folk culture also suggests an understanding of race as something that is ascribed to individuals as a social construction rather than something rooted in biology. For example, when his publisher Horace Liveright admonished him not to "dodge" his "colored blood," Toomer responded by writing "my racial composition and my position in the world are realities which I alone may determine."[25] In the same letter to his publisher, Toomer assumes the paradoxical position of claiming to be a "Negro" in his published writings, while maintaining a kind of racial neutrality in person: "As a B[oni] and L[iveright] author, I make the distinction between my fundamental position and the position which your publicity department may wish to establish for me in order that *Cane* reach as large a public as possible."[26] Toomer's willingness to identify himself as a "Negro artist" was a practical decision, at least from his standpoint as an aspiring Black artist in the 1920s. He knew that the "Negro" was in vogue, especially at a time when "Harlem" was synonymous with "hip," making it beneficial for artists to be associated with anything Black. Yet, his unwillingness to identify himself as a "Negro person" suggests the more general symbolic rift between Black artists and intellectuals and Negro folk culture. The emerging racialism of the period was for Toomer an opportunity to explore similar themes in his literature; beyond this immediate aesthetic project, however, Toomer viewed race and racial categories as anachronistic to human development.

Toomer adopted the persona of a racial outsider, even as a distinctive coterie of Black authors was coming to prominence in the decade of the Harlem Renaissance. He becomes in many ways the literal embodiment of Johnson's ex-colored man, neither affirming his racial commitments nor entirely denying them altogether. Ironically, in a letter to James Weldon Johnson, Toomer refused the former author's request for material to be included in his upcoming anthology of Black writers. Toomer offered this explanation: "As regards art I particularly hold this view. I see our art and literature as primarily American art and literature. I do not see it as Negro, Anglo Saxon, and so on . . . Accordingly, I must withdraw from all things which emphasize or tend to emphasize racial or cultural divisions. I must align myself with things which stress the experiences, forms, and spirit we have in common."[27]

Despite his constant hedging, Toomer felt himself "spiritually" compelled as an artist to identify with some aspect of his African American linage, although he would continue to express mixed feelings about his role as a writer of Negro culture and experience. Toomer's first visit to the South exposed many of the internal conflicts that would continue to manifest themselves in the author's personal life and in his literature. Toomer more than once wrote about the spiritual awakening he experienced during his visit

to Sparta, Georgia, in 1921. He served as substitute principal at Sparta Agri-
cultural and Industrial Institute, where he wrote a number of the Southern
sketches that would later comprise *Cane*.[28] After his short stay in the South,
Toomer believed he was indelibly linked in spirit to a distinct "Negro" experience—an experience that unavoidably began to shape his writing and would
become the inspiration for *Cane*. However, despite his desire to define himself
as simply an "American," Toomer would admit something of the opposite in
an August 19, 1922, letter to *Liberator*'s editor, Claude McKay. The account he
provides therein reveals an artist torn between the social acceptance of the
"other" and the "rich dark beauty" of Black Southern culture:

> Within the last two or three years . . . my growing need for artistic
> expression has pulled me deeper and deeper into the Negro group.
> And as my powers of receptivity increased, I found myself loving it in
> a way that I could never love the *other*. It has stimulated and fertilized
> whatever creative talent I may contain within me. A visit to Georgia
> last fall was the starting point of almost everything of worth that I
> have done. I heard folk-songs come from the lips of Negro peasants.
> I saw the *rich durk* [sic] beauty that I had heard many false accents
> about, and of which till then, I was somewhat skeptical. And a deep
> part of my nature, a part that I had repressed, sprang suddenly to life
> and responded to them. Now, I cannot conceive of myself as aloof and
> separated. [emphasis mine][29]

Toomer's awakening to Black culture came at a time when Harlem writers
were also looking to the South in search of a usable past. And, like Toomer,
many of these Black artists were similarly torn between their obligation to
portray the "Negro" in his own terms while also representing the lived experience of Black people as art for mass consumption. Alain Locke described the
revisionist work of these authors as "a revaluation . . . of the Negro in terms of
his artistic endowments and cultural contributions, past and prospective."[30]
Richard Wright would later describe the work of Black authors during the
Harlem Renaissance in decidedly more derisive terms. As Wright quipped,
these authors "entered the court of American public opinion dressed in the
knee pants of servility."[31] Reflecting both positions, *Cane* reveals the necessary
tension that informs the project of representing Black vernacular culture as
a product of the rural South even as it was transformed (in both theory and
practice) in the urban spaces of the North. The Northern influence on Black
vernacular culture (re)shaped vernacular forms and practices such as Jazz
and the Blues. The cultural influence of places like Chicago, Washington, DC,

and New York City on Black vernacular culture was both undeniable and multifaceted. On the one hand, Black artists, writers, and musicians flourished in these places, most notably in Harlem, a place that had inspired the New Negro movement and the Harlem Renaissance. On the other hand, the "prurient demand" of the masses also meant that Black culture was a source of entertainment for scores of white patrons who frequented these places. The dilemma this created for Black artisans and writers was whether to portray Black people as authentically as they could or to trade on the racial stereotypes that white audiences demanded.

Toomer's personal experience of visiting the South serves as a model for his portrayal of Southern Black culture in *Cane*. Toomer believed he came to the South too late in history to experience Black folk culture for himself, a similar plight for his characters who find themselves in a Southern setting where Black vernacular culture has receded into distant memory. Indeed, Toomer's description of the Southern landscape evokes images of death and blight. His portrait of the land is elegiac in tone and finite in scope. Gone are the Black folk who endured slavery while singing songs of hope and freedom. They have been replaced by a generation of Black migrants no longer moored to a Southern Black vernacular experience, no longer hopelessly working the land in order to get ahead. Indeed, they are frustrated sharecroppers, scorned lovers, exploited women, and restless youth, all hoping to get out, to get away. They are portrayed as constantly in motion, but their momentum is always carrying them away from the South, away from an ideal of "home" rooted in the historical practices and way of life that once defined Black culture there. However, while they cannot marshal an authentic Black Southern experience in the receding cultural landscape of the South, they can (re)appropriate the symbolic terms of that experience in the ghetto pastoral spaces of the Northern city. Like the author of *Cane*, they too must reconfigure the symbolic terms of their racial and cultural identity, beginning with the shattered pieces of a bygone Black vernacular culture in the South. Their experience as Black migrants is, therefore, replete with endless placards that denote the symbolic vestiges of a Southern rural and Black vernacular culture in the Northern city. Indeed, like the sign that punctuated my experience in Chicago by encouraging people to "eat at the Mississippi Café," these symbolic signposts recall a familiar if also tumultuous past reminding us of the contested quality of Black migrant experience.

The Southern landscape in the Georgia section of the novel symbolizes a way of life that is gradually coming to an end. The blighted soil of the South can no longer provide an adequate means for growth and renewal. The Southern landscape, always a potent symbol of pastoral growth and renewal, is described in elegiac terms signifying death and decline. For instance, the central image of cane fields in the Southern section of the novel is emblematic of the declining system of agriculture in the South of the 1920s. The domestic sugar cane industry in the United States had steadily declined during the period between 1919 and 1921. In fact, when *Cane* was published in 1923, sugar cane prices had plummeted from fourteen cents a pound to a little less than four cents a pound.[32] Appropriately, the core image around which the novel revolves is marked by social and economic decline. Indeed, the image of cane fields reveals the duality of Southern Black life—a life that was as much deformed by the cycles of planting and harvesting as it was sustained by them. Prior to the Great Migration, agriculture was both a source of labor and a way of life for Black Southerners. The cultivation of cotton and various other cash crops had given to Southern life a natural order upon which Black people attempted to find meaning and purpose in their lives. The cry from an earlier generation of southern Black people for "forty acres and a mule" idealized a desire for Black self-determination rooted in the very soil of the South. However, just as that slogan reminded Black Southerners of the failures of Reconstruction, so too had the realities of Southern agriculture reminded them of their subjugated place in the "New South." The decline of Southern agriculture during this period because of economic factors such as the boll weevil and because of social factors arising from unscrupulous sharecropping practices, frustrated any sustained vision of Black self-determination.[33]

Reflecting this history, the stories of this section reveal the plight of women whose lives are barren and unyielding like the land. "Becky" is the story of a white woman who gives birth to two "Negro sons." Because she has violated the taboo of miscegenation, both the Black and white people in the rural Southern community ostracize her. The story reveals the shared values of Black and white folk that give rise to racial norms in the South. It also demonstrates the instability of those racial norms as both Black and white people in the story attempt to deny the impact of Becky's transgression in this Georgia community. The story of "Carma" is "the crudest melodrama," as it invokes the common theme in Black literature of marital infidelity and domestic instability (15).[34] Carma, a woman "strong as any man," is unfaithful to her lover while he is away working for a contractor (16). When he returns to find rumors of the affair circulating around town, he exacts vengeance on the nearest man he believes to be the culprit. The story demonstrates the conflict that arises from the permanent displacement of Black men in the domestic space of the home and within the larger community, as well as the permanently diminished status of Black women in both spheres of existence.

The remaining stories of this opening section ("Fern," "Esther," and "Blood Burning Moon") focus on the circumscribed lives of women torn between their sexual roles and their desire for self-recognition.

The male perspective registered in this section is more hopeful of realizing the pastoral dream symbolized by the Southern landscape. The speaker of the poem "Song of the Son" is a migrant returning home to dusky Georgia. As one of its prodigal sons, the narrator returns to the soil of his birth only to find a "parting soul in song" lamenting the passing of a people and its way of life (17). The narrator has returned in time to witness the last vestiges of this life but not in time to prevent its inevitable passing:

> O land and soil, red soil and sweet-gum tree,
> So scant of grass, so profligate of pines,
> Now just before an epoch's sun declines
> Thy son, in time, I have returned to thee
> Thy son, I have in time returned to thee.
> In time, for thought the sun is setting on
> A song-lit race of slaves, it has not set;
> Though late, O soil, it is not too late yet
> To catch thy plaintive soul, leaving, soon gone,
> Leaving, to catch thy plaintive soul soon gone. (17)

The hope that something remains of this passing life is registered in the narrator's first apostrophe. The "soil" sends forth its "plaintive soul" even though the culture that once planted its roots there has all but passed away. The narrator's second apostrophe evokes the image of "Negro Slaves," painting them in this earthly portrait as "dark purple ripened plums," whose fruit bears the memory of that ancestry. In this last image of the fruit bearing plum tree, there is hope that a life that once was will forever be; the seed it sends forth becomes for the narrator: "An everlasting song, a singing tree, / Caroling softly souls of slavery, / What they were, and what they are to me, / Caroling softly souls of slavery" (17). While the life of a "song-lit race of slaves" has forever passed away, the Southern landscape provides its memorial and attests to its lasting influence. The fading away of this "song-lit race of slaves" from a practical way of life into an ethereal symbolic presence is indicative of Toomer's elegiac pastoral vision. The novel registers here an implicit hope that this lasting folk song may provide a cultural basis for ordering the lives of Black people following the social and economic upheavals of the 1920s.

This pastoral vision of Black Southern life, however, completely unravels in the last story of the Georgia section, where the impending doom of the "blood moon" becomes a powerful symbol of disorder and chaos. The atmospheric symbolism of the story constantly gestures toward the macabre and the tragic: "Up from the skeleton stone walls, up from the rotting floor boards and the solid hand-sewn beams of oak of the pre-war cotton factory, dusk came. Up from the dusk the full moon came. Glowing like a fired pine-knot, it illumined the great door and soft showered the Negro shanties aligned along the single street of factory town. The full moon in the great door was an omen. Negro women improvised songs against its spell" (39). The tragedy implicit in this stark imagery will mean the death of two men, Bob Stone and Tom Burwell, both of whom love the same woman, Louisa. Bob Stone, a white man, loved Louisa, and "by the way the world reckons things, he had won her" (39). Tom Burwell, a Black man, also loved her, "but working in the fields all day, and far away from her, gave him no chance to show it" (39). The dilemma this creates for both men comes to a head when each man learns of the other's affection for Louisa. Toomer figures this climactic moment of recognition for each man as signaling the loss of a natural pastoral order: "[Bob Stone] got to his feet and walked calmly to their meeting place. No Louisa. Tom Burwell had her. Veins in his forehead bulged and distended. Saliva moistened the dried blood on his lips. He bit down on his lips. He tasted blood. Not his own blood; Tom Burwell's blood. . . . Chickens cackled. Roosters crowed, heralding the bloodshot eyes of southern awakening. Singers in town were silenced. They shut their windows down" (46). What is lost in this moment is not only an overarching pastoral order but also the contrived narrative of race that defines the lives of both men.

The image of Tom Burwell standing beside the well as if "rooted there" is a final symbol of Black agency and pastoral transcendence (48). However, this statuesque image of strength is horribly perverted when Tom is burned alive by a white lynch mob after he kills Bob Stone in self-defense: "His face, his eyes were set and stony. Except for irregular breathing, one would have thought him already dead. Torches were flung onto the pile. A great flare muffled in Black smoke upward. The mob yelled. The mob was silent. Now Tom could be seen within the flames. Only his head, erect, lean, like a *Blackened Stone*" (49; emphasis added). The description of Tom's burned corpse as a "Blackened Stone" inextricably links both men. Indeed, Tom becomes a "Blackened" version of Stone in that his death is also the result of masculine pride and racial norms. The last image of Tom's death also reveals the distance that now separates him from the pastoral landscape of southern Georgia as he is taken from his place beside the well and burned alive beside the mill, itself a symbol of the commercial forces that diminish the land by extracting materials from it for profit. The last image of the full moon, the great omen of chaos and disaster, completely reverses the transcendent pastoral vision that began the Georgia section of the novel.

From the "Pine Matted Hillock in Georgia" to "Seventh Street"

The problem that the novel poses in its Northern section is how to appropriate a Southern pastoral vision as a way of attending to the urban displacement of Black folk in the city who possess the spirit of the "harvest song" (95). The novel approaches this problem through the symbolic formation of ghetto pastoral spaces in which the potent pastoral vision of the Georgia section might be reappropriated in the city. Therefore, if the Georgia section of the novel represented the erosion of a pastoral ideal that had shaped Southern Black life, the Northern section of the novel attempts to (re)configure that ideal in the urban spaces of the city. *Cane* (re)presents the symbol of the South as a potential source of pastoral transcendence but also as a source of contestation. Thus, rather than an idealized view of the past or a nostalgic return to a rural way of life, the ghetto pastoral mode of representation in the Northern section of the novel frames Black culture as a liminal experience shaped by conflict between rural and urban.

"Seventh Street," the prose poem that opens the Northern section of the novel, demonstrates this thematic pattern. Seventh Street is figured as a contested space that contains at once the external forces of urban decay and the internal cultural practices of a diverse Black population. Seventh Street is the result of "Prohibition and the War," an urban space formed out of economic struggle and social deviance (53). The life that is revealed there reflects impoverished circumstances, where "Money burns the pocket, pocket hurts," or the illicit activities of "Bootleggers in silken shirts" (53). The contested values ascribed to this space are those of both workers and criminals. Yet between these two realities is another portrait of Seventh Street that stands almost as liminal testimony to the vast potential of this urban space: "A crude-boned, soft skinned wedge of n----r life breathing its loafer air, jazz songs and love, thrusting unconscious rhythms, black reddish blood into the White and White-washed wood of Washington" (53). This description of Seventh Street is literally wedged between the two repeated stanzas that describe the harsh urban realities of Washington, DC. Within this larger urban frame, we find resonances of the past registered in the everyday spaces of lived experience that constitutes this portrait of Seventh Street.

These "unconscious rhythms" of Seventh Street are the symbolic patterns of experience that form a basis for a whole way of life. These are the subtle rhythms of everyday life—embedded in the social, cultural and spiritual practices of the people in rural places and spaces far removed from the theaters and boulevards of Washington, DC, Chicago, and New York. The repeated phrase "who set you flowing?" is the narrator's attempt to apprehend the source of this experience and the sense of loss it has invoked—to institute modes of perception that could mitigate the trauma of the past and the stark reality of the present. After the phrase is repeated a third time, it is extended to encompass the various urban spaces that make up Seventh Street: "Who set you flowing? Flowing down the smooth asphalt of Seventh Street, in shanties, brick office buildings, theatres, drug stores, restaurants, and cabarets? Eddying on the corners? Swirling like a blood red smoke up where the buzzards fly in heaven?" (53). These varied spaces reveal the composite nature of Black urban life as representing a distinctive folk character while also encompassing every aspect of urban life in the city. This fact further motivates the initial question "who set you flowing?," for it implies the potency of folk culture and the need for African Americans to sustain some vestige of folk identity in Northern cities. The problem in the prose narrative is the task of bridging the gap between the most salient aspects of Black Southern folk culture and the social dynamics of urban experience. Farah Griffin's study of African American migration narratives, *"Who Set Your Flowin?,"* describes the thematic significance of communal spaces such as those contained in Toomer's "Seventh Street." Griffin describes these as "safe spaces" where "the ancestor," or the symbolic presence of folk culture, is invoked: "These spaces are often sites where the ancestor is invoked; at other times they are sites from which he or she is banished . . . The ancestor in turn is a site of negotiation for the construction of a new self."[35] Griffin is right to interpret Black migration narratives as stories of transformation and resistance, but I would like to complicate her reading as it pertains to the novel. If Toomer's version of the Black migration narrative portrays the "construction of a new self," it is a liminal self formed at the intersection of the old and the new.

The story "Avey" represents the dialectical tension at the center of *Cane*'s ghetto pastoral narrative. Avey is a sexually precocious adolescent who is the object of the protagonist's desire. He pines for her although she remains largely indifferent toward him. From afar, he and his friends entertain their pubescent fantasies about Avey, although it is rumored that her mother will force her to marry "that fellar on the top floor" with whom she has been sexually active (59). The social and sexual distance between Avey and the protagonist is analogous to the disjuncture between the urban life of the North and the rural, pastoral experience of the South. Like the other women of the Northern section of the novel, Avey embodies a certain ideal of rural life—a life that is attuned to the natural and the everyday, a life that stands in stark contrast to the formally structured experience of urban life.

Toomer's protagonist is unable to access the pastoral ideal embodied in the symbolic figure of Avey: "I wanted to talk. To explain what I meant to her. Avey was as silent as those great trees whose tops we looked down upon" (60). In this sense, Avey is the embodiment of a pastoral experience, an experience formed at the intersection between the natural world ("the simple beauty of another's soul") and the world of material contrivances ("the arch lights of U street") (63, 62). The problem that this invokes is how to reconcile urban and pastoral modes of experience. Thus, "Avey" introduces the rural and urban conflict that shapes the thematic structures of the remaining stories in the novel. The story "Avey" culminates with the protagonist's attempt to figure a ghetto pastoral space in which his desire for Avey can take definitive shape and meaning. The city park then functions for the protagonist as a site of ghetto pastoral memory, evoking images of a Southern past while ascribing new meaning(s) to the realities of the urban present. The ghetto pastoral space of the park offers a kind of conceptual high ground in which the urban landscape of the city is illuminated and invested with new meaning. The light that emanates from the park onto the "darkened sky" of the city also provides a counterpoint to the bleak atmospheric imagery of the Georgia section. His description of the city park is worth quoting at length here:

> I have a spot in Soldier's Home to which I always go when I want the simple beauty of another's soul. Robins spring about the lawn all day. They leave their footprints in the grass. I imagine that the grass at night smells sweet and fresh because of them. The ground is high. Washington lies below. Its light spreads like a blush against the darkened sky. Against the soft dusk sky of Washington. And when the wind is from the South, soil of my homeland falls like a fertile shower upon the lean streets of the city. Upon my Soldier's home. (63)

The figuring of the city park as ghetto pastoral space establishes an initial point of departure in the northern section of the novel. It conveys a spatial ideal that involves, on the one hand, a tacit acknowledgment of the viability of Black folk culture and, on the other hand, a realization of the unique and sometimes disparate practices that define Black urban experience. For the protagonist, both modes of experience converge in the park, producing a charged ghetto pastoral experience: "I began to visualize certain possibilities. An immediate and urgent passion swept over me" (64). He envisions a "larger life" than the proscribed and cramped life that emanates from the city—a larger life out of which a new art would be born, "an art that would open the way for women the likes of [Avey]" (64). The potent ideals reflected in this ghetto pastoral space represent a counterpoint to the barren spaces of the Georgia section of the novel.

However, the birth of this new art depends on a consummation of rural and urban modes of experience, ideals that both the protagonist and Avey respectively embody. The protagonist's failure to engage Avey romantically in the park (she falls asleep in his arms) indicates the ongoing conflict between both ideals. While the pastoral space of the park provides a liminal point in the narrative where both ideals come into contact, the conflict of rural and urban meanings remains unresolved. Though the story holds out the promise of a new art, one in which rural and urban ideals could be integrated, it is a promise that is in the last instance deferred indefinitely. As this would indicate, the ghetto pastoral spaces that comprise the novel's cityscape contain the promise of a rural-urban synthesis but do not provide an immediate means of achieving it.

"Bona and Paul," the longest story of the Northern section, continues this pattern of deferment in which the promise of ghetto pastoral spaces is frustrated by rural and urban conflict. Paul, who is Black, attends a predominantly white school in Chicago. He agrees to a date that his roommate, who is aptly named Art, has set up with Bona, a doting white girl filled with romanticized notions of Paul's Blackness. For Bona, "[Paul] is a harvest moon. He is an autumn leaf" (97). Both of these pastoral descriptions of Paul culminate with her admission that he is also a "n----r," thereby revealing that the pastoral values ascribed to him are racialized. The exoticism ascribed to Paul's Blackness and the natural quality of the pastoral images that he comes to embody provide a sharp contrast to the images of drilling students and precise movement that describe the school. As is the case throughout this Northern section, a Black migrant is thrown in sharp relief to the urban spaces that he occupies and that provide him no immediate sense of belonging.

Paul's perception of his own place in this cityscape is informed by the rural, urban conflict that shapes his experience as a Black migrant. The tenement where he lives functions as a spatial metaphor that dramatizes the nature of this conflict. The section of the story that describes this space is worth quoting at length here:

Paul is in his room of two windows. Outside, the South-Side L track cuts them in two. Bona is one window. One window, Paul. Hurtling Loop-jammed L trains throw them in swift shadow. Paul goes to his. Gray slanting roofs of houses are tinted lavender in the setting sun. Paul follows the sun, over stock-yards where a fresh stench is just arising, across wheat lands that are still waving above their stubble, into the sun. Paul follows the sun to a pine-matted hillock in Georgia. He sees the slanting roofs of gray unpainted cabins tinted lavender. A Negress chants a lullaby beneath the mate-eyes of a southern planter. Her breasts are ample for the suckling of a song. She weans it, and sends it, curiously weaving, among lush melodies of Cane and corn. Paul follows the sun into himself in Chicago. He is at Bona's window. With his own glow he looks through a dark pane. (99)

Bona and Paul embody the separate windows that face North and South from the tenement apartment. As David Nicholls has observed in his reading of this imagistic scene, Toomer turns the earth literally on its axis to have the sun set in the South, Paul's birthplace.[36] Although the pastoral imagery of the South provides an appealing alternative to the "fresh stench" of the Chicago stockyards, Paul realizes that the sun has literally set on that bygone world of "pine-matted" hills and "unpainted cabins." He must "wean" himself of that life, as it has sent him forward into this new world of L-tracks and tenements. Closing the curtain on that life, Paul now turns to look into the "dark pane" of Bona's window and into the uncertain urban future that it symbolizes. Like the other displaced Black characters of the Northern section, Paul's perception is shaped by the conflict between rural and urban ways of life. The ghetto pastoral mode here functions as a means of mitigating such conflict. The ghetto pastoral mode that shapes Paul's perception is made apparent in the narrator's description of downtown Chicago: "The Boulevard is sleek in asphalt, and, with arc-lights and limousines, aglow. Dry leaves scamper behind the whir of cars. The scent of exploded gasoline that mingles with them is faintly sweet. Mellow stone mansions over-shadow clapboard homes which now resemble Negro shanties in some southern alley" (103). As this passage reveals, the city undergoes a symbolic transformation, so that the Boulevard is "aglow," as though bathed in the diffuse light of dusk; "Dry leaves scamper" as though they were moved by soft Southern winds rather than the "whir of cars"; the smell of "exploded gasoline" is "faintly sweet" like the odor of fresh pine sap; and perhaps the most radical transformation, the "clapboard homes" have now become "Negro shanties."

In this conceptual geography, the Crimson Gardens is transformed into another ghetto pastoral space. At this restaurant club, where Bona and Paul engage in a suggestive dance, the pastoral imagery of the previous scene takes on both sexual and racial connotations here. Toomer again evokes the imagery of blood circulation, thus recalling similar descriptions in the prose narrative "Seventh Street," by describing the dance floor as a place where "blood flows to a clot" (107). Indeed, the resulting scene is a confluence of disparate symbolic elements. Though the "crash" of urban jazz fills the scene, Paul imagines that he is listening as "a Negress chants a lullaby beneath the mate-eyes of a southern planter," a description that foreshadows the image of a "pregnant Negress" that figures prominently in the novel's final section (106). Paul ascribes to the club the vitality of this pastoral image, seeing in the people there "flushed faces" and in Bona "eager brilliant eyes" (106).

However, the idealism of Paul's pastoral vision is undercut when the scene changes to purple, the color of dusk. This atmospheric change follows from Paul's realization that his presence in the club is not welcomed, as evidenced by the white couples leaving the dance floor. Paul sees the failure of his dream registered in the eyes of the Negro doorman:

> As the black man swings the door for them, his eyes are knowing. Too many couples have passed out, flushed and fidgety, for him not to know. A strange thing happens. He sees the Gardens purple, as if he were way off. And a spot is in the purple. The spot comes furiously towards him. Face of the black man. It leers. It smiles sweetly like a child's. Paul leaves Bona and darts back so quickly that he doesn't give the door-man a chance to open. He swings in. Stops. Before the huge bulk of the Negro. (109)

Paul appeals to the unwitting doorman by saying that "something beautiful is going to happen." Paul associates the dusky imagery that shrouds the Crimson Gardens with the "dark faces" of Black folk. This image has now descended on the faces of the white folk, which he figures as a "bed of roses." He then imagines himself as a "gather" of petals, ascribing to himself the role of racial mediator, or someone who will penetrate the "dark pane" that separates the races (109). The symbolic confluence of racial images in the story gestures toward the resolution of racial conflict that is at the center of the ghetto pastoral narrative. However, this possibility is finally shot through when he returns to the spot where he and Bona were standing only to find that she is gone.

"Kabnis Is Me"

The last section of the novel comes full circle (completing the circle frag-ments that intersperse the text) as it returns to the South and to the source of Black cultural and racial identity. "Kabnis," the eponymous prose nar-rative that completes the circle, reflects the artistic vision that shapes the entire novel. Kabnis views the problem of cultural displacement from the perspective of the artisan. In describing the story, Toomer wrote to his friend and mentor, Waldo Frank, that "Kabnis is Me," an indication of the author's distance from the narrator of the Southern section and his affinity with the more disaffected Ralph Kabnis.[37] In the novel, Kabnis wants to "feed the soul," not with ornamented words but "misshapen, split-gut, tortured, twisted words" (156). The problem of representation the story poses then is how to represent in art a Black vernacular culture that is receding into memory.

The short drama "Kabnis" provides, on its surface, a simple resolution to this problem of representation. Through the inclusion of symbols of sunrise and rebirth, the story points to the possibility of saving what Toomer referred to as the "rich dusk beauty" of Black Southern folk culture—recording it in art, and giving to it an aesthetic if not physical reality.[38] Beneath its sur-face, however, is a story whose understanding of Black culture and lived experience is as divided as its title character. Ralph Kabnis is a reluctant witness to the potency of Southern folk culture and, in this sense, he most resembles Toomer himself. Indeed, Kabnis is the inevitable product of his-tory, a Northern-born Black man in search of his cultural roots, hoping to find himself in a Southern landscape replete with cultural remnants of the past but no practical means of sustaining the lives of Black people.

The opening scene of the story positions its titular character Kabnis at the historic crossroads between rural and urban, Southern and Northern modes of experience. Unlike Black migrants who ventured North in search of a bet-ter life, Kabnis is a Black migrant of a different sort. Like Toomer himself, Kabnis is a Northern-born migrant who has come to the South as a teacher hoping to find himself within a potent but proscribed Black Southern culture. Unlike Toomer, however, Kabnis cannot comprehend a Southern landscape that constantly frustrates him with beauty that can only be registered in the most ambivalent terms. In an ironic gesture of both self-description and self-deprecation, Kabnis ruminates on his precarious position as Black man who is both inside and outside of a rich Southern landscape and culture:

> Ralph Kabnis is a dream. And dreams are faces with large eyes and
> weak chins and broad brows that get smashed by the fists of square

faces. The body of the world is bull-necked. A dream is a soft face that fits uncertainly upon it . . . *God, if I could develop that in words. Give what I know a bull-neck and a heaving body, all would go well with me, wouldn't it, sweet-heart" If I could feel that I came to the South to face it. If I, the dream (not what is weak and afraid in me) could become the face of the South. How my lips would sing for it, my songs being the lips of its soul. Soul. Soul hell. There aint no such thing. What in hell was that?* [emphasis mine] (114)

Toomer figures Kabnis as a tortured version himself, a liminal character torn between his Northern sensibilities and the cultural meanings embedded in a Southern landscape that could otherwise provide him with a sense of identity and belonging were he able to relate to it in any meaningful way. Instead, he recoils at the Southern landscape and its "radiant beauty" that at once "touches and tortures" him. And yet, when Kabnis considers Washington, DC, and New York City as alternatives to his existential dilemma in the South, he is gripped by an "impotent nostalgia" for the people of those places "whom he had always half despised." Instead, he attempts to find solace in the everyday lived experience of Black folks in the South, in the quotidian immediacy of their existence wherein "They farm. They sing. They love. They sleep" (117).

In the end, however, the austerity of Black Southern life is far too restrictive for Kabnis, who drinks and smokes himself out of his job as a schoolteacher. When he is evicted for these infractions, he is forced to move into the shop dwelling of Fred Halsey. The workshop recalls another time and place, a theme that reverberates throughout the story. The building itself is covered in an "age-worn cement mixture" and the "considerably crumbled" facade is covered with musket shot. Ironically, Halsey assures Kabnis, who believes he is a potential target of racial violence, that "These ain't the days of hounds an Uncle Tom's Cabin," instead pointing out that "If what they wanted was t get y, they'd have just marched right in an took y where y sat" (122). Although Halsey recognizes the passing of the Old South into memory, he has not been able to avoid the negative effects of this social change. For this reason, the space inside Halsey's shop is a mixture of antiquated and broken items. The "variety of wood-work tools" in the shop indicates the obsolescence of the work done there. The unfinished projects strewn about the shop are a further indication of the failure of his business and livelihood. The symbolism here harkens back to the images of a blighted landscape and social decay that characterized the stories in the opening Southern section of the novel. However, where the opening Southern section of the novel ends in scenes of death, this last Southern section ends with symbolism that is suggestive of cultural rebirth. It is this final evocation of a Black cultural ideal that provides a resolution to the ghetto pastoral tension that structured the southern and northern sections of the novel.

The penultimate section of the story opens with the figure of a "pregnant negress," symbolizing the potency of Toomer's aesthetic vision in the novel to bring to birth social and cultural change. This imagery also attests to the dialectical quality of Black culture and lived experience after the Great Migration—an experience that drew its cultural inspiration from the rural South as it also sought to establish the material basis for a new cultural experience in the urban North: "Night, soft belly of a pregnant Negress, throbs evenly against the torso of the South. Night throbs a womb-song to the South. Cane- and cotton-fields, pine forests, cypress swamps, sawmills, and factories are fecund at her touch. Night's womb-song sets them singing. Night winds are the breathing of the unborn child whose calm throbbing in the belly of a Negress sets them somnolently singing" (146).

The passage reveals at once the promise of cultural uplift and rebirth rooted in the South as well as the competing forces of history and migration that constantly challenged that ideal. This symbolism of birth and renewal culminates in the figures of Carrie K and "Father John," whose "gray-bearded," "gray-haired," and "prophetic" appearance foreshadows his pronouncement of white hypocrisy by the end of the story. His condemnation of the sin white folks "'mitted when they made th Bible lie" provides a symbolic basis for a kind of cultural salvation for Black folks. Indeed, the racist discourse condemning Black people in Southern religious mythology is countered here by images of their cultural salvation and rebirth. Although a gospel of white supremacy denied Black people salvation, the Southern landscape itself is made here to symbolize their cultural rebirth as new creatures. When Carrie and Father John step outside of the shop after an evening of revelry and drinking, they immediately bear witness to a sublime Southern landscape now set in sharp contrast to the images of blight and decay that characterized the opening section of the novel: "Outside, the sun arises from its cradle in the tree-tops of the forest. Shadows of pines are dreams the sun shakes from its eyes. The sun arises. Gold-glowing child, it steps into the sky and sends a birth-song slanting down gray dust streets and sleepy windows of the southern town" (165).

While the opening section of the novel laments the passing of a "song-lit race," this passage conveys a prophetic hope that something borne of that expression remains. The collective experience of Black people suppressed by a history of racism is reconfigured here through the promise of cultural rebirth and the "birth-song" of a "gold-glowing child," the novel's final images of renewal and hope. Carrie K emerges in this symbolism as a Black Madonna figure. Unlike the women of the Southern section of the novel, Carrie is imbued with agency as a kind of midwife who ushers the birth of a proverbial "gold-glowing child." Her abbreviated surname is suggestive of a symbolic relationship to Kabnis. Like the titular character, she too must make sense of this prophetic vision while also conveying its message to the world despite the "misshapen, split-gut, tortured, twisted words" that necessarily speak the truth behind it. Both are given a prophetic view from the mountaintop overlooking the cultural promised land that awaits Black folk. However, that promised land is more spiritual than spatial, more rooted in cultural thought than in material practice. For this reason, the elusive ideal of the promised land is figured in the novel as existing neither in the North nor in the South. Rather, Toomer's ghetto pastoral story of Black migration positions that ideal in a liminal space betwixt and between North and South, within the cultural interstices of Black migrant experience, somewhere between "Seventh Street" and the "pine matted hillock in Georgia."

Cane's final movement back to the South is indicative of its ghetto pastoral vision, as it reveals the liminal position of Black vernacular culture after the Great Migration and the social movements of the 1920s. Like Toomer's title character, a generation of Black novelists and poets sought to represent Black culture and lived experience with "misshapen, split-gut, tortured, twisted words" in places and spaces far removed from the South. Toomer's accomplishment in *Cane* reveals the inherent tension at the core of that artistic project. As Toomer undoubtedly understood, Black folk in the 1920s stood at the proverbial crossroads of Southern folk culture and an emergent urban consciousness. It is precisely his foregrounding of this tension in *Cane* that marks it as a ghetto pastoral narrative. The same thematic tension would define Black migration novels in the decades to come. As Black migration authors continued to grapple with issues ranging from racial deracination to urban industrialization, their novels would become touchstones for racial uplift (a prominent theme of the early Black novel) and would signal the hope of transforming America into a more equitable society (a progressive theme that anticipates the proletarian fiction of the 1930s following the Great Depression). Indeed, Toomer's novel was a beacon for Black authors hoping to slip the yoke of the "plantation tradition," a burden that Toomer's predecessor Paul Laurence Dunbar knew all too well. And yet, *Cane*'s ghetto pastoral model was also a tacit challenge to a generation of Black authors who, like Toomer, regarded race itself with a great deal of ambivalence. If the literature of the New Negro movement was to expand definitions of what it might mean to be Black in the Northern city, it would presumably need to reconsider what it meant to be racialized in the first place.

Chapter Three

THE GHETTO PASTORAL AND DOMESTIC SPACES OF BLACK FEMALE DESIRE IN THE CITY

"You have everything here [in Harlem]: shops and theatres and churches and libraries . . ."

"And cabarets," added Mary. "You should have mentioned them first.

"Well, they are an essential part of our life, I suppose."

—CARL VAN VECHTEN, *NIGGER HEAVEN*

When Claude McKay published *Home to Harlem* in 1928, the much celebrated author of "If We Must Die" could not have anticipated the vitriolic reaction of W. E. B. Du Bois, who in his review of the novel wrote that it "for the most part nauseates me, and after the dirtier parts of its filth I feel distinctly like taking a bath."[1] In contrast to his scathing critique of McKay's novel, Du Bois extols the literary merits of another novel in the same review, a work entitled *Quicksand*, written by a then-obscure author named Nella Larsen. Du Bois extends his highest praise to Larsen's novel, announcing it "the best piece of fiction that Negro America has produced since the heyday of Chesnutt."[2] Both exaggerated claims reveal something about the dual quality of urban life in Black Harlem. Harlem of the 1920s was home to nearly two-thirds of all Black people living in New York City[3] and was rapidly becoming a city within a city viewed by many as the Black capital of the world. It was also a popular place for white folk who came in droves to experience the Harlem nightlife, complete with its jazz music and exotic people. Thus, while Harlem had become a cultural space that signified "all things black," it had also become a space of consumption for white bohemians who liked to watch the "natives" sing and dance. The "prurient demand on the part of white folk," Du Bois writes, is "for a portrayal in Negroes of that utter licentiousness which conventional civilization holds white folk back from enjoying."[4] Where McKay's novel failed, according to Du Bois, was is in its eager willingness to cater to this demand for the primitive and exotic, while Larsen's novel, on the other hand, succeeded by painting a more complex portrait of Harlem that reveals the "curious cross currents that swirl about the black American."

Du Bois's reading of *Home to Harlem* misplaces its angst in emphasizing the role of the primitive and exotic in that novel. To be sure, McKay's novel revels in the seamier side of Harlem, its prostitution and drunkenness, and presents it in a celebratory albeit also ironic tone. But what sets *Home to Harlem* apart from the primitive homage of Van Vechten's more controversial novel, *Nigger Heaven,*[5] is the way in which the novel foregrounds the problem of establishing a place for oneself in the city even as it acknowledges the always already tenuous quality of urban spaces where Black folk resided in Harlem. While McKay's novel centers on the "lower strata" of Black Harlem, it provides a relatively complex portrait of that experience. The culturally valorized spaces of Harlem—its streets and cabarets—are presented in the novel as false substitutes to the ideals of home and community. Ironically, given its title, the idea of home is contested in the novel for its protagonist Jake, who eagerly returns to his "brown" Harlem after going AWOL in Europe. The Harlem that Jake returns to is now shaped in part by the "downtown white trade," the whites who patronize the cabarets and clubs of Harlem. This image of Harlem is not created entirely by or for Black folk, and this is precisely the point the novel is making. In other words, the "Harlem" represented in the novel is a place where the "prurient demands of white folk" along with the "curious cross currents that swirl about the black American," come together to create an urban space in which Black folk are ironically displaced in their much-acclaimed Harlem, their urban "home" away from home.

This reveals the central complication in the novel and indeed in much of Black migration literature of the period—the public spaces of Harlem providing what many saw as an urban Black mecca also seemed to deny the possibility of establishing *real* or authentic homes in the city. The problem posed by these "primitive and exotic" public spaces in Harlem was merely incidental, perhaps even antithetical, to the more important problem for McKay's characters to establish a place of belonging and an enduring sense of community in the city. One way of understanding this complication is to view it as a function of the ghetto pastoral mode. What sets McKay's novel apart from earlier Black ghetto pastoral fictions is the bifurcated space of Harlem itself—its dialectical quality that produces yet another source of thematic tension in the text. The already liminal Black migrant characters of these fictions who necessarily moved between rural and urban modes of existence are divided as well within an urban space that reveals at once the cultural value of Black lived experience and the "prurient demands of whites" who went slumming there. If the haunting presence of the South necessarily complicated earlier Black migration novels, migration novels like McKay's set in Harlem were further complicated by the problem of Harlem itself.

This chapter responds to that problem as it relates to the representation of "Harlem" in two Black migration novels of the period, Nella Larsen's *Quicksand* (1928) and Walter White's *Flight* (1926). Both novels reveal the metafictional problem for authors who sought to harness the potent symbol of Harlem as a capacious signifier of Blackness, but who also sought to reveal the material realities of Jim Crow segregation and exploitative primitivism that also defined the city once called the "Black Mecca." Larsen's and White's novels offer this dialectic representation of Harlem as a function of the ghetto pastoral mode. The female protagonists in both novels struggle to achieve an elusive ideal of domesticity in response to their contested racial status as Black migrants in New York City's Harlem neighborhood. In turn, these migration novels figure the trope of Harlem as a dialectical space constructed, on the one hand, as a public space of consumption in which white people ascribe primitive meanings to Black urban experience, and on the other hand, as a private space of production in which Black female characters struggle to define domestic spaces that can reflect the values and ideals of Home. In ghetto pastoral novels, the ideal of home is necessarily fraught with the material realities of urban space in general and Harlem in particular. For this reason, the conventional ideal of domesticity is necessarily complicated in *Quicksand* and *Flight* by the general problem of social displacement and the objectification of Black female sexuality in the urban setting of the Northern city. My readings of both novels will thus reveal the ways in which they attend to the complication(s) of the ghetto pastoral, Black migration novel through the interpretative framework of the domestic narrative of ascent.

The domestic narrative of ascent, based on an ideal of home, is necessarily complicated in both novels by the challenges Black migrant women encountered in establishing their own domestic spaces. In addition to the material challenges they faced, such as housing discrimination and low wages, the very ideal of home itself was fraught with negative meaning for Black women. Where white women benefited from a domestic tradition that provided them with agency within the sphere of the home, Black women were in turn objectified in the very same domestic traditions that often reduced them to racial stereotypes. Lisa Boehm's recent ethnographic study of Black female migrants reveals the fraught quality of domestic labor for these Black women. For these Black women, writes Boehm, "work did not constitute a 'liberating' experience the way it would for the white, middle class housewives influenced by Betty Friedan's 1963 *The Feminine Mystique*"[6] Indeed, the "problem" of rethinking one's relationship to patriarchal authority for white women paled in comparison to Black women's struggle to overcome "the vicious myths that cast black women into such negative roles as the ever competent 'mammy,' the scheming 'Jezebel,' and the lazy 'welfare mother.'"[7] The more recent Black female migrants of Bohem's study are part of a long history of Black women struggling for recognition within the domestic traditions that privilege the experiences of white women. Larsen's and White's novels reflect this history of Black migrant women struggle for agency and belonging.

Home and Harlem

As New York's Harlem neighborhood emerged as the Negro capital of the world, much of the literature that revolved around the image of Harlem reflected an urban space fraught with contradictions. As Rudolph Fisher once observed, Harlem of the 1920s was undergoing a "change of complexion," as white patrons went in droves to the largely segregated cabarets of Harlem.[8] Fisher's observation qualifies the cultural ideal that Black authors of the Harlem Renaissance posited in the image of Harlem, which envisioned it as an urban space signifying a progressive ideal of Blackness. If Harlem was indeed the source of Black cultural expression in the 1920s, it was also a place shaped in part by the demands of white folk whose consumption of Black culture influenced the artistic production of Black authors and artists. These "new negroes," Alain Locke's moniker for this emergent class of Black middle-class cultural elites, were also bringing their own influence to bear on Harlem. Peter M. Rutkoff and William B. Scott describe the cultural project of these "new negroes" in their book *Fly Away* as involving a collaboration between the wealthy "downtown white folk" who drove Harlem's culture industry and an emergent Black middle class:

Disdainful of rural southern black culture, by 1925 Harlem's New
Negroes understood their fate was intertwined with poor southern
migrants. The Great Migration had redefined their status, from a small
and isolated group of northern Negroes, who provided menial services
to wealthy whites, into the leaders of a large and increasingly powerful
racial class, answerable only to its own people. In the 1920s Harlem's
Old Settlers formed migrant assistance organizations, recruited
migrants to their churches, and provided newcomers legal, medical,
dental, beauty, and funeral services. They advised migrants on appropriate dress and hygiene and served as their formal and informal
teachers. Old Settlers, now New Negroes, became Harlem's leaders.[9]

The triangulation of these complimentary interests in Harlem—Black
middle-class cultural elites, the Black migrant population, and white benefactors—made Harlem a unique point of inflection for Black cultural expression.

The Black migration novels set in Harlem of the 1920s necessarily figure
Harlem as a contested space—divided, on the one hand, between the ideals
of Black cultural expression and, on the other, the "prurient demands" of
white folk. The characters of these fictions are often represented as having
to negotiate a space of belonging that is determined by both factors. The
"Harlem" that was a racial and cultural signifier for Black people in the
1920s was also a brutal city of fact, an urban space with its own peculiar
history written by the effects of Black migration, white racism, and urban
industrialism. The Black exodus of the Great Migration coincided with the
collapse of the housing boom in Harlem, leaving scores of vacancies that
would eventual give home to thousands of Black migrants at the turn of
the century.[10] This influx of Black migrants into the once predominantly
white sections of Harlem was met with opposition from white homeowner
groups who vehemently urged property owners not to rent to Black people.
There were Black led companies that fought to bring fair housing to Black
people, although these real-estate groups, such as Philip A. Payton's "Afro-
American Realty Company,"[11] were forced to rent to Black tenants at much
higher rates than their white counterparts, and Payton's company, like many
others, folded as a result. These "housing wars" were racially motivated and
led to racial antagonisms that would fuel a series of race riots beginning in
1900, peaking with the Red Summer riots of 1919 and continuing into the
1920s. After Harlem's emergence in this period as the "black capital," its story
would be one of racial strife and contested urban space(s). Despite these
racist and violent conflicts, Black migrants did manage to find a permanent
place in Harlem, albeit it one fraught with social and economic ambivalence.

Harlem, the Black city within a city, affirmed Black subjectivity at the turn of the century, and gave place to the cultural life that would define what it meant to be Black in the twentieth century. As Charles Scruggs writes, "The city as a symbol of community, of home—this image lies beneath the city of brute fact in which blacks in the twentieth century have had to live."[12]

Harlem Renaissance authors and artists inscribed domestic ideals of home as a response to the historic alienation of Black folk in the urban spaces of the Northern city in general and Harlem in particular. For this reason, where early migration novels had appropriated the symbol of the city as connoting fragmentation and discontinuity, the migration novels set in Harlem began to at least imagine the possibility of establishing homes and communities in the city despite the material realities that alienated and displaced Black folk there. Indeed, the possibility of realizing an ideal of home is necessarily complicated in these novels by the more general problem of Harlem itself. Harlem of the 1920s signified an urban experience where Black subjectivity was circumscribed by cultural and material practices that produced competing images of Blackness. Some of these practices celebrated African American culture and lived experience, while others made a mockery of it. For example, the ubiquitous Harlem nightclub, frequently valorized as a progressive signifier of Black cultural life and experience, is often figured in Black migration novels (including both considered here) as a contested space of Black performance and racial exploitation. The clubs and cabarets of Harlem offered jazz music and other indulgences for white and Black audiences. However, these nightspots were often segregated,[13] and many promoted so-called jungle themes that showcased primitive portrayals of Black folk. The historian Gilbert Osofsky describes this culture of primitivism centered in Black Harlem:

> Popular images of the Negro were portrayed to New Yorkers in the numerous vaudeville and minstrel shows which regularly appeared in the city. New York City was the theater capital of America at the turn of the century and Negro vaudeville reached the height of its popularity then. Many of the performances, including the Creole shows which specialized in presenting scantily clad and beautiful Negro women, were hits. The hackneyed themes running almost without exception through all these plays were, in exaggerated form, a reflection of the generally accepted attitudes of white America toward Negro life.[14]

The space inside the club reveals the ironic shape of Black culture and urban experience in Harlem. White audiences were enthralled by the

primitive depictions of Blackness on vaudeville and cabaret stages, its atavistic portrayal of Black thought and expression, and the sexual abandonment
that such images gave them purchase to.[15] The exotic musical and theatrical
offerings of Harlem gave to white audiences a unique glimpse into their own
psyche, although their gaze projected it back onto Black bodies. In this sense,
white people encountered urban Black culture in Harlem nightclubs as voy-
euristic spectators. The exotic image of Blackness that emanated from many
Harlem stages was at once an object of desire and a stamp of degradation.

The racial exploitation that the Harlem stage produced was for many a
mark against the race. The meteoric ascendancy of Harlem into the national
spotlight in the 1920s was a boon for Black art and literature, but equally so,
the Harlem world of the "night club" and "cabaret" cast aspersions on the
ideal of the "New Negro," the literary representation of upwardly mobile
Black people in the city. This dual aspect of urban Black culture suggested
for some that two Harlems existed at once—one for Black people and one for
white people. This idea gained currency among those who increasingly came
to view Harlem as a dialectical cultural space that was at once a signifier of
Blackness and a product of white paternalism.[16] This dual aspect of Harlem
was for others an indication that the urban neighborhood that came to be
known as "Negro Heaven" was really a scene of racial exploitation that could
not be held up as the apex of Black culture. In an article entitled "Where Is
the Negro's Heaven" (1926), published originally in *The Opportunity*, Kelly
Miller provides sociological evidence to refute the claim that Harlem should
be viewed as the "Negro capital of the world." Miller claims that the facile
image of Harlem made popular in literary works such as Van Vechten's *Nigger
Heaven* belied the more serious aspects of Black culture that were best represented in the culture of Washington, DC:

> The mad quest for "kicks" and thrills, the saturnalia of song, dance
> and wine, the revelry of the cabaret are merely outbursts of Negro
> nature which would break forth at any place and time under like pro-
> vocative conditions. The so-called Negro art is merely the Negro soul
> turning itself wrong side out for white people to weep over and laugh
> at. The Negro life in Harlem is mainly effervescence and froth without
> seriousness or solid supporting basis. The riot of frolic and frivolity
> is characteristic of Babylon on the verge of destruction rather than of
> Heaven, the blissful abode of tradition.[17]

Concluding that Washington, DC, rightfully deserves the distinction
of "Negro Heaven," Miller writes that "the capital city furnishes the best

opportunity and facilities for the expression of the Negro's innate gayety of soul."[18] Miller argues this on the basis that Black people in Washington, DC, in contrast to those in Harlem, possessed greater self-determination in their political and cultural institutions. As Miller observes, "The Washington Negro has the only complete school system in the country practically under his own control."[19] In short, if Harlem was the popular seat of Black culture, it was not a culture in which common Black folk could equally participate. Langston Hughes's reflections of Harlem almost a decade later would seem to corroborate Miller on this point.[20]

Reflecting the contested status of "Harlem," the migration novels of this period set in Harlem figured it as a dialectical space that was racially divided. For instance, where the Harlem night club was often for white New Yorkers a site charged with disarming primitive meaning, it was often for Black attendees a site of racial orientation and recognition that figured Blackness as positive meaning over and against the racist connotations imposed by "whiteness." In this sense, the Harlem nightclub is often figured as a modernist space that can reflect the experience of the "other" against prevailing racial norms and values. For example, in "How It Feels to Be Colored Me," Zora Neale Hurston describes the "tonal veil" that marks her as "colored" in a Harlem night club in contrast to her fellow white club goers:

> [. . .] when I sit in the draft basement that is The New World Cabaret with a white person, my color comes. We enter chatting about any little nothing that we have in common and are seated by the jazz waiters. In the abrupt way that jazz orchestras have, this one plunges into a number. It loses no time in circumlocutions, but gets right down to business. It constricts the thorax and splits the heart with its tempo and narcotic harmonies. This orchestra grows rambunctious, rears on its hind legs and attacks the tonal veil with primitive fury, rending it, clawing it until it breaks through to the jungle beyond. I follow those heathen—follow them exultingly. I dance wildly inside myself; I yell within, I whoop; I shake my assegai above my head, I hurl it true to the mark yeeeeooww! I am in the jungle and living in the jungle way. My face is painted red and yellow and my body is painted blue. My pulse is throbbing like a war drum. I want to slaughter something—give pain, give death to what, I do not know. But the piece ends. The men of the orchestra wipe their lips and rest their fingers. I creep back slowly to the veneer we call civilization with the last tone and find the white friend sitting motionless in his seat, smoking calmly.[21]

The primitivism that marks Hurston's self-identification is ascribed positive value in her account. Although Hurston's tone in the essay is decidedly tongue in cheek, her point is clear. Her identity is both the product of the racial exoticism that had become a popular feature of Harlem culture and her own complex subjectivity as an individual whose uniqueness belies racial categories. In an ironic flourish, she describes the "tonal veil" that is torn asunder by the symbolic force of the music inside the club thereby rupturing the thin veneer of a civilization that would otherwise deny her an essential quality of her being. The racial romanticism of Hurston's account "makes" this essential quality a thing in itself whose reified form is manifested in the status of being "colored." In contrast, her white counterpart cannot engage the "primitive" as anything but a detached spectator. As Hurston points out, it is at this moment of recognition inside the club that her Blackness becomes a thing—that she is immediately made to feel "*so* colored." But it is also in this moment of recognition that Hurston ascribes positive value to her "colored self." In this sense, her status as a colored person is not merely a negative sign of racial difference, but also a signifier of some ancestral link (real or imaginary) to an original experience rooted in Africa. Her final description of herself as a bag containing "brown miscellany" conveys the full complexity of her identity, a complexity that belies the racial exoticism of white consumer culture in Harlem.

The literary turn toward primitivism was for some authors of the Harlem Renaissance a progressive response to the displaced status of Black culture in America. Primitivism was in many cases fertile ground for the exploitation of Black culture and experience. But as Brian Dorsey points out, "primitivism also meant a search of black people for their African ancestry and roots."[22] From that search, "a huge reservoir of inspiration was to be found in the unabashedly unsophisticated treasure-trove of folk tales, conjure stories, and other African remnants remaining in spite of centuries of white-imposed civilization."[23] In other words, while racial exoticism in Harlem could become a form of social mockery for Black people, it could also provide them with the raw materials for refashioning their racial selves. Insofar as the Harlem nightclub was an immediate source of this racial primitivism, it came to be seen as the proverbial seat of Black culture and urban life. Yet, the cultural prominence of the Harlem nightclub ironically reveals the more general problem of making spaces that can sustain Black lived experience. That sort of intimate experience would presumably need to emanate from privileged domestic spaces. It was therefore incumbent on authors of the Harlem Renaissance in general, and migration novelists in particular, to envision the ideals of home and family in their fiction.

Stories of Black female experience, including both novels considered here, have their roots in the post-Reconstruction domestic novels of Black women.[24] Claudia Tate defines this genre of writing about Black women, which emerged during the last decade of the nineteenth century, as works that "constitute a specific category of African-American fiction in which a virtuous heroine generally undergoes a series of adventures in route to marriage, family happiness, and prosperity."[25] Tate locates in these fictions privileged domestic spaces where Black female political desire is both imagined and mobilized in the interests of the race. These domestic spaces necessarily reflected the cultural and ideological assumptions of the mostly white middle-class readers of these fictions. As Tate points out, the domestic values that informed these fictions afforded their Black heroines a means of establishing "racial prosperity within a matrix of sanctioned Victorian social, political, and economic viewpoints."[26] Following this thematic structure, these novels were able to sustain their polemical and ideological force by appealing to the accepted discourses of "home" and "family," couching in these domestic ideals the political concerns of racial uplift and social equality for Black people.

As Tate observes, these fictions figure the domestic ideal of "Home" as a unique countercultural space in which Black female desire is mobilized within mainstreams values and norms, while in turn the political nature of that desire challenges those same values and norms. These domestic fictions figure the "Home" as a space where "self-naming" can occur—as a transformative space where Black heroines can negotiate an identity for themselves. In this sense, the ideal of home provides the terms for imagining and understanding racial prosperity and social mobility for Black women. Tate reads these domestic fictions as "allegories of black political desire, public and private."[27] She remarks that these works "depict an ideal black family formation in which the realization of the heroine's conjugal happiness and personal fulfillment parallels community prosperity in the context of an equitable society."[28] Thus, the domestic spaces in these novels provide an idealized point of reference against which the racist and sexist values of the larger society can be interpreted and contested.

Similarly, the spatial trope of home in *Quicksand* and *Flight* offers a kind of domestic, countercultural space that lies in distinction to the exotic public image of Blackness that had gained currency in Harlem of the 1920s. But what sets these novels apart from the domestic fiction that Tate identifies is the fraught image of home they both represent. The ideal of home in both novels, and the domestic spaces where that ideal is located, provides a means of achieving social mobility for the novels' female protagonists. Yet, the contested nature of those domestic spaces in both novels reflects the

ghetto pastoral tension at the core of these domestic stories of Black migration. In *Flight*, the female protagonist of that novel, Mimi Daquin, must
"pass for white" in order to achieve what is for the Black female migrant
an elusive ideal of domesticity. However, the social ascent made possible
by her Washington Square home parallels her descent into a conformity
of white middle-class values, which ultimately leads to the negation of her
racial identity. A similar kind of tension emerges in *Quicksand* when the
novel's protagonist, Helga Crane, is driven into an unfulfilling domestic life of
unrelenting childbearing and hollow religiosity. Therefore, unable to realize
the domestic ideal of home and belonging in the North, Helga returns to the
South and to the circumscribed domestic life it offers. While the alternative
to this fraught ideal of domesticity in both novels is signified in the space of
the cabaret and the public image of Blackness it connotes, it too is fraught
with the ambiguities of race and the specter of Black primitivism. In this
sense, where earlier migration narratives portrayed the conflict between rural
and urban spaces, these later migration novels set in Harlem foreground a
specific version of this conflict by highlighting the tension between privileged domestic spaces of female empowerment and public spaces of racial
primitivism and exploitation.

The Promise of Domesticity: Walter White's *Flight*

Walter White's career as a novelist parallels his social activism and his prominent involvement with the NAACP. White is perhaps best known for his
activist work, but what distinguishes him as an author is what he perceived
as the role of his fiction in advancing the causes of Black folk. His first novel,
Fire in the Flint (1924), received modest critical acclaim, although Sinclair
Lewis went further than most in his praise of the novel, comparing it in a
letter to White to E. M. Forster's *Passage to India*.[29] Lewis was willing to
read past the formal mistakes of White's inaugural work, focusing instead
on the powerful theme of lynching that energized the narrative.[30] Lewis and
others seemed willing to make this concession based on the political and
social relevance of the novel and its direct link to the activism of its author.

For many critics, White's second novel *Flight* (1926) was not a stylistic
improvement over his first.[31] Its thematic scope set it apart from *Fire* and
the political concerns that had earlier sparked the interests of White's critics.
However, while *Fire* explored the problem of racial violence in the South, he
directed his social critique above and below the Mason–Dixon line in his
second novel. Indeed, what makes *Flight* a different sort of polemical novel

than its predecessor is its commentary on the general problem of establishing viable domestic spaces in the city for Black migrants, an issue that is the defining conflict for the novel's protagonist. As a migration novel, *Flight* can be viewed as a logical progression for White, who had already exposed the problem of lynching and racial violence in the South and was now exploring themes related to the subsequent migration of Black people to the North. The Southern section of the novel reprises the racial violence of *Fire*, but it does so to establish the circumstances that motivate the novel's protagonist to migrate to the North, where she faces a different set of problems. The problem of establishing a place for herself in the city turns on the practical issue of urban housing and the possibility of establishing a comfortable middle-class home in the city. In this sense, the novel reflects Victorian novels that center on the trope of domesticity, but it differs in that it presents that domestic ideal as something unattainable for its Black female protagonist. Those critics who voiced a cooler opinion of White's second novel, especially those who argued that the novel was too "white," were perhaps unwilling to allow White the "race man" to venture into this sort of thematic territory.

Despite the tendency of some critics to reduce his fiction to mere political propaganda, White continued to view his fictional work as an aesthetic expression as well as an extension of his political activism. He believed his charge as an author was to produce an accurate account of Black experience. "Writing about Negro life as it really exists," according to White, was a literary field, "which is as yet practically untouched."[32] *Flight* was his attempt to bridge the gap between the practical concerns of Black folks (which were necessarily political and racial concerns) and their representation in literature. True to its title, *Flight* moves beyond the sectional problem of racial violence in the South (although it addresses that issue as well), to consider the broader social concerns that Black Southerners faced after migrating to Northern cities. Just as the problem of establishing a home is a central thematic concern in the novel, it was of paramount concern for White as a NAACP leader and activist. Writing several decades after the publication of *Flight*, White surveyed the progress that Black people had made in securing adequate urban housing and the general attitude of white people as it related to the issue of housing integration:

It has been demonstrated over and over that two factors have played a most important part in racial prejudice in America: reasoning, often faulty, based on economic factors, and the ignorance of many who unthinkingly follow the lead established by others. In no manifestations of the ugly phenomenon have these factors been more clearly demonstrated than in those that have made it impossible for the overwhelming majority of Negro Americans to have the freedom of choice in housing which their white contemporaries enjoy. Two of the most commonplace of all clichés uttered by American white people are these: "Sure, I like so and so" . . . "he's different from most of them," and, "Not that I have any prejudice, but I wouldn't want to have a Negro live next door to me because it would lower the value of my property."[33]

Flight dramatizes the problem of creating domestic spaces in the city that can reflect the values of home for its Black migrant character. It centers on one of the complications of ghetto pastoral novels, namely, negotiating the problem of cultural displacement while constructing a viable ideal of home and belonging. The novel's title provides an ironic statement on the ideal of home in that its protagonist is constantly in "flight" or movement, unable to find a place of belonging in the South or the North. As a migration novel, *Flight* does not make any significant revision to that genre as much as it supplements the form. Where the migration novels already discussed imagined no immediate place of belonging in the city for its migrants, *Flight* offers at least the possibility of establishing a home in the city, although one that represents a contested ideal in the novel.

We first encounter the novel's protagonist, Mimi (Annette Angela) Daquin, when she is eleven years old and living with her widower father, Jean, in New Orleans. Her father eventually marries Mary Robertson, an ambitious social climber from Chicago. Unsatisfied with the "backwardness" of life in New Orleans, Mary convinces Jean to move the family to Atlanta, Georgia, where Jean takes a position in his father-in-law's insurance company. Mimi rapidly ascends in her new social setting, while Jean languishes in Atlanta's urbane society. Mimi's social ascent is further facilitated by her friendship with Hilda Adams, who introduces her to the privileged class of Black people in Atlanta. Although Mimi rejects the sordid values of Atlanta's Black elite, she does not possess what may be described as race or class consciousness. The first important shift in her development as character occurs when she witnesses a race riot and the murder of a Black man:

A Negro was seen walking down Marietta Street, one of the five thoroughfares focusing in Five Points, unaware apparently of the scene he was approaching. Mimi saw him and wanted to shout a warning to him. It would have been fruitless—the roar was too great and her voice would have been as the falling of a single drop of water on the shore

while near-by boomed the surf. It would have been almost suicidal—
the pack might easily have turned on them. Nevertheless, she wanted
to cry out to this unknown man to flee. It was too late. One man in
the crowd spied him just as Mimi saw him, just as she uttered a little
scream of terror. Up went the roar, "There's a n----r now!"

Too late the Negro saw his danger. He turned to flee but before he
had gone many yards the pack was upon him. Mimi saw him strike out,
dodge, attempt to elude his attackers. It was useless. Down he went and
a great bellow of hatred, of passion, of sadistic exultation filled his ears
as he died. Mimi covered her eyes with her hands and pressed close to
Jean as she saw the flashing jack-knives. (73)[34]

This experience shades Mimi's character by providing the occasion for
the formation of her racial consciousness. From this point on, she identifies
with all things Black, casting her lot with her own people. Describing this
transformation, White writes, "To Mimi there was no more fascinating thing
in the life she saw around her than the song, the laughter, the deep religious
faith and the spontaneous humanity of the people of whom she was now
a part" (91). As this passage indicates, the lasting impression of the riot on
Mimi is that it imbues her with a sense of racial pride, a reaction that sets
her apart from Johnson's ex-colored man, who upon witnessing the lynching
of a Black man feels nothing but shame. Mimi emerges from the experience
of the riot as someone keenly aware of her contested racial status and the
possibilities this conscious awareness affords her.

Making her race a conscious thing follows the conventions of the "passing figure," the tragic mulatto figure who consolidates her racial identity in
similar moments of social recognition. But what distinguishes Mimi from
the standard trope of the mulatto is her valorized perception of Black life as
something that exists solely for itself without the need for social legitimization
through white approval. Appropriately, White has Mimi's love interest, Carl
Hunter, recite lines of poetry from Paul Laurence Dunbar. Mimi responds
approvingly to this recitation of dialect verse, seeing in it an indication of the
"rhythm and instinct" that shapes Black expression. White is not valorizing
Blackness through his protagonist so much as he is setting the table for the
conflict of racial values that will attend Mimi's social ascent in the North.

Her subsequent experience of Black life in Atlanta resembles a similar
portrait of Black expression. Her gaze is conspicuously focused on what
Hughes called the experience of the "low-down folks," those Black people
whose experience is born directly out of the race struggle. Mimi's valorization of Black everyday experience extends to this lowest stratum of Black

experience, thus signaling her turn away from the pretentious society of Black elites. She responds to the spectacle of a Black chain gang in much the same way she would a musical recital:

> The day when a convict gang began to repair the street in front of their home was one Mimi never forgot. She awoke hearing a wild, plaintive, poignantly simple melody so strange she thought herself yet asleep.....
>
> Mimi's heart beat faster and faster as she watched and listened. She sensed that the song carried the toilers far above their miserable lot. For them the toil and sweat, the louring guards who shouted staccato commands or flung crisp oaths when one of the convicts slackened or appeared to slacken in his labour, did not exist. She began to comprehend the thing Carl had said to her of the "over-soul" the Negro possessed. (91, 93)

Already established for Mimi is this symbolic quality of Black experience as something that is both immediate and transcendent. The brutal simplicity of the chain gang obscures an essential meaning that is rooted in some collective black experience. Her deep-seated desire to tap into the reservoir of this common experience enables her to construct an ideal of Blackness that belies the material conditions that otherwise suppress it. Her symbolic identification with the chain gang is a further recognition of her personal investment in the race struggle. In this sense, the concept of the "over soul" connotes a collective experience that presumably extends to all Black people regardless of social class or material conditions.

However, Mimi's racial awakening in the Southern section of the novel is challenged by the conflict of ideals that attends her social ascent in the Northern section. Her romantic ideals of the race as such run up against both the competing versions of Blackness that Harlem signifies as well as the ideals of domesticity and home that are largely unavailable to Black people in the city. This conflict motivates her decision to "pass as white," a decision she makes in order to escape the fraught images of Blackness that Harlem projects and to establish a domestic space of belonging in the city. The hard-boiled portrait of Harlem that begins the New York section of the novel reflects her optimistic belief in the transformative quality of the urban life that exists there: "For here was a new life, teeming, exotic, individual. Hurrying along the streets, coming out of restaurants, standing in doorways and on street corners were groups of Negroes, well dressed, jubilant, cheerful. Here and there hurried coloured men in twos and threes, clad in smartly fitting dinner jackets, snow-white bosoms peeping from heavy overcoats, musical instruments, violins, saxophones, mandolins in cases clutched in their hands" (186).

While such urban encounters typically initiate a series of displacements for the characters of Black migration narratives, Mimi is "ushered" into this urban life through the domestic figure of Aunt Sophie: "The new life she was ushered into through Aunt Sophie seemed by comparison with her experiences since she left Atlanta almost idyllic to Mimi" (192). Aunt Sophie and her home signify the domestic ideal to which Mimi aspires throughout the Northern section of the novel. In *Fiction of the Home Place*, Helen Levy defines the trope of "home place" as "an ideal pastoral domestic setting," that is usually "presided over by an elder wise woman who embodies the care and wisdom associated with maternity."[35] Levy describes domestic fictions that construct the ideal of home place, and thereby establish for their female protagonists a domestic space in which they may assert an authority that is otherwise denied them outside the home. For Mimi, the domestic space inside Aunt Sophie's home functions as a site of cultural mediation where she may order her post migration, urban identity through a familiar—if substitutive—home place. It also signifies an ideal domestic space that signals the goal of the Black female migrant—to establish homes that symbolize a viable place of belonging in the city.

Aunt Sophie's home also reflects the extended family networks that migrants necessarily accessed as a means of establishing a place of belonging in the city. In this sense, the ideal of domesticity was a more fluid concept for Black migrants who necessarily had to establish a homeplace wherever they could find it—often with other family members. In his study of the migration patterns of Black families, Earl Lewis assesses the central role of kinship networks in the North that migrants accessed through visitation and extended residence in the homes of their relatives. As Lewis points out, these Northern visits allowed Black migrant families an opportunity to reaffirm family ties that were strained or lost because of the breakup of extended family structures in the wake of the Great Migration. In addition, these visits afforded recently migrated families the opportunity to participate in the domestic spaces created by Black families in Northern cities. These visits also presented the possibility of establishing similar domestic spaces for themselves. In assessing the importance of these family visits, Lewis writes,

> Of course, it is impossible to construct an emotional index for visits, but we can map their importance. Such a mapping underscores the enduring importance and multi-layered character of "home." In the Afro-American cultural vernacular home was always more than the

house in which one lived. Home was the household and the community; home was a shared culture and a shared culture of expectations;
home was the community of origin and the community of residence;
home was a state of mind and the link between the past, the present,
and the future.[36]

As Lewis's observations reveal, the ideal of home in the collective imagination of Black migrants signified something not merely denoted by a physical
structure. Rather, "home" signified an ideal rooted in a collective experience
that extended beyond individual spaces and often included the experience
of the entire community. Insofar as these homes were the meeting places
for recently migrated families and their relatives already living in the city,
they provided a symbolic link between a recent rural past and an unfolding
urban present. More importantly, these homes signified a domestic ideal that
held the promise that Black migrants could make a better life for themselves
in Northern cities.

The novel's plot also reveals another aspect of the general problem that
Black migrants faced as they struggled to achieve the elusive ideal of domestic fulfillment in the city. When Mimi leaves Philadelphia for New York City,
she is forced to leave her infant child in the care of a Catholic orphanage,
where he would remain "until she had accumulated enough to assure herself
and him freedom from their more immediate wants, and then get him again
when she had gained her objective" (182). While this practice reflects one of
the hardships endured by Black migrants, it also reveals the profound desire
of Black migrants to establish viable domestic spaces in the city that could
provide a better life for themselves and their families. This practice was pervasive and, as Darlene Clark Hine points out, an option that many women
had to exercise: "Although greater emphasis has been placed on men who
left families behind, black women, many of whom were divorced, separated,
or widowed, too left loved ones, usually children, in the South when they
migrated." [37] The novel remains remarkably true to the documented patterns
of black migration occurring in the 1920s. This historical specificity in the
novel distinguishes it from that romantic genre of Black middle-class fiction
that dominated at the turn of the century.[38]

The conflict between material aspirations and racial values drives the
Northern section of the novel. When Mimi's tawdry past is discovered, she
leaves Harlem and the cultural life it represents, a disavowal of the past that
links her story to Dunbar's Black migrants. For Mimi, as for Dunbar's black
migrants in *Sport*, the past is a constant source of trauma that prevents
her from realizing her dream of domestic fulfillment. In response to her

predicament, she decides to "pass as white," a decision that initiates her social ascent in the city and enables her to marry a white man, Jimmie Forrester, who provides her with the domestic life she has long sought. White's description of the Forrester home conveys an idyllic domestic space: "The Forrester house sat on the north side of Washington Square. Its high ceiling walls and hand-carved wood work, its air of mellowed age were all redolent of days when coaches-and-fours rolling easily through the Square sent flocks of broad-winged pigeons fluttering to safety on the huge, clumsy arch which took its name from the Square" (262). The house "spoke to her in tender tones of the days of splendor it had seen," speaking as it where to Mimi in the language of domesticity, drowning out the otherwise discordant tones of her racially proscribed existence. Her selective hearing [read perspective] obscures the reality of her marriage not to mention her husband's comment that "these kikes and Catholics and n----rs got to be kept under control," to which Mimi offers no response, "in fact, did not hear him" (265).

The domestic life that Mimi achieves in the novel is immediately undercut by the self-negating values associated with it. Because she must "pass as white" in order to achieve this domesticity, she must disavow her racial identity and everything associated with her past, including her child. Rather than affirm her identity as a woman, the traditional function of such domestic spaces, Mimi's identity is subverted and contradicted in the setting of her own home. Indeed, she too must actively subvert her own Blackness, for as White suggests, "when coloured persons went white, in order to prove their whiteness, they were more anti-Negro than anybody else" (240). Her domestic life, although replete with the comforts of her Washington Square home, becomes a source of racial conflict. Unlike Johnson's ex-colored man, she cannot entirely repress the racial values that form her identity; in other words, her agonizing silence in the face of her husband's racism is the price she must pay for domesticity.

The alternative is registered in the vibrant space of the Harlem nightclub. The exotic public image of Blackness generated there provides a point of contrast to Mimi's conventional domestic life. Where Mimi experiences a racial awakening in the Southern section of the novel, she experiences inside the club a kind of sexual awakening: "The music had a strange effect upon her. Analyzed, it was all wrong when judged by conventional musical standards. Taken as a whole, it formed a weird and oddly exciting cacophony of chords and exotic rhythms. A muted cornet sent forth hair-disturbing peals like an eerie sound heard in a graveyard after midnight. The saxophone *grunted* and *slid up and down* a facile scale of gurgling harmonies. Drums and the piano *pounded a steady beat* that had in them all the power and mystery and *inflaming* beauty of the tom-tom" [emphasis mine] (293). These overt sexual images conflate Mimi's conscious transformation with her burgeoning sexuality, a sexuality heretofore repressed by her sterile domestic life at home.

The novel concludes with Mimi walking out her Washington Square home, presumably in the direction of Negro Harlem, which she now sees with "new eyes." But the ending reflects neither a complete denial of conventional domestic values nor an uncritical acceptance of the racial exoticism rooted in Harlem. Rather, the novel suggests that Black migrants like Mimi must establish a symbolic space of mediation between both concepts—that is, between the conventional domestic values that reflect an essential aspect of social life and the exotic image of Blackness that reflects an essential aspect of Harlem's (America's) cultural life. Nevertheless, the ending is problematic in that it does not precisely envision such a space for its protagonist. For this reason, Laurence Rodgers argues that the novel ultimately fails in its conclusion because it "yields to a temptation," in that it "inscribes an unambiguous happy ending, taking for granted the presence of a viable post migration Northern setting that will accommodate Mimi."[39] Yet the fact that Mimi must turn away from a comfortable middle-class home is meant to be read as both tragedy and sacrifice. Instead of "selling her birthright for a mess of pottage," she takes the path of greater resistance. In this sense, the novel leaves open the question of whether conventional domestic spaces are available to Black New Yorkers and, if so, what sort of values and meanings they might privilege.

The Price of Domesticity: Nella Larsen's *Quicksand*

Similarly to White's novel, Nella Larsen's *Quicksand* dramatizes the problem of realizing female desire within conventional domestic spaces. Larsen also explores the problem of displacement in the context of female agency and sexual desire. As a ghetto pastoral expression of domesticity, *Quicksand* problematizes the quest for female agency and sexual fulfillment as a function of establishing domestic spaces of belonging. Indeed, like *Flight*, Larsen's novel reveals the cost that women must often pay in establishing domestic spaces of belonging as a requisite for self-fulfillment. Both novels reveal the pitfalls of conventional domestic spaces as well as the inability to realize any viable idea of female agency outside of such domestic spaces. As expressions of the ghetto pastoral form, neither novel offers an easy solution to this problem. To be sure, the ending of Larsen's novel represents a more realistic and more tragic outcome of this problem for Black female migrants.

In her quest for self-realization, the novel's Black migrant protagonist, Helga Crane, bears a strikingly resemblance to the author. Charles Larsen, Nella Larsen's biographer [no relation], describes her early life as "mysterious," and admits "The scanty facts that can be validated (and they are only a handful) are like a series of lights interspersed along a dark, underground tunnel."[40] As Charles Larsen points out, most of what is known about Larsen's early life comes from her own embellished accounts in the biographical information she provided for publishers and magazine editors.[41] In these various addenda to her fiction, "she rewrote her early life as if it were one of her novels."[42] Like Helga Crane, the past was for Larsen something that held anxiety and uncertainty, especially as it related to her racial linage. As to her ethnic background, her father was a Black man from the Virgin Islands, and her mother a woman of Danish descent. She visited her mother's family in Denmark at the age of sixteen but never established a lasting relationship with them. Similarly, her protagonist Helga Crane travels to Copenhagen in search of family roots only to find a greater sense of displacement and alienation than she had known in America.

A concern that figures both Larsen's personal life and her fiction is the problem of imagining domestic spaces that can provide a place for the realization of Black female desire. Once again, Larsen's own life provided a ready source for her fiction. Her father's death when she was two years old and her publicized divorced from physicist Elmer S. Imes were both sources of domestic disillusionment for Larsen, a tragic concern she would represent in her fiction. The epigram from Langston Hughes's poem that begins the novel laments the plight of the tragic mulatto, but it may equally relate to the author as well:

> My old man died in a fine big house.
> My ma died in a shack.
> I wonder where I'm gonna die,
> Being neither white nor black.

The Hughes epigram reveals one of the tragic circumstances surrounding the mulatto figure; namely, the racial conflict that attends the mulatto character prevents her from establishing a domestic space of belonging. Similarly, for Helga Crane, the tragic circumstance of her family origin (her father was a "gay suave scoundrel" who abandoned her Scandinavian mother) prevents her from ever inhabiting a conventional domestic space. However, her goal of recovering this lost birthright is constantly frustrated in the novel because of the social factors that constantly beset her as a Black woman.

Helga Crane is neither white nor Black but a "despised mulatto," a racial stigma that also complicates her goal of domestic fulfillment. Her displaced status is evident in the Southern section of the novel, where her proscribed environment provides her no immediate place of belonging. The fictional town of Naxos provides the Southern setting for the novel and introduces the initial conflict of values that forces Helga to migrate to the North. The town itself, and the Negro vocational school where Helga teaches, embody the conventional domestic values that Helga rejects from the outset. Indeed, "Naxos," the name of the town, is an anagram for "Saxon." The implication is that Helga's world, although ostensibly black, tacitly acknowledges the primacy of all things white. Against this social backdrop of conventionality and racial conformity, Helga stands out as a figure of sexual vitality and radical individualism. Larsen presents her in a "vivid green and gold negligee," an apt portrait of a lady whom the narrator describes as profoundly "attractive." Helga's glowing quality stands in stark contrast to her "schoolteacher paraphernalia of drab books and papers," (4) implements of the "cruel educational machine" (17) that employs her and threatens to rob her of individuality.[43] Her physical beauty, however, is also the source of her alienation, as her *mixed* racial status is a constant reminder to those around her of her illegitimate family origin.

The conflict that shapes Helga's experience in the South is not merely the result of race but also involves the accepted sexual mores and domestic values of Naxos. Cheryl Wall writes, "Helga is divided psychically between a desire for sexual fulfillment and a longing for social respectability."[44] Helga believes that her family circumstance prevents any chance of social respectability in the South. Dr. Anderson tries to convince her to stay in Naxos rather than leave for the North, remarking "You're a lady. You have dignity and breeding," to which she responds with presumptive guilt: "If you're speaking of family, Dr. Anderson, why, I haven't any. I was born in a Chicago slum" (54). That she identifies with her urban birthplace complicates the traditional migrant narrative form in that she is already displaced in the rural setting of Naxos, thus leaving open the possibility that the North will provide her with a place of belonging. Like in previous migration narratives, the North is figured in the novel as an urban space of possibility. It is a space where the past as it relates to family origin is effectively suspended. Thus, migration to the North offers Helga the possibility of domestic and sexual fulfillment that is denied to her in the South.

The immediate irony of Helga's venture north to Chicago, her birthplace, is that she is displaced there from the outset. Larsen writes, "Helga Crane, who had been born in this dirty, mad, hurrying city, had no home here" (59). Her sense of "homelessness," both literally and figuratively, is reinforced when she attempts to reconnect with her uncle. The pall of race immediately settles around her as she encounters her mother's side of the family for the first time. Upon discovering that her uncle is away, she is forced to endure the cold rejection of his wife: "Mr. Nilssen has been very kind to you, supported you, sent you to school. But you mustn't come here anymore. It—well, frankly, it isn't convenient. I'm sure an intelligent girl like yourself can understand that" (61). This final dissolution of family ties—for she has no knowledge of her father's folk—renders her completely alone. In this sense, she becomes the epitome of the displaced and alienated Black migrant figure.

Her journey farther into the heart of the city, however, reveals yet another possibility. Amid the anonymous crowd of people, she nevertheless feels an effusive sense of belonging:

> She stood intently looking down into the glimmering street, far below, swarming with people, merging into little eddies and disengaging themselves to pursue their own individual ways. A few minutes later she stood in the doorway, drawn by an uncontrollable desire to mingle with the crowd. The purple sky showed tremulous clouds piled up, drifting here and there with a sort of endless lack of purpose. Very like the myriad human beings pressing hurriedly on. Looking at these, Helga caught herself wondering who they were, what they did, and of what they thought. What was passing behind those dark molds of flesh? Did they really think at all? *Yet*, as she stepped out into the moving multicolored crowd, there came to her a queer feeling of enthusiasm, as if she were tasting some agreeable, exotic food—sweet breads, smothered with truffles and mushrooms, perhaps. And, oddly enough, she felt, too, that she had come *home. She, Helga Crane, who* had no home. [emphasis mine] (63)

Unlike earlier migration novels, where the initial encounter of the urban landscape is typically marked by a sense of immediate displacement, Helga at least *feels* at home in the city. Simply put, her perceptive sense of belonging in the city belies her physical displacement there. What she finds in Black Harlem is a kind of self-recognition that derives from a sense of belonging: "Again she had had that strange transforming experience, this time not so fleetingly, that magic sense of having come home. Harlem, teeming Black Harlem, had welcomed her and lulled her into something that was, she was certain, peace and contentment (75)." The emotion that Black Harlem incites for Helga, as did Chicago before, is the "joy at seeming at last to belong somewhere" (75). She had in her own words "found herself."

The problem of her physical displacement is resolved when she enters into the service of Mrs. Hayes-Rore, a prominent social activist and women's rights advocate. In the context of the Black female migration narrative, Mrs. Hayes-Rore embodies the maternal figure that presides over the ideal domestic space that Helga hopes to establish for herself. Her urban ascent is marked physically by her transition from relative homelessness to a place of belonging in the Hayes-Rore home: "Ever afterwards, on recalling that day on which with well-nigh empty purse and apprehensive heart she had made her way from the Young Women's Christian Association to the Grand Boulevard home of Mrs. Hayes-Rore, always she wondered at her own lack of astuteness in not seeing in the woman someone who by a few words was to have a part in the shaping of her life" (69).

As her hyphenated name also suggests, "Mrs. Hayes-Rore" also embodies the independent woman that Helga aspires to be. Her identity as a woman is not subsumed by the institution of marriage. Instead, she enjoys the domestic fulfillment of marriage without the obligation to conform to gender norms that subjugate women in the home place. In this sense, Hayes-Rore's marriage reflects an egalitarian model of domesticity that, ironically, will prove elusive for Helga Crane.

Helga's sense of place in the city is informed by her desire for an ideal domestic space of belonging. When the issue of her lodging arises again, she quickly discounts the possibility of living at the YMCA as "too bare, impersonal, and restrictive," "nor did furnished rooms or the idea of solitary or a shared apartment appeal to her" (76). Instead, she opts to live in the home of Anne Grey, an acquaintance of Mrs. Hayes-Rore who employs Helga when she arrives in New York. Larsen writes, "Anne's home was in complete accord with what [Helga] designated as her 'aesthetic sense'" (76). Larsen's subsequent description of Anne's home figures it as an ideal domestic space:

> Even Helga Crane approved of Anne's house and the furnishings which so admirably graced the big cream-colored rooms. Beds with long, tapering posts to which tremendous age lent dignity and interest, bonneted old highboys, tables that might be by Duncan Phyfe, rare spindle-legged chairs, and others whose ladder backs gracefully climbed the delicate wall panels. These historic things mingled harmoniously and comfortably with brass-bound Chinese tea chests, luxurious deep chairs and davenports, tiny tables of gay color, a lacquered jade-green settee with gleaming black satin cushions, lustrous Eastern

rugs, ancient copper, Japanese prints, some fine etchings, a profusion of precious bric-a-brac, and endless shelves filled with books. (76)

The domestic space inside the home is an assemblage of high cultural artifacts from both Western and Eastern traditions. Its cultural refinement attests to the possibility of urban ascent for the Black women who reside there. Claudia Tate's discussion of the post-Reconstruction domestic novels of Black women is again illuminating. As Tate points out, the bourgeois decorum represented in these fictions constituted the symbolic basis for black female social ascent. She writes, "post-Reconstruction black women writers . . . maintained that genteel class membership as a lady or gentleman was based more on individual virtue, dignity, and decorum than on construc- tions of noble black heritage arising from a racially mixed ancestry."[45] Helga Crane's racially mixed ancestry is the source of her domestic displacement. Conversely, the domestic accoutrements of Anne Grey's Home provide her with a basis for self-recognition—a kind of domestic self-recognition that Helga seeks for herself throughout the novel. Each item of the home, each elaborate furnishing, provides both a sense of identity and belonging for its owner. In this sense, the promise of domestic fulfillment in the novel is both the object of female desire as well as a potential source of racial identity.

Because Anne Grey's husband is deceased, her home signifies a feminine model of domesticity where the male figure is entirely displaced. Her name, Anne Grey, also has symbolic resonance: her surname, "Grey," suggests a kind of hybridity that reflects her unique place in the domestic space of the home. Anne's home is devoid of the traditional male figure of authority, making her the de facto "man of the house," although she does not entirely accept the role for herself. In fact, she turns Helga into a sort of surrogate male figure in the home. Larsen's description of their relationship conveys the subtle hint of homoeroticism: "Between Anne Grey and Helga Crane there had sprung one of those immediate and *peculiarly sympathetic* friend- ships" [emphasis mine] (75). Larsen's subsequent description of Anne paints her as a golden Madonna, an image that suggests her respective role as a presiding maternal figure in the idealized domestic space of her home. If Helga becomes a kind of surrogate male in this symbolic economy, Anne becomes a kind of surrogate mother.

Outside of the idealized domestic space of Anne's home, the urban space of Harlem provides for Helga a symbolic buffer between her new life and other spaces in the city occupied by influential and powerful white people. In this sense, Black Harlem is figured as the source of a more vibrant experience that resists the otherwise deadening and subjugating features of urban life in New York. Helga's description of Anne and the place she has established for herself in Harlem makes this important distinction:

> But, while the continuously gorgeous panorama of Harlem fascinated her, thrilled her, the sober mad rush of white New York failed entirely to stir her. Like thousands of other Harlem dwellers, she patronized its shops, its theaters, its art galleries, and its restaurants, and read its papers, without considering herself a part of the monster. And she was satisfied, unenvious. For her this Harlem was enough. Of that white world, so distant, so near, she asked only indifference. No, not at all did she crave, from those pale and powerful people, awareness. Sinister folk, she considered them, who had stolen her birthright. Their past contribution to her life, which had been but shame and grief, she had hidden away from brown folk in a locked closet, "never," she told herself, "to be reopened." (77)

It is within the image of this Harlem, set apart from the urban spaces occupied by white people, that Helga hopes to achieve the elusive goal of domesticity. Unlike the drab suitors who attended on her in Naxos, Harlem provides an array of possible suitors who can presumably provide her both domestic as well as sexual fulfillment: "Someday she intended to marry one of those alluring brown or yellow men who danced attendance on her. Already financially successful, any one of them could give to her the things which she had now come to desire, a *home* like Anne's, cars of expensive makes such as lined the avenue, clothes and furs from Bendel's and Revillon Freres, servants, and leisure" (77). It is amid this urban scene that "Helga Crane meant, now, to have a home and perhaps laughing, appealing dark-eyed children in Harlem" (77). This domestic dream "sprang from a sense of freedom," an indication that its content reflects the healthy (and egalitarian) models of domesticity presented in the homes of Mrs. Hayes-Rore and Anne Grey. Helga's dream is that she will marry an "alluring brown or yellow" man who will provide her with an ideal domestic space in the city, thus enabling her to realize her migrant goal of urban ascent, but one who will not saddle her with the traditional female domestic role. It is the disillusionment of this dream, and the redaction of "Harlem" as a signifier of urban possibility, that marks the tragic circumstance of the novel.

The disillusionment of the dream owes in part to the dual quality of Black life in Harlem. The Harlem described in the novel is replete with the best and the worst of Black urban life: "Everything was there, vice and goodness, sadness and gaiety, ignorance and wisdom, ugliness and beauty, poverty and richness" (78). However, Helga experiences the urban life of Harlem with intellectual detachment, viewing it as though it were a painting on a canvas rather than actual lived experience. In this sense, she experiences Black life in Harlem from a liminal perspective, torn as it were between the racial exoticism of the place and the conservative (read white) values that inform her ideal of domesticity: "While proclaiming loudly the undiluted good of all things Negro, she yet disliked the songs, the dances, and the softly blurred speech of the race. Toward these things she showed only a disdainful contempt, tinged sometimes with a faint amusement. Like the despised people of the white race, she preferred Pavlova to Florence Mills, John McCormack to Taylor Gordon, Walter Hampden to Paul Robeson. Theoretically, however, she stood for the immediate advancement of all things Negroid, and was in revolt against social inequality" (80).

Helga's intellectual detachment from Black urban life belies her spiritual attachment to it. She is "entertained" by the performance of Black urban life on the Harlem stage, but not drawn to participate in it as yet another racial actor for the amusement of whites. It is with increasing scorn that Helga regards the "serene tan and brown faces" that populate Harlem, seeing in their visages a "carefree quality" that "roused in her the desire to scream at them" (84). Her "unreasoning protest" against the urban Black life in Harlem sets her apart from the traditional mulatto character who finds in Black life both an ideal source of racial pride and inspiration, as well as an undeniable affinity for a group of people entirely unlike herself except where race is concerned. Describing Helga's uneasiness among Black Harlemites, Larsen writes, "life became for her only a hateful place where one lived in intimacy with people one would not have chose had one been given choice" (84). Her shame of being "yoked to these despised black folk" is not merely a rejection of Black Harlem but rather reflects her rejection of race as a defining concept. Her disillusionment/realization is followed by an epiphany as to the source of her own identity: "She didn't, in spite of her racial markings, belong to these dark segregated people. She was different. She felt it. It wasn't merely a matter of color. It was something broader, deeper, that made folk kin" (86).

The conventional cabaret scene in the novel reinforces Helga's resolve to cast off the aspersions ascribed to her because of race. The cabaret is not figured in the novel as a place of racial redemption, as it had been in White's novel *Flight*, but as a place of damnation, "one of those places characterized by the righteous as a hell" (89). The spatial motif of the cabaret, whose long hallway leading into a larger anterior space usually symbolizes a kind of spiritual (re)birth, is more likened here to death rather than life. Helga descends into the Cabaret as a kind of Black Virgil, bearing witnesses to its exotic allures but in the end rejecting its damning influence. Her atavistic experience inside the cabaret recalls Zora Neale Hurston's similar account in "How It Feels to Be Colored Me," as she momentarily rejects the respectability of domestic life for the moral inhibition of this sexually charged space. Larsen's description is worth quoting at length here:

> They danced, ambling lazily to a crooning melody, or violently twisting their bodies, like whirling leaves, to a sudden streaming rhythm, or shaking themselves ecstatically to a thumping of unseen tomtoms. For the while Helga was oblivious of the reek of flesh, smoke, and alcohol, oblivious of the oblivion of the other gyrating pairs, oblivious of the color, the noise, and the grand distorted childishness of it all. She was drugged, lifted, sustained, by the extraordinary music, blown out, ripped out, beaten out, by the joyous, wild, murky orchestra. The essence of life seemed bodily motion. And when suddenly the music died, she dragged herself back to the present with a conscious effort; and a shameful certainty that not only had she been in the jungle, but that she had enjoyed it, began to taunt her. She hardened her determination to get away. She wasn't told herself, a jungle creature. She cloaked herself in a faint disgust as she watched the entertainers throw themselves about to the bursts of syncopated jangle, and when the time came gain for the patrons to dance, she declined. (90)

Helga experiences a sudden transformation in the Cabaret, colored by the same "jungle" imagery and sexual abandon that Zora Neale Hurston conveys in her description of the New World Cabaret in "How It Feels to Be Colored Me." However, rather than formulate a sense of her racial identity as existing outside of this facile portrayal of Blackness, something Hurston ultimately professes in her essay, Helga's experience inside the cabaret leads her to reject race altogether, as well as the symbolic spaces of Harlem that produce the exotic image of Blackness she so vehemently detests. She migrates again, this time to Copenhagen, in hopes of reconnecting with her mother's family and finding a permanent place of belonging there. Her hopes are initially confirmed in Copenhagen. Larsen writes, "Helga Crane's new existence was intensely pleasant to her; it gratified her augmented sense of self-importance" (104). But when she attends a vaudeville house featuring the performance of two "cavorting" Negro dancers, she is thrown back into a realization of her racially marginalized status. This newest disillusionment hardens her against the possibility of establishing a domestic space of belonging in Denmark. When Axel Olsen, an aspiring artist, asks her to marry him, she rejects him outright. In response to his proposal, Helga remarks, "You see, I couldn't marry a white man. I simply couldn't. It isn't just you, not just personal, you understand. It's deeper, broader than that. It's racial. Someday maybe you'll be glad. We can't tell, you know; if we were married, you might come to be ashamed of me, to hate me, to hate all dark people. My mother did that" (118).

Unable to achieve the elusive ideal of domesticity in Europe, Helga returns to America and to the urban scene of Harlem. Helga's return to Harlem occasions yet another shift in her flittering racial consciousness. Resembling the classic tragic mulatto figure,[46] she experiences a kind of spiritual rebirth as a bona fide member of the Negro race. The fervor that marks her reattachment to the "dark hordes" of Harlem is expressed in nearly atavistic terms: "*These* were her people. Nothing, she had come to understand now, could ever change that. Strange that she had never truly valued this kinship until distance had shown her its worth. How absurd she had been to think that another country, other people, could liberate her from the ties which bound her forever to these mysterious, these terrible, these fascinating, these lovable, *dark hordes*. Ties that were of the spirit. Ties not only superficially entangled with mere outline of features or color of skin. Deeper. Much deeper than either of these" [emphasis mine] (125).

However, her renewed sense of urban optimism is short-lived as she once again fails to achieve the elusive ideal of domesticity. This last failure marks the movement in the novel toward her final disillusionment. The first such indication of this is her rejection of James Vayle's marriage proposal. Helga recoils at Vayle's proposal in part because with it comes the obligation of child rearing. To Vayle's questioning of her intent to ever marry, Helga responds with marked ambivalence: "Someday, perhaps. I don't know. Marriage—that means children, to me. And why add more suffering to the world? Why add any more unwanted, tortured Negroes to America?" (132). Her rejection of Vayle leaves her with the prospect of initiating an affair with Dr. Anderson, a married man. Her motives for this are directly linked to her unwillingness to endure the high cost of marriage for the rewards of domestic stability. The possibility of an affair with Dr. Anderson appeals to her precisely because it will not require of her the traditional duties of a wife, although it will presumably give her access to some version of the domestic ideal to which she aspires. Anderson's rejection of her signals the end of her domestic dream and the expression of female desire attached to it.

Ironically, the failure of Helga's domestic dream is confirmed by her marriage to Reverend Green. Her decision to marry Reverend Mr. Pleasant Green, a Southern-born minister who eventually takes her back to the South, initiates a downward spiraling of events. The ideal of domesticity is finally shot through in this last section of the novel, where the impoverished circumstances and unrelenting childbearing of her marriage relegate her existence to a domestic hell. The description of the Green home stands in stark contrast to the ideal domestic spaces presented in the Northern section of the novel. The bleak circumstances of her domestic life are exacerbated by the frequent absences of her husband from the home: "Helga, looking about in helpless dismay and sick disgust at the disorder around her, the permanent assembly of partly emptied medicine bottles on the clock shelf, the perpetual array of drying baby clothes on the chair backs, the constant debris of broken toys on the floor, the unceasing litter of half-dead flowers on the table, dragged in the toddling twins from the forlorn garden, failed to blame him for the thoughtless selfishness of these absences" (151).

The novel ends with Helga giving birth to yet another child, her fifth, an ironic image of life in the midst of what is for Helga a kind of spiritual death. Her failure to establish a domestic space of belonging in the city attests to the contested status of Blackness in the urban spaces of the North, particularly in Harlem. The tragic plight of Larsen's protagonist points to the conflict between prevailing racial norms and conventional domestic values. Where the urban spaces of Harlem often exoticize Black experience, representing it as a primitive thing, the idealized domestic spaces in the novel represent the same experience as culturally and intellectual dynamic. For this reason, the problem of imagining spaces of domestic fulfillment in the novel turns on the question of racial authenticity—that is, what counted (or could be counted) as Black identity in Harlem of the 1920s. What the novel reveals in this regard is that the exotic public image of Blackness focused in 1920s Harlem far outshone the middle class, domestic image of Black people that might have otherwise gained cultural normalcy and social legitimacy. For this reason, the question of whether such domestic spaces could exist at all for Black people was foreclosed by the prevailing exotic public image ascribed to Black experience in Harlem.

The contested image of Harlem in *Flight* and *Quicksand* revealed a marked shift in the representation of urban spaces in the black migration novels of the period. The city no longer merely symbolized a space of infinite possibility—a place where Black migrants were either corrupted or saved, depending on their moral or practical choices. The Northern city is portrayed in both novels, like Harlem of the 1920s, as an overdetermined space with its own set of racial and social proscriptions in place of those located in the South that Black migrants knew all too well. Indeed, Harlem of the 1920s possessed its own unique racial character, one that was not exclusively Black. As Du Bois attested to, many of Harlem's cultural institutions, ostensibly rooted in African American culture and lived experience, were also influenced by the "prurient demands" of white folks. The exotic public image of Blackness that gained currency in Harlem was necessarily a product of both influences. Therefore, the urban settings figured in the Black migration novels of the period were frequently portrayed as spaces of cultural and racial ambivalence. This necessary tension at the center of Black migration novels set in Harlem reflects the dialectical function of the ghetto pastoral mode. Places like Harlem were figured in these novels as contested spaces where Black migrants vie for the simple right to live in peace and for a measure of social recognition that would acknowledge them, in the words of W. E. B. Du Bois, as "contributors in the kingdom of culture." The ghetto pastoral impetus on adapting "old world tongues" to meet the demands of a new urban environment is represented in both novels as a struggle to articulate the terms of domesticity in response to urban displacement and deracination. The constant frustration of that struggle to establish viable homes that could reflect the ideal of domesticity is registered here as a failure to overcome the structures of inequality Black migrants found in Northern cities.

Both novels also reflect the material realities of black migration and the failed promises of 1920s "Jim Crow" American society. The ideal of the promised land in Black migration novels, much like the promise of America in urban naturalist fictions of the period, is always fraught by the material uncertainties of urban spaces and the exigencies of race. In this sense, the promised land was never an ideal actually borne out in reality but was rather always an elusive concept fraught by the countervailing forces of race, class and gender. Just as Ralph Ellison would remark of Harlem decades later, the promised land was "nowhere" except in the imaginations of Black people who "lived as they must" in spite of the material realities of their urban environment. Therefore, to simply articulate the terms of belonging for displaced Black migrants in Northern cities was for the authors of Black migration novels a conscious effort to rewrite the standard narrative of race in American society—that is, to imagine for Black people an ideal of home and community still yet to be sanctioned as "safe space" in a segregated America.

Chapter Four

"HARLEM IS NOWHERE"

Blues Expression and the Ghetto Pastoral Mode in Ralph Ellison's *Invisible Man*

The blues is an impulse to keep the painful details and episodes of a brutal experience alive in one's aching consciousness, to finger its jagged grain, and to transcend it, not by the consolation of philosophy but by squeezing from it a near-tragic, near-comic lyricism. As a form, the blues is an autobiographical chronicle of personal catastrophe expressed lyrically.

—RALPH ELLISON, *SHADOW AND ACT*

And so I play the invisible music of my isolation . . . Could this compulsion to put invisibility down in black and white be thus an urge to make music of invisibility?

—RALPH ELLISON, *INVISIBLE MAN*

Billie Holiday's haunting rendition of "Strange Fruit" marked an important shift in the musical career of the famed singer. Despite repeated warnings against recording the provocative song, Holiday embraced the song, making it one of her signature performances.[1] Although Black and white folk were certainly aware of the horrors of lynching, no one before Holiday had made the horrific practice the subject of mainstream musical expression. Indeed, when Holiday first performed the song in 1939 in Greenwich Village, it was met with cautious concern if not outright shock by many of her adoring fans.[2] Her performance of the provocative classic became a nightly ritual as audiences (mostly white) encountered images of the most egregious form of domestic terrorism the country has ever seen. The song is recognized today as one of the most influential songs in the American musical tradition. But while its most powerful expression is undeniably the symbolism it evokes of "strange fruit hanging from the Poplar trees," its rhetorical power as social protest comes from its disruption of the Southern pastoral narrative. The second stanza begins "pastoral scene of the gallant South / bulging eyes and twisted mouth," thereby evoking at once the myth of the "gallant South" as ironically juxtaposed with the horrible reality of the perverted "pastoral scene" unfolding there.[3] The remaining verses, "scent of Magnolia sweet and fresh, / And the sudden smell of burning flesh," further underscore the distance between the Southern pastoral ideal, figured in the effervescent scent of the Magnolia, and the human tragedy of lynching with its countervailing imagery, "the sudden smell of human flesh," signaling the disruptive narrative that *suddenly* intrudes an otherwise bucolic, pastoral scene.[4]

It may well be argued that Holiday's performance of "Strange Fruit" possessed the unique ability to evoke such a provocative message precisely because of its mastery of human suffering as a meaningful expression of human agency and social protest. Although Holiday's "Strange Fruit" is not a blues song, it certainly belongs to a blues tradition that masters the pain of Black lived experience as a defiant musical expression of resilience. The blues tradition from which Holiday took much of her inspiration possesses the paradoxical quality of expressing a profound sense of human agency within the throes of human suffering. I believe the reason for this is attributable to what Ralph Ellison describes as the "near tragic, near comic lyricism" of the blues.[5] In that ambiguous configuration, the blues becomes a capacious signifier of Black lived experience, an expression that endeavors "to finger the jagged grain" of an experience that is at once tragic and comic; one that requires a double consciousness to adequately express and to apprehend. It is this "music of invisibility," as Ellison would also call it in his novel *Invisible Man*, that marshals this kind of bivocality, which mitigates the pain of suffering even as it provides a powerful and poignant means of expressing it. But it is also this feature that allows the blues artist to deliver their message in a way that is both disarming and cathartic.

The capacity of the blues to interpret African American culture and lived experience is powerfully expressed in Ralph Ellison's modernist take on the black migration novel, his seminal masterpiece *Invisible Man*. Although the novel's relationship to jazz has been the subject of several critical studies, the blues is present throughout the novel both literally as a musical form of expression and figuratively as symbolic way of representing the struggle of Ellison's invisible man.[6] In what Ellison calls the "music of invisibility," the "turgid blues" reminds his nameless invisible man of the incongruities of his experience—an experience that finds its register in the "lower frequency" of the human condition, in a subaltern place represented by the underground cellar where the protagonist resides beneath the streets of Harlem. Ellison, who once quipped that the novel's ironic description of this finite space as "full of infinite possibilities" was not lost on him, understood the profound possibilities of a blues perspective that could find meaning in a dark and damp hole. This symbolic space is a place of refuge for his embattled protagonist, but it also represents the bivocality of Black expression, symbolizing its simultaneous message of despair and hope in the phonographic recording that renders this space "full of sound." In this framing of the novel, Ellison announces the blues perspective that will provide the basis for interpreting the contradictory world above his protagonist's head—registered poignantly in the jazz lamentation "Black and Blue." Much like Holiday's "Strange Fruit," Armstrong's song is not a traditional blues, but the song does belong to a blues tradition that masters Black suffering as a response to racial oppression. Ellison's novel thus reveals the ways in which Black people have marshaled this "music of invisibility" in establishing their own sense of place and identity.

Invisible Man is for this reason the aesthetic and critical culmination of the Black migration novel as a genre—the modern expression of perhaps the most important subgenre of fiction in African American literary history. At the thematic center of the ghetto pastoral mode expressed here is a blues symbolism that figures the ubiquitous crossroads of Black cultural life where race and place intersect. Ellison's protagonist emerges in this symbolic configuration as the liminal figure par excellence; the postmodern Black Übermensch through which an entire tradition of Black writing and collective struggle finds its most powerful and profound expression.

Ellison wrote *Invisible Man*, according to Ken Warren, "just in the nick of time," an indication that the novel resonated when it was published in 1953, but would have been less relevant were it to have appeared later that decade.[7] Indeed, the decade that saw the beginning of the end for Jim Crow segregation provided an appropriate backdrop for a novel focused on themes of racial alienation, especially as it relates to the geographic displacement of individuals in the racially segregated spaces of the North. Ellison's framing of the narrative inside the symbolic space of the underground cellar does the metaphorical work of establishing a ghetto pastoral perspective. In this expression of the ghetto pastoral mode, the central source of meaning is the blues, the "music of invisibility" embodied in the figure of Louis Armstrong whose slow tempo rendition of "Black and Blue" provides the figurative soundtrack for the novel. The ghetto pastoral expression of the blues turns on the pain and struggle brought about by the urban displacement of Black folk after the failures of the migration. At once, the symbolic figure and expression of the blues in the novel also establishes a basis for finding meaning in the Black migrant's struggle for belonging. Rather than an acceptance of racism and oppression, the blues perspective at the center of the novel imagines a liminal position for displaced Black migrants betwixt and between the displaced folk culture of the South and the racially restrictive spaces of the North.

From the opening pages of *Invisible Man*, Ralph Ellison's singular literary masterpiece, the symbolic meanings that Black people often ascribe to urban spaces in the city are revealed. Ellison's unnamed protagonist inhabits what he ironically describes as a space of "infinite possibilities" in what is actually a coal cellar beneath the streets of New York City. It is from this underground vantage point that he becomes the fictional author of his story. "Full of light," this space beneath the bustling city above ground denotes possibility and prophesy, as his last words in the novel reveal: "who knows but on the lower frequencies I speak for you." Like so many other scholars of Ellison's masterpiece, I have attempted to decipher the meaning of this potent spatial symbol, at times with the certainty of having interpreted once and for all its cryptic messages, for example, reconsidering the exactly 1,369 lights that fill it with light or the music of Louis Armstrong that fill it with sound. My present effort at interpretation rests on an examination of the blues perspective that Ellison's protagonist creates within this liminal space. While some critics of the novel have emphasized the symbolic role of jazz in the novel, it will be my contention that the novel frames Black lived experience in a way that is analogous to the unique perspective of the blues performer. Indeed, Ellison's symbolic mapping of Black experience in the novel rests on a blues perspective that imagines Black folk as always already standing at the proverbial crossroads of cultural meaning—between a traditional folk sensibility and a nascent urban consciousness. Within the various liminal spaces figured in the novel (i.e., the underground cellar, Jim Trueblood's cabin, "Pete Wheatstraw's" corner, and Mary Rambo's apartment), Ellison maps the experience of his protagonist and by extension African American lived experience by marshaling a symbolic blues perspective in framing the contradictory lives of the dispossessed and displaced. This blues perspective operates as a function of the ghetto pastoral mode in the novel, thereby framing the experience of Ellison's protagonist in a way that reveals at once his "indebtedness" to a Southern Black vernacular tradition (the "old world tongues" that continue to shape his experience) and his struggle to navigate an urban environment that is fundamentally (re)shaping what it means to be Black.

The central complication in the novel is the conflict produced by the cultural and geographic displacement of migration. The story that Ellison tells through his invisible man reflects the larger historical narrative of Black migration in the first half of the twentieth century. When the novel was published in 1953, the Great Migration had already forever reshaped Black culture and lived experience by making it synonymous with urban culture and society. However, this historical narrative of Black ascent in Northern cities was also shaped by cultural displacement and deracination. It is against this historical backdrop of Black migration that Ellison's invisible man struggles to gain recognition in a society that refuses to see him. As a Black migrant character, his struggle in the novel also parallels the struggle of Black migrants forced to leave the South in the early part of the twentieth century in hopes of gaining social recognition in the North. What he finds in the cold urban landscape of New York, however, also reflects the harsh reality of the Great Migration. Many who left the South in droves hoping to find a better life for themselves in the promised land of the North found even greater deprivation in the form of urban poverty, social neglect and systematic-institutionalized racism. Where the Jim Crow South imposed a brutal racial order, the Jim Crow North imposed its own oppressive practices (e.g., red-line housing segregation, restrictive covenants, and exorbitant rents for Black residents) that systematically eroded the promise of Black ascent in Northern cities.

Ellison's novel then stands at a historical crossroads between an earlier vision of Black migration as a social movement and the emerging realities of the mid-twentieth century, a cold war period that would be an era of inner-city urban decay and decline. In his essay "Harlem Is Nowhere," Ellison describes the "psychological character" of the urban scene in Harlem as one that "arises from the impact between urban slum conditions and folk sensibilities."[8] Ellison's essay anticipates the theme of cultural displacement that frames his novel. This problem, according to Ellison, adversely affects the psyche of black Harlemites, placing them "out of synch" with their urban environment. Ellison writing in the late 1940s was witnessing the effects of almost two decades of steady urban decline in Northern cities. By this time, the reality of urban slum conditions and pervasive black unemployment had already supplanted the myth of the Great Migration shared by an earlier generation of black migrants.[9] For Ellison, the way in which Black people experienced life in the city seemed devoid of the recognizable patterns of experience and social institutions that pointed up to a viable way of life. Regarding these necessary structures of everyday lived experience, Ellison notes the failure of the urban scene to yield suitable alternatives for northern

Black folk: "But without institutions to give [the black individual] direction, and lacking a clear explanation of his predicament—the religious ones being inadequate and opportunistic—the individual feels that his world and his personality are *out of key*" [emphasis mine].[10]

Ellison's use of a musical metaphor—the condition of being "out of key"—to express the urban displacement of Black folk in the Northern city signals the important relationship in Black culture between Black vernacular forms (such as blues, jazz, and spirituals) and the establishment of communal spaces.[11] For Ellison, if Black people felt culturally displaced in Northern cities after the Great Migration, it was (at least in part) because they had lost contact with their music. Ellison goes on to describe the changes to Black musical forms—most notably folk jazz—that shaped the culture of 1940s Harlem: "The lyrical ritual elements of folk jazz—that artistic projection of the only real individuality possible for him in the South, that embodiment of a superior democracy in which each individual cultivated his uniqueness and yet did not clash with his neighbors—have given way to the near-themeless technical virtuosity of bebop a further triumph of technology over humanism."[12]

For Ellison, the spontaneity and intimacy associated with the culture of the South in general and with Black folk musical forms in particular were not always common features of urban life in Harlem. He writes of the typical Black Harlemite, "his speech hardens; his movements are geared to the time clock; his diet changes; his sensibilities quicken and his intelligence expands."[13] In short, the detached routine of urban life had supplanted the sensuousness of everyday lived experience rooted in Southern folk culture—an experience that had been for Black folk profoundly shaped by their musical expression. It is not surprising then that *Invisible Man* opens with a scene that reveals the central importance of music in Black culture. When Ellison's invisible man listens to a recording of Armstrong, he clearly expresses an affinity with the famous trumpeter and singer. The symbolic portrayal of the blues in this scene functions as a capacious signifier of Black culture and lived experience. Ellison's musical expression allegorizes the suffering of a displaced people even as it provides Ellison's protagonist with a means of apprehending his own erasure as an invisible man.

The novel marshals this blues perspective from the very outset in its representation of the underground cellar as a liminal space both part and apart from the teeming life of the city above it. The rest of the story is told as a recounting of events that mark the development of the protagonist's burgeoning consciousness of that life and his relative place in it. Ellison establishes a pattern of initiation from which his protagonist encounters people and places

in the city that harken back to Southern culture. His encounter with the street
vendor selling candied yams, his reluctance to order pork chops at the city
dinner, his rumination on the blues in Mary Rambo's apartment, his comments after hearing a "turgid blues" near the novel's conclusion—all reflect
the novel's deep investment in a ghetto pastoral mode of representation that
has the symbolic figure of the blues at its center. These crucial moments in
the novel reveal the critical tension between what Ellison referred to as the
"folk sensibilities" that informed Black lived experience in Northern cities
and the "urban slum conditions" that Black communities faced in the wake
of inner-city urban decay. The experience of his protagonist in the novel
also reveals the unique position of many second-generation Black migrants,
the sons and daughters of Black migrants who made the journey decades
earlier, who had to negotiate a place for themselves in the only home they
have ever known. The blues perspective that Ellison marshals in the novel
then represents the mastery of the ghetto pastoral form as his invisible man
is the figurative embodiment of the dialectical tension always at the center of
Black migration novels. Indeed, Ellison demonstrates through his portrayal
the Black migrant's ability to stand at the proverbial crossroads of Black lived
experience, between "folk sensibilities" and "urban slum conditions," while
finding meaning and purpose in his liminal subject position.

Criticism of the novel has often emphasized its relationship to musical
expression, more often as it relates to jazz rather than the blues.[14] For example, Horace A. Porter's reading of *Invisible Man* as a "jazz text" centers on
the formal structure of the novel. Porter writes "[the novel] consciously riffs
upon or plays countless variations on familiar literary and cultural themes."[15]
Porter views this formal structure as indicative of the protagonist's oscillating
perspective that flitters from one cultural form to the next. For Porter, this
"jazz perspective" represents the protagonist attempt to ascribe meaning
and substance to his otherwise marginalized existence. He does so through
a kind of symbolic improvisation, thereby creating a coherent self-identity
out of disparate fragments of his past and the disordered events of his present
circumstances. In other words, jazz as a narrative form becomes a basis for
establishing a sense of place and identity for Ellison's displaced and "invisible" Black migrant character.

Indeed, while the formal structure of the novel can certainly be viewed
in relation to jazz expression, its thematic structure is better understood in
relation to the blues. Porter rightly emphasizes the improvisational form of
the novel as analogous to the structure of jazz. But the way in which the novel
conveys meaning centers on a blues perspective. Indeed, the blues perspective
in the novel is analogous to the way in which musical expressions of the blues

attempt to make meaning out of human suffering. The musical expression of the blues punctuates the disconnection between the painful murmurings of the blues singer and the lyrical mastery achieved by the performance itself. Thus, the blues presents itself as a contradiction, what Ellison once referred to as the "near-tragic, near-comic lyricism" of human experience. It is precisely this construction of Black experience that Ellison's protagonist embodies as an "invisible man." His invisible man is simultaneously an active agent in constructing his own narrative while also embodying the erasure of a society that refuses to acknowledge his existence in any meaningful way. He embraces this reality—indeed, he appropriates it as a basis for understanding and expressing his contested identity. In short, he is a blues man writ large.

The blues gives Ellison's displaced migrant a means of articulating his place in a society that refuses to see him even if it cannot change his immediate circumstances. This power of the blues to give meaning to the suffering of Black people stems in part from its popular mass appeal. Although the blues performer stands at the proverbial crossroads amid endless possibilities, they do not stand alone but rather appeal to a larger Black experience. Farah Griffin argues that this communal ideal registered in the blues parallels a central theme of Black migration fiction. Griffin describes the communal ideal that blues singers such as Bessie Smith were able to create through their charged and intimate performances. She writes of Smith, "While the blues performance did not serve as a worship ritual, Smith's performance was more than mere entertainment. It acted as a means of convening community, of invoking common experiences and values. Though not necessarily a resistant space, it was a space where migrants could let their hair down, be themselves, and have a good time. As such, it was healing space."[16]

Griffin's description of the blues as constituting a "healing space" is instructive in gauging its function in Ellison's migration novel. The moments in the novel when Ellison's invisible man encounters the blues are therapeutic in mitigating his initial sense of displacement in the city. However, responding to Griffin's interpretation, I would add that the blues also foregrounds conflict and unresolved pain. While blues expression may represent a "healing space," it also represents a site of psychological struggle and painful introspection. The bivocal quality of the blues is central to its function as reflected in the blues spaces represented in the novel. The symbolic spaces in the novel formed around the trope of the blues (i.e., the underground cellar, Jim Trueblood's cabin, "Pete Wheatstraw's" corner, and Mary Rambo's apartment) foreground the conflict of rural and urban (past and present) experience that is at the center of Black migrant experience. It is this conflict that defines the expression of the blues performer who must simultaneously register joy in the midst of pain.

Ellison's artistic vision acknowledged such a blues perspective. In his famous essay, "The World and the Jug," Ellison describes Black lived experience as circumscribed by racial segregation but also charged with symbolic potential. Ellison asserts that Black folk occupy marginalized spaces in American society from which they have had to cultivate a unique blues perspective—a perspective that effectively enables them to manage psychological pain and social alienation. Ellison is worth quoting at length here:

> For even as his life toughens the Negro, even as it brutalizes him, sensitizes him, dulls him, goads him to anger, moves him to irony, sometimes fracturing and sometimes affirming his hopes; even as it shapes his attitudes toward family, sex, love, religion; even as it modulates his humor, tempers his joy—it *conditions* him to deal with his life and with himself. He must live it and try consciously to grasp its complexity until he can change it; must live it as he changes it. He is no mere product of his socio-political predicament. He is a product of the interaction between his racial predicament, his individual will and the broader American cultural freedom in which finds his ambiguous existence. Thus he, too, in a limited way, is his own creation. [emphasis mine][17]

It is precisely this sort of blues perspective that enables Ellison's invisible man to ascribe meaning to himself and to the environment around him. He is "invisible" only because a racist society refuses to see him. The fictional frame narrative that structures the novel is his attempt to write himself into existence, and it is from the liminal/blues space of his underground cellar that he sets out to do this. Ellison's symbolic treatment of this urban space is especially important, and parallels Baldwin's treatment of a similar space, the "threshing floor" of the storefront church, in his novel *Go Tell It on the Mountain*. Both spatial representations foreground the competing terms of black migrant experience, combining symbolic forms of musical expression (e.g., jazz, blues, and gospel) in a unique place of cultural mediation and urban initiation. These spaces are sites of rural and urban conflict, but they are also places in which cultural forms and practices are brought to bear in reconciling the competing terms of Black lived experience—an experience formed at the confluence of Southern folk culture and urban spaces in the city. These are not idyllic spaces but are rather sites of physical and psychological struggle. From this perspective, these urban spaces are more dialectical than didactic—that is, they reflect the harsh wilderness instead of the proverbial promised land.

In his seminal work, *The Urban Revolution*, Henri Lefebvre describes the "urban form" in similar terms. There he writes, "The urban is . . . pure form: a place of encounter, assembly, simultaneity. This form has no specific content but is the center of attraction and life. It is an abstraction, but unlike a metaphysical entity, the urban is a concrete abstraction, associated with practice. Living creates, the products of industry, technology and wealth, works of culture, ways of living, situations, the modulations and ruptures of the everyday—the urban accumulates all content."[18] Lefebvre's conception of the urban space as a ubiquitous form reflects its symbolic function in Ellison's novel. The urban spaces depicted in the novel are primarily places of commerce and consumption; the invisible man's underground dwelling is foremost a coal cellar. This fact underscores the material function ascribed to urban spaces. However, such spaces also acquire symbolic meaning in the novel through the invocation of a blues perspective. For example, the invisible man inhabits a space of "infinite possibilities," an ironic description for his subterranean, alienated existence. Yet, what allows him to describe his existence in these terms is the blues perspective he marshals in this urban space. As he listens to a recording of Louis Armstrong in his underground cellar, this circumscribed space is figuratively transformed into a site of identity formation, a veritable blues space in which the so-called music of invisibility ironically provides a basis for self-recognition in an urban environment that systematically denies any such self-identification.

Ellison's marshaling of this blues perspective in his Black migration novel is the culmination of the form precisely because it figures urban spaces as ubiquitous signifiers of meaning. His protagonist adeptly manipulates not only his identity but also the spatial signifiers around him that shape his self-identity. The underground cellar functions in this sense as a capacious signifier that exemplifies the varied meanings associated with urban spaces in the city. What makes his "hole" a ghetto pastoral space is the "infinite possibilities" it represents. The symbolic possibilities registered in this space set the tone for the rest of the novel where Ellison's invisible man enters into and out of urban spaces that both empower and delimit his sense of subjectivity. His ability to not only adapt to these spaces (as Johnson's ex-colored man does) but also to interact with these spatial forms as an interpreter and as a producer of meaning is a key thematic element that fundamentally sets him apart from an entire tradition of Black migrant characters. As such, Ellison offers up a prophetic vision of the future for Black folk generally who stood betwixt and between their Southern folk roots and a nascent modern consciousness—at the proverbial crossroads of the social movement began earlier that century with the first influx of Black migrants seeking a better life for themselves in the Northern city.

How Far Is the Promised Land?

The Black migration novels of the 1950s were set against much more difficult historical circumstances than their literary predecessors. Foremost among the historical factors that shaped the period were the expansion of urban ghettos and the growing housing crisis in Northern cities.[19] Paradoxically, however, the 1950s saw a renewed optimism among Black Southerners to migrate north in search of a better life. Manning Marable has described this decade of the 1950s as a "second reconstruction" period for the country.[20] Just as the first Reconstruction period occasioned both the optimistic discourse of racial uplift and the failed dream of "forty acres and a mule," this period of social and economic prosperity for the country obscured many of the urban realities that black folk were encountering in Northern cities. Marable notes the economic factors that were pushing Black people out of the South even as the social and economic fabric of Black life in the North was steadily declining. Marable is worth quoting at length on this point:

> The mechanization of southern agriculture was a decisive reason why the black migration north continued. From 1940–50, the number of non-southern blacks increased from 2.4 million to 6.4 million. In most industrial cities in the Midwest, the black population growth rate was between 500 to 1,000 percent above that for whites. The drive to the North was inspired also by the promise of higher wages and better working conditions; but these factors were dependent upon the availability of employment. During the last five years of Truman's administration, non-white unemployment had jumped to 9.3 percent v. 4.5 percent for whites. In 1954, 16.5 percent of all non-white youths in the job market were unemployed. The black ghettoes of the North, first taking shape with industrial demand for Negro labor a half century before, where beginning to become stagnant centers for joblessness and despair.[21]

These conditions occasioned a profound change in the symbolic value ascribed to the character of the city. The new face of the city was more gritty than cosmopolitan and reflected the bleak visage of the underclass of Black folk residing in the once industrial centers of Northern cities. These Black urban sections, such as Chicago's "Black Belt" district, had become notorious slum areas by the late 1930s.[22] If "Black" had been a euphemism for urbanism during the great migrations of the 1920s, it was increasingly coming to symbolize by the 1940s the worst of urban life in the North. In short, the blasted ghetto landscapes of the postindustrial North became synonymous with the Black life that endured there.[23] The negative value ascribed to urban places in the North, most notably places like New York's Harlem neighborhood and Washington's Seventh Avenue, signaled the end of an era for Black folk in general and for the culturally valorized representations of such places in particular.

The romantic view of the city, rooted in the optimistic discourse of Black migration at the turn of the twentieth century, gave way to more realistic representations of urban life that emphasized the oppressive structures and institutions that characterized the postindustrial cities of the North. Often referred to as "protest fiction," stories portraying the working-class struggle became popular between the decades of the 1930s and 1940s. These decades saw the wide publication of so-called radical novels, novels that were informed by Marxist and socialist philosophies, and that centered on questions involving economic and social inequality.[24] Novelists such as Pietro Di Donato, John Dos Pasos, and Richard Wright conveyed socialist realist themes in their fiction.[25] These novelists, especially Wright, emphasized the structures of inequality that shaped the urban landscape of America, most notably racial segregation and class stratification.

While Ellison's literary predecessors sought to reconcile the promise of the North with the socioeconomic realities of the country, Ellison embarks on a much different task as an author. He writes his novel during a period when the disillusionment of black urban life revealed the stultifying conditions in big cities across the country. It is out of desperation not hope that Ellison's protagonist leaves the South. Indeed, he believes his northward migration is merely a stop gap until he has raised the funds necessary to return to the Tuskegee like Southern school that various extenuating circumstances have forced him to leave. The North is less a "promised land" for him than it is a brief respite from the troubles he faces in the South. By revising the thematic trajectory of the traditional migration novel, Ellison forces his protagonist to (re)consider his place in a Southern culture and society from which Black migrants had historically sought to escape. His always imminent return to the South (a return home that is permanently deferred in the novel) means that he is already in a liminal position—neither displaced in the northern city (because he does not view himself as belonging there in the first place) nor enamored with a Southern home that refuses to acknowledge any aspect of his existence except his "social responsibility" in maintaining the prevailing racial hierarchy. As the ubiquitous blues figure at the proverbial crossroads, he finds a sense of belonging not in a particular place but in the interstices between places—between normative standards of living and radical ways of knowing.

Ironically, the problem that attends the representation of his symbolically potent underground home is the countervailing reality of urban life that exists above it. This becomes the central complication in the novel. The ideals ascribed to the symbolically charged space from which the story is set—ideals such as "placeness," "identity," "hopefulness"—are constantly challenged by the disordering, displacing quality of the urban spaces he encounters in the story. The contrast between the symbolic space of the underground cellar and the urban spaces of the city is the tension at the center of Ellison's ghetto pastoral narrative. For Ellison's protagonist, the harmony of sound emanating from his underground cellar is always juxtaposed with the "discordant voices" of the city. These urban spaces are represented as sites of conflict wherein the Black migrant must marshal the symbolic forms and practices there as a means of articulating (or imagining) a sense of place of belonging in the city. Thus, the cultural forms operative in these spaces— e.g., blues and spirituals—are transformed into a language of the displaced and dispossessed precisely because they endeavor to "finger the jagged grain" of that experience in hopes of finding something meaningful in it.

"Blues People"

In his commentary on LeRoi Jones's *Blues People*, Ralph Ellison writes of the vivid complexity of the blues form in depicting the triumph and tragedy of black life. Ellison describes the "aesthetic nature" of the blues—its formal aspect as art rather than a political (as Jones would have it) category of cultural expression. Ellison's account of the blues—which one may very well read as a thematic epilogue to his novel *Invisible Man*—is worth quoting at length here: "The blues speak to us simultaneously of the tragic and the comic aspects of the human condition and they express a profound sense of life shared by many Negro Americans precisely because their lives have combined these modes. This has been the heritage of a people who for hundreds of years could not celebrate birth or dignify death and whose need to live despite the dehumanizing pressures of slavery developed an endless capacity for laughing at their painful experiences."[26]

Ellison's marshaling of the blues form in *Invisible Man* reflects his understanding of the role of musical culture in the symbolic formation of "place."

Indeed, for the dispossessed Black folk who were not able to "celebrate birth or death," the blues was a means of expressing through music a sense of shared experience. It becomes for Ellison's Black migrant protagonist a means of articulating identity and place in an urban environment that denies him both—indeed, an environment that renders him virtually invisible. Similar to Lefebvre's conception of the urban as a place of "simultaneity," Ellison figures the blues as a capacious signifier of Black lived experience, encompassing within its symbolic structure the contradictory terms of Black lived experience. Indeed, the figure of the blues in the novel signifies the paradoxical quality of Black migrant experience, as it invokes an ideal of collective experience that is both a source of social conflict and cultural affinity. In this sense, Ellison figures his protagonist as a blues man at the proverbial "crossroads," permanently displaced from home and community, but ever creating a sense of place(ness) from the fragments of his discarded past.

Ellison appropriates the blues form as signifying both the promise of the city—registered in the ideal of establishing a sense of place and belonging—as well as the rural and urban conflict that complicates the fulfillment of that promise for his Black migrant protagonist. The invisible man stands at the crossroads of Black migrant lived experience between Harlem, the brutal city of fact, and an elusive vision of the promised land. He occupies a symbolic space that is the product of both things—a liminal space of "infinite possibilities." Ellison's nameless protagonist sets out to write the story of his life from his underground cellar, where he has fashioned a surreal existence that symbolically underscores his liminal status in a society that refuses to see him. Ironically, his "hole" becomes a symbolic figure of the enduring quality of Black urban life inasmuch as it represents Black folk's ability to overcome oppressive structures in order to create a whole way of life. Indeed, the underground existence he has forged for himself can be understood as representing a blues sensibility. Just as the blues musician makes art out of the *everyday*, he discovers in Louis Armstrong's song "(What Did I Do to Be So) Black and Blue" an articulation of his own place and identity in the city, an evocation of the absurdity of his existence, and the means to make sense of it all. Thus, in what he calls the "music of invisibility," the protagonist sees a reflection of his own condition as a Black migrant, exiled and displaced beneath the streets of New York City.

Ellison's protagonist migrates to the North, although not by choice. He is forced to leave school when he makes the mistake of driving a white trustee of the college, Mr. Norton, into the old slave quarters where he hears Jim Trueblood's tale of incest. As punishment for his transgression, Mr. Bledsoe, the president of the college, asks him to leave school "temporarily." He sets out for New York City in hopes of earning enough money to eventually return to school. In wandering the streets of Harlem in search of work, Ellison's protagonist resembles the classical Black migrant character—displaced from home and community, betwixt and between rural and urban modes of experience.[27] He eventually falls prey to a series of misadventures in the city; he searches for work only to find that the "recommendation letters" given to him by Bledsoe are actually warnings to potential employers. He becomes involved with the Brotherhood, a quasi-communist organization, only to find that their commitment to the "Negro Problem" is disingenuous. Indeed, the central complication of the novel is figured in the haunting phrase Ellison's protagonist hears in a dream: "Keep this n----r boy running." This ominous warning foreshadows the permanent displacement that Ellison's protagonist experiences in the city.

Even before his migration to the city, the traditional scene of displacement in the Black migration novel, Ellison's protagonist is displaced from the outset in a Southern society that has not evolved an adequate place for him. His first realization of this occurs when he is asked to give a speech before the town's influential white men. Before he can give his speech, however, he is forced to participate in the "Battle Royal," a boxing free-for-all pitting the town's Black boys against one another. Having fought and paid the proverbial "price of ticket" in the form of a violent beating, he is allowed to give his speech in which he extols the virtues of Black humility. But when he mistakenly utters the phrase "social equality" instead of his intended phrase, "social responsibility," he is immediately forced to retract his words. Reminded in this instance of his proscribed place in Southern society, he humbly accepts the gifts the white men bestow upon him—a leather brief case that "will someday contain important documents pertaining to his people" and a scholarship to the local "Negro college." Both items, ironically, will eventually underscore his displaced status in the Northern city.

The Southern section of the novel begins with this violent scene of initiation and figures Ellison's protagonist as a displaced black migrant par excellence.[28] For not only is he displaced within a society dominated by powerful white men, but he is also without a sense of home and belonging among black folk as well. His sense of belonging within a well-defined cultural context and social order is immediately shot through by the figure of his grandfather, whose deathbed confession calls into question the very nature of Black experience in the South: "Son, after I'm gone I want you to keep up the good fight. I never told you, but our life is a war and I have been a traitor all my born days, a spy in the enemy's country ever since I give up my gun back in Reconstruction. Live with your head in the lion's mouth. I want you to overcome 'em with yeses, undermine 'em with grins, agree 'em to death and destruction, let 'em swoller you till they vomit or bust wide open" (16).[29]

The narrator's predicament is embodied in the central figure of his grandfather. The figure of the grandfather, with whom "the trouble all began," calls attention to a contrived social order that assigns arbitrary racial value to people. His haunting words reveal for the protagonist—in what is for him an initial moment of recognition—the nature of a society that has failed to provide an adequate place for him and, indeed, for all Black people. Thus, the grandfather's perspective gestures toward the social recognition and social consciousness that eventually drives Ellison's invisible man underground. His deathbed confession becomes in this sense a great commission, to which Ellison's apostolic protagonist is compelled to fulfill. Yet, it is with a great deal of reluctance that he does so. For this reason, the grandfather's confession becomes for the protagonist a blessing and a curse as it constantly challenges him to look beyond the appearance of things in order to forge a new reality.

The grandfather's passive resistance to the racial status quo functions as both a model of racial subversion and as a rhetorical basis for establishing a sense of place and identity. For the perspective he reveals calls upon the invisible man to make sense of the contradictory aims and values that define his place (or lack thereof) in American society. It is a perspective that acknowledges the contradictions that underscore the experience of Black folk, and in doing so, ascribes its own meaning to that experience despite the veritable absurdity that perpetually attends it. It is, in short, a kind of "blues perspective," reflecting both the incongruities of Black experience as well as the meaning(s) embedded in that experience. Yet, it is only at this final moment of death that the subterfuge is revealed and the meaning behind the grandfather's "blues sensibility" can be expressed. Like a "spy in the enemy's country," he has had to pretend to be something that he is not. Although the grandfather embodies a "blues perspective," it is a perspective that can find only limited expression in the social context of the South. He and other Black people can only speak to white people in the language of "yeses and grins," a fact that Ellison's protagonist attests to after the ordeal of the "Battle Royal." Thus, the blues form functions in the social context of the South as a kind of racial performance designed to assuage white people and comfort Black people.[30]

Houston Baker's reading of the novel describes this function of the blues in the context of the South. His view of the novel as expressive of a blues aesthetic stems in part from his reading of the "Trueblood episode," a story conveyed in the Southern section of the novel describing a Black sharecropper who commits incest by sleeping with his daughter. After impregnating both his wife and daughter, Trueblood is ostracized by the local black community, but finds favor among the white folk who give him money in exchange for his lurid tale. Trueblood's tale of incest conveys an almost triumphant tone as he affirms his stark resolve in the face of seeming disaster: "I make up my mind that I ain't nobody but myself and ain't nothing' I can do but let whatever is gonna happen, happen" (62). Baker reads Trueblood's statement of self-affirmation as expressive of a blues aesthetic. He writes,

> The farmer's statement is not an expression of transcendence. It is, instead, an affirmation of a still recognizable humanity by a singer who has incorporated his personal disaster into a code of blues meanings emanating from an unpredictably chaotic world. In translating his tragedy into the vocabulary and semantics of the blues and, subsequently, into the electrifying expression of his narrative, Trueblood realizes that he is not so changed by catastrophe that he must condemn, mortify, or redefine his essential self. This self, as the preceding discussion indicates, is in many ways the obverse of the stable, predictable, puritanical, productive, law-abiding ideal self of the American industrial-capitalist society.[31]

Baker's reading notwithstanding, one must make the important distinction between Trueblood's marshaling of the blues form in a rural-Southern context, and the narrator's subsequent encounter with the blues form in an urban-Northern context. It is within this urban context that the narrator relates his story. It is also within the context of the city that his blues expression assumes a particular form that I would argue distinguishes it from its rural-Southern iteration in the novel. The "self" that Trueblood's blues constructs is one that has "survived" the disaster of incest, a self that speaks the "unspeakable" in order to avoid its own destruction. But it is also an expression of the "self" that is privileged (and, indeed, made possible) by the racist values of a Southern society. Trueblood is able to trade on his tragic circumstances precisely because his self-degradation reinforces the social norms and expectations of white supremacy. He is made a symbol by white people who, like the white men in the novel that constantly remind invisible man of his place, seek to uphold the racial hierarchy that posits whiteness as a normative ideal and Blackness as negative value. Trueblood becomes an object of curiosity for white folks because his tale of incest confirms their racist assumptions about the degradation of Black people, while also affording them a vicarious fulfillment of their repressed sexuality. In this sense, Trueblood's "singing of the blues" imagines a self that is certainly "the obverse of the stable, predictable, puritanical, productive, law-abiding ideal self of the American industrial-capitalist society," but it is also one that is obverse to any positive ideal of Blackness.

Ellison's portrayal of Trueblood—as well as his portrayal of the protagonist's grandfather—functions as a thematic point of departure for his invisible man, who must necessarily move beyond the proscribed modes of existence (and expression) in the South. For this reason, I would argue that the expression of the blues as means of accessing both place and identity assumes a unique form in the northern section of the novel, where the protagonist must affirm a positive identity for himself despite an urban environment that renders him "invisible." Baker's reading obscures this thematic progression in the novel along with the rural and urban conflict that produces it. The urban variant of the blues, and its function as a symbolic means of establishing place and identity in the city, is shaped in part by migration and the rural-urban conflict associated with it.

In contrast to Trueblood's self-negating expression of the blues, the protagonist's encounter with a man named "Pete Wheatstraw"—a blues singing, homeless wanderer on the streets of Harlem—reveals the self-affirming function of the blues in the urban context of the Northern city. The protagonist's hearing of the blues in the streets of Harlem becomes a Proustian reminder of the Southern culture from which he is displaced: "Close to the curb ahead I saw a man pushing a cart piled high with rolls of blue paper and heard him singing in a clear ringing voice. It was a blues, and I walked along behind him remembering the times I had heard such singing at home. It seemed that here some memories slipped around my life at the campus and went far back to things I had long ago shut out of my mind. There was no escaping such reminders" (173). The performance of the blues functions as a signifier of collective experience and as a symbolic means of establishing a sense of place and belonging in the city. The name "Pete Wheatstraw" was a common pseudonym used by blues performers in the early 1930s.[32] Thus, the man in the street is representative of an entire tradition of blues performers as he marshals past lived experience. Exemplifying both critic and connoisseur of such a tradition, "Pete Wheatstraw" implores his interlocutor to drop his pretensions and engage in a verbal game of signifying. His constant refrain "who got the dog" is meant to elicit from the protagonist a codified response that utilizes the language of the vernacular. When the protagonist refuses to do this, the man on the corner appeals to shared experience: "Now I know you from down home, how come you trying to act like you never heard that before! Hell, ain't nobody out here this morning but us colored—why you trying to deny me?" (173). What, indeed, the protagonist denies him is a symbolic exchange that posits an ideal of collective experience—in other words, a codified form of expression—what the protagonist refers to at the outset as the "music of invisibility"— that can mitigate the culturally displaced status of Black folk in the city. Despite his misgivings about the past, and his reluctance to acknowledge the vernacular forms embodied in the figure of "Pete Wheatstraw," Ellison's protagonist locates in this "blues man" an ideal of "home" and "belonging": "I wanted to leave him, and yet I found a certain comfort in walking along beside him, as though we'd walked this way before through other mornings, in other places" (175).

Ellison's urban "blues man" signifies both the enduring ideal of place that Black folk established in the city as well as the perpetual sense of displacement that undercut such ideals. In the context of the city, the blues signifies a sense of place (and collective experience) even as it also acknowledges the urban displacement of Black people in the city and the failed promise of the North. Pete Wheatstraw's description of Harlem figures it simultaneously as a dangerous place and as the "only place" for Black folk: "Man, this Harlem ain't nothing but a bear's den. But I tell you one thing . . . it's the best place in the world for you and me, and if times don't get better soon I'm going to grab that bear and turn him every way but loose!" (174). The description of Harlem as a "bear's den" recalls the protagonist's description of himself as "jack the bear," as well as his description of living in an underground cellar as a "hibernation." If Harlem is a veritable "bear's den" emblematic of the failed promised of Black migration, within the expression of the blues is a symbolic means of negotiating the contradictory terms that define urban spaces in the city. Thus, the blues form is figured here as a symbolic means of negotiating place and identity in the city.

Charles Keil, in his seminal study *Urban Blues*, describes the urban blues as functionally distinct from its rural iteration. Describing the blues as foremost a "migratory music," Keil delineates its particular iterations in both rural and urban contexts:

> . . . a blues man in the country or for the first time coming to grips with city life sings primarily to ease his worried mind, to get things out of his system, to feel better; it is of secondary importance whether or not others are present and deriving similar satisfactions from his music. It is a source of encouragement to know that your complaints and grievances are shared by others, but such support is not essential. An urban bluesman senses a broader and deeper obligation to the community or, rather, to Negro communities across the country, since the urban blues singer is practically by definition itinerant.[33]

Keil's general description of the urban blues singer emphasizes the thematic importance of establishing a sense of place and belonging in this urban variant of the blues. For the "itinerant" blues man, the reestablishment of place through the expression of the blues is the thematic impetus behind his music. In this sense, the thematic impetus behind the blues is analogous to the promise of black migration in that both seek to locate a "place of belonging" for the otherwise displaced figure.

For Ellison's invisible man, it is this symbolic expression of place and identity that holds the key to fulfillment of the promise of Black migration. To put it another way, the expression of the blues signifies a symbolic mediation (if not a complete transcendence) of the absurd and contradictory circumstances that define the experience of black migrants in the city. As to this possibility, the narrator ruminates on the old man's blues expression as he watches him disappear into the city:

> "So long," I said and watched him going. I watched him push around the corner to the top of the hill, leaning sharp against the cart handle, and heard his voice arise, muffled now, as he started down.
> *She's got feet like a monkeee*
> *Legs*
> *Legs, Legs like a maaad*
> *Bulldog . . .*
> What does it mean, I thought. I'd heard it all my life but suddenly the strangeness of it came through to me. Was it about a man of about some strange sphinxlike animal?
> . . . I strode along, hearing the cartman's song become a lonesome, broad-toned whistle now that flowered at the end of each phrase into a tremulous, blue-toned chord. And in its flutter and swoop I heard the sound of a railroad train high-balling it, lonely across the lonely night. He was the Devil's son-in-law, all right, and he was a man who could whistle a three-toned chord . . . God damn, I thought, they're a hell of a people! And I didn't know whether it was pride or disgust that suddenly flashed over me. (177)

The protagonist's initial rush of pride and nostalgia is undercut by his final expression of ambivalence. This and other similar moments in the novel represent the incessant conflict of rural and urban meanings that define his experience as a Black migrant. The invocation of the blues foregrounds this conflict even as it also provides a brief respite from his feeling of displacement in the city. Thus, the invocation of the blues, while providing the protagonist with a symbolic space of memory and self-recognition, also forces him to recognize his displaced status as a Black migrant in the city.

His encounter with a man selling hot candied yams becomes another instance in which the cultural materials and practices of a displaced rural past rub against the environment and circumstances of the city. Another Proustian reminder of his displaced cultural status as a Black migrant, the odor of the yams evokes in him "a stab of nostalgia." This description suggests the pain of memory registered in his eating of the yam, an otherwise mundane act in the social and cultural context of the South, transformed here into an expression of "freedom" in the urban environment of the city. The pain of remembering stems from the racial stereotypes associated with such things as "yams," "chitterlings," and "pork chops," and the stigma they have acquired as popular food items among southern Black folks. Where Ellison's protagonist had once shunned these things, he now views them with new eyes in the city. For this reason, his eating of the yam evokes in him a sense of newfound freedom: "I walked along, munching the yam, just as suddenly overcome by an intense feeling of *freedom*—simply because I was eating while walking along the street" [emphasis mine] (264).

His experience in the streets of Harlem generates a wistful nostalgia for life "down home." Yet the terms of that nostalgia are immediately undercut by the immediate recognition that such comforting reminders cannot entirely mitigate his profound sense of displacement in the city: "Continue on the yam level and life would be sweet—though somewhat yellowish. Yet the freedom to eat yams on the street was far less than I had expected upon coming to the city. An unpleasant taste bloomed in my mouth now as I bit the end of the yam and threw it into the street; it had been frost-bitten" (267). The "frost-bitten" yam becomes a symbol of rural and urban conflict; the "unpleasant taste" blooming his mouth is an indication of his growing disillusionment in the city. The brutal cold that ruins his yam symbolizes the physical forces he faces as a black migrant in the city, while the yam itself symbolizes a sense of wistful nostalgia for home and place that is inadequate alone to mitigate his growing sense of displacement. Thus, the ideal of home and place—symbolized in food, music, and the blues—is complicated in the novel by the urban realities of the city.

Against the brutal backdrop of the city, however, Ellison's protagonist finds a brief respite from his feelings of displacement in the apartment of Mary Rambo. Mary's apartment is representative of the ideal domestic spaces that were so important in the Black migration novels of the 1920s.[34] Mary herself comes to represent an ideal of collective experience that is expressed once again in the form of the blues. It is the perspective of the blues that enables her to make a place for herself despite the transient quality of her existence and the ever-present threat of eviction. The protagonist describes her demeanor as he listens to her sing the blues: "Then from down the hall I could hear Mary singing, her voice clear and untroubled, though she sang a troubled song. It was the 'Back Water Blues.' I lay listening as the sound flowed to and around me, bringing me a calm sense of my indebtedness" (297).

Her ability to maintain an "untroubled" demeanor while singing a "troubled song" is a testament to the enduring quality of her blues perspective. Mary's singing of this particular blues signifies her enduring sense of home and belonging despite the constant threat of her displacement. She may well be displaced (evicted) from her physical place of belonging—a reality that the song laments—but she cannot be displaced from her sense of symbolic belonging. She has made a place for herself in an urban environment that has not evolved a permanent place for her. Hearing her blues evokes in Ellison's protagonist a "calm sense of [his] indebtedness," a description that suggests a reconciliation (although momentary) of the rural and urban conflict that defines his experience as a black migrant. What he feels "indebted" to is the collective experience that Mary's "blues" signifies, an experience he unconsciously rejected while growing up in the South but now finds greater connection to in the North. And yet, this moment of recognition, initiated by another symbolic invocation of the blues, is undercut by his compelling desire to go back out into the city. Ellison's protagonist is torn, as it were, between a longing for home (and community) and the irresistible allure of the city.[35]

In this sense, the domestic space of Mary's apartment is represented here as a dialectical space signifying both an ideal of place and belonging—the proverbial promise of the North—as well as the incessant conflict of rural and urban meanings that defines Black migrant spaces in the city. The novel pivots on this symbolically charged space and, with the exception of the underground cellar, it is perhaps the most important expression of the ghetto pastoral mode in the novel. Drawing on this episode in the novel, Laurence Rodgers agues "the principal imperative of the African-American migration novel can be viewed as a century-long attempt to reconvene the family mealtime gathering in the heart of the modern city."[36] Rodgers is right in acknowledging the central task of "place making" in Ellison's novel, but his interpretation does not account for the conflict of rural and urban experience at the center of stories of Black migration. Indeed, the trope of "place making" in Black migration novels, the "attempt to reconvene that family mealtime gathering in the heart of the modern city," must also necessarily involve an engagement with this conflict of rural and urban experience. Ellison's protagonist must first attend to this conflict before he can figure a place for himself in the city. In a heightened moment of introspection, he resembles a Black Hamlet in his attempt to reconcile these contradictory terms of his existence:

> One moment I believed, I was dedicated, willing to lie on the blazing coals, do anything to attain a position on the campus—then snap! It was done with, finished, through. Now there was only problem of forgetting it. If only all the contradictory voices shouting inside my head would calm down and sing a song in unison, whatever it was I wouldn't care as long as they sang without dissonance; yes, and avoided the uncertain extremes of the scale. But there was no relief. I was wild with resentment but too much under "self control," that frozen virtue, that freezing vice. (259)

His desire to reconcile this conflict—to establish a harmonious lived experience in the city—is the principal imperative of the novel. Ellison again expresses the problem of urban displacement in musical terms. The "self control" that inhibits his ability to appropriate the cultural materials of the past (of the South) recalls Ellison's description of the cultural attitudes of Black people in Harlem. Like the permanently displaced Harlemites Ellison describes in "Harlem Is Nowhere," his protagonist finds himself "out of sync" with the humanistic forms of expression such as the blues that could provide a basis for home and belonging in the city. Similarly, Ellison's protagonist refers to the innumerable masses of Black migrants in Harlem as "men of transition whose faces were immobile," (440) seeing in them a reflection of his own condition. For they too are cut off from the cultural forms that would enable them to express a sense of self and place in an urban environment that has denied them both. Witnessing the Black masses of Harlem, he evokes what becomes the central question in the novel: "I moved with the crowd, the sweat pouring off me, listening to the grinding roar of traffic, the growing sound of a record shop loudspeaker blaring a languid blues. I stopped. *Was this all that would be recorded? Was this the only true history of the times, a mood blared by trumpets, trombones, saxophones and drums, a song with turgid, inadequate words?*" [emphasis mine] (443).

The blues, with its "turgid, inadequate words," becomes in this instance a language of the displaced and dispossessed. The blues provides a kind of soundtrack for the teeming masses of Harlem, recording in "inadequate words" a tenuous sense of place and belonging. Ellison's protagonist, however, questions its lasting effect. His ambivalence again underscores the precariousness of his existence and the perpetual displacement he experiences as a black migrant. Ultimately, Ellison's invisible man appeals to a broader sense of place and identity; his last words—"who knows but that, on the lower frequencies, I speak for you"—gestures toward an ideal of universal experience. This becomes the real "moment of arrival" for Ellison displaced protagonist who resolves to quit his underground cellar because "even an invisible man has a socially responsible role to play" (581). However, his decision to end his "hibernation" does not foreclose the conflict and contradiction that have defined his experience as a displaced, Black migrant in the city. He concedes this fact when he admits, "I'm shaking off the old skin and I'll leave it here in the hole. I'm coming out, no less invisible without it, but coming out nevertheless" (581). Ever the blues man, he presses forward despite the incongruity of his existence. He is "no less invisible," an indication of his permanently liminal status, but his recognition of this fact coupled with his ability to now utilize his newfound double consciousness brings the narrative full circle, back to the very outset where he is the fictional author of this metanarrative.

In the end, Ellison's invisible man embodies the linguistic agency that an entire tradition of Black authors sought to invest in their characters, an artistic and political goal they could not fully achieve because of the historical exigencies of a society that did not acknowledge the social existence of such a thing as a "black writer." Ellison's protagonist is the ironic culmination of that rhetorical history, a Black migrant who finds his voice in an underground coal cellar beneath the streets of New York City, who gives meaning to a Black experience formed at the crossroads of history between "strum und drang."

"The Little Man at Chehaw Station"

Perhaps the most salient expression of the artistic and political vision of Ellison's classic novel is conveyed in his seminal essay "The Little Man at Chehaw Station." An essay that ostensibly turns on the metaphoric figure of "the little man behind the stove," Ellison sets out to explain the challenges of the artist/author who must always be mindful of the "mixed background and general character of his audience."[37] For the American artist/author must, in Ellison's view, approach their work as both an act of rhetorical skill and "an act of democratic faith."[38] For in the latter is revealed the tenuous relationship between the author and her audience, a relationship that always already turns on a general assumption of mastery, where the writer as a deft manipulator of linguistic tools and the reader as a competent if not adept interpreter of the written word are both concerned. While that dynamic may well hold sway on most occasions, it does not always. The complexity of the crowd is the fly in the rhetorical ointment so to speak, and for the artist/author, this means a tacit recognition that "any American audience will conceal at least *one* individual whose knowledge and taste will complement, or surpass, his own."[39]

This linguistic agent, this connoisseur of the written word, this "little man behind the stove," embodies the democratic spirit of a society where even the least of us can avail herself as a cultured aficionado. But what sets Ellison's metaphoric conceit apart from its not-so-distant cousin, Antonio Gramsci's organic intellectual whose rational prowess springs from the depths of the working class, is the social contradiction it highlights. While Gramsci's folk genius is not only comfortable among "the people" but distinctly visible among them as well, Ellison's "little man" is set apart by his uncommon character, his "personal uniqueness," and his "democratic anonymity which makes locating him an unending challenge."[40] In a passage that may as well describe his invisible man, Ellison explains the liminal status of his "little man" who stands betwixt and between normative social standards and radical ways of knowing: "Drawn to the brightness of bright lights, he cloaks himself in invisibility—perhaps because in the shadow of his anonymity he can be both the vernacular cat who looks at (and listens to) the tradition-bound or fad-struck king *and* the little boy who sees clearly the artist-emperor's pretentious nakedness."[41] A figure who seeks the "brightness" of the light even as he "cloaks himself in invisibility" would seem at first glance a contradiction in terms. But the tension inherent to this liminal figure is more a reflection of the society that refuses to see him than it is an expression of personal ambiguity. In other words, like his fictional invisible man, the metaphoric figure of the "little man" is an expression of the enduring thought and experience of individuals forced to live on the margins of society—but individuals who nevertheless find agency in the critical recognition of their own complex social position.

The problem for Ellison is how then to locate oneself as an author in relation to this displaced figure whose critical perspective is always reciprocal. It would be quite easy to identify Ellison's protagonist as the fictional embodiment of this "little man." Yet, another way of reading the trope of the "little man" in relation to the novel is to understand Ellison's protagonist as the fictional embodiment of the Black author writ large. We do after all find him engaged in writing his tome at the very outset of the novel, and the action that follows we are to assume comes from the very pages he has presumably set about composing. If he is indeed a composite figure of sorts, a placard for the vernacular tradition itself, he is not the best that tradition has to offer. He is not represented as an exemplar of Black letters, nor are his underground ruminations presented as a virtuoso performance. Rather his attempt to find a voice amid a polyphony of blues expressions is representative of the collective struggle of the Black artisan. It was this struggle that Du Bois described in *The Souls of Black Folk* where he laments the "double aims" every Black author must pursue.[42] It is precisely this problem the Black artist encounters as she must tailor her writing to the collective interest (and needs) of the masses while also (and at once) attending to the proverbial "little man behind the stove."

Ellison's ghetto pastoral expression of the blues is an appropriate narrative for attending to this problem. His nameless, "invisible" protagonist attempts to respond to the challenge posed by a diverse audience whose varied sensibilities reflect the range of thought present in a democratic (if also racially segregated) society. The profound import of his final words—"who knows but on the lower frequencies I speak for you" —certainly appeals to a universal sensibility; but just as well his last words also speak to an unspoken (if not unspeakable) expression of the unique complexity of black folk who have historically found themselves permanently located at a proverbial crossroads. It is no wonder that Ellison believed his novel to be timely in its outlook and perspective written just in time before the promise of Black migration gave way to the promise of integration. The promise of integration, if not the actual reality of an integrated society, would forever transform the symbol of the Northern city as a proverbial promised land. Those vibrant Black migrant communities in the North had their share of poverty and struggle. But they retained a share of a Black cultural heritage brought by scores of southern Black migrants who saw themselves as the heirs of a new social reality in the North, where they could perhaps avail themselves as both Black and as citizens of the republic. Racial integration with its promise of inclusion lacked the practical means to ensure economic and social development in those communities once hailed as bastions of Black progress. And since de facto segregation prevented an overwhelming majority of Black folk from leaving those now impoverished communities, the so-called promised land now signified stagnation and entrapment.

"Harlem Is Nowhere," Ellison's negative description of the permanent displacement of Black folk in Northern ghettos, defines what was once the epicenter of black cultural life as a liminal space of uncertainty and ambiguity. No longer a destination, Harlem becomes in Ellison's construction emblematic of the proverbial crossroads itself—the iconic blues expression of the indeterminacy of Black life, the symbolic expression of the permanent displacement of Black people in a society that had not evolved an adequate place for them. Much like the symbolically charged description of Chehaw Station, where the metaphoric "little man" resides, Harlem, the once held promised land, is transformed into an interstitial space of arrivals and departures, where the varied forces of history bear down on an entire people. And while the metaphoric figure hides behind the stove, Ellison's invisible man hides beneath the streets of the teeming city as a figure that at once embodies and responds to the metaphoric "little man." The reflexive quality of Ellison's invisible man represents the very mastery of the ghetto pastoral mode.

Especially for this reason, Ellison's novel was timely, written after the social transformations brought about by the Great Migration but just before the racial integration of the 1960s civil rights movement. It is a transitional text that embodies in its liminal perspective the proverbial crossroads of blues expression. Like the ghetto pastoral stories of Black migration that preceded Ellison's novel, *Invisible Man* foregrounds the conflict at the center of Black migration, thereby figuring it as a subversion of geographic boundaries and racial meanings. Ellison's mastery of the form is realized in his use of Black vernacular forms of expression to bridge the symbolic and physical gap between the culturally charged spaces of the South and the racially fraught spaces of the North. Through his marshaling of the blues as a symbolic (if also textual) point of reference, he taps into a vernacular tradition that celebrates even as it laments the collective struggle of Black people. He articulates that struggle from an ironic position as an invisible man writing on the margins of society. But he also does so as someone in control of his narrative perspective—as someone with the ability to transform this music/perspective of invisibility into a message of hope. And this is really the culmination of the genre—a Black migrant speaking truth to power precisely because of his liminal status and the unique perspective it affords him. It is this mastery of form that the novel represents in its final declaration, "I am coming out. . . ."

WHERE IS THE PROMISED LAND?

Claude Brown's autobiographical novel, *Manchild in the Promised Land*, is prefaced with a disquieting question: "For where does one run to when he's already in the promised land?"[1] Indeed, this question reverberates throughout his powerful work and provides a rather appropriate epilogue to the genre of the Black migration novel. To revise that question as it pertains to my critical project, it might well read, "How does one assess the legacy of the Black migration novel as it relates to the triumphs and failures of Black migration and urbanization?" In other words, did the "promised land" exist in any material reality beyond the mythos and idealism ascribed to Northern cities during the Great Migration? The answer, it would seem, can found in the novels themselves. I have argued in this book that Black migration novels figure the Northern city as a dialectical space wherein Black migrant spaces become ghetto pastoral sites of rural and urban conflict. This conflict precludes the possibility of (re)inscribing a folk past as a means of urban assimilation and social ascent. Instead, Black migrant characters are represented as having to negotiate a liminal conception of urban spaces betwixt and between the country and the city. Thus, the ideal of the folk, as well as the ideal of the "promised land" itself, is suspended in these novels. As to Brown's question—"where does one run to when he's already in the promised land"—the answer gleaned from the migration novels considered here reveals an alternative conception of place and belonging in response to the problem of urban displacement. That conception of place is defined by the liminal spaces of existence wherein Black migrants find themselves (ironically speaking) as new creations, neither here nor there but betwixt and between categories of race and place.

Indeed, the Black migration novels considered here can be read as revising the terms of Black subjectivity and place in response to the displacement brought about by the Great Migration. These novels figure Black migrant spaces at the proverbial intersections of rural and urban consciousness. These contested spaces foreground the competing terms of Black migrant experience in the city—an experience formed at the interstices of cultural practices and Black lived experience. As dialectical spaces (e.g., urban pastoral spaces, alternative domestic spaces, and blues spaces) these discursive settings fundamentally resist static conceptions of Black subjectivity and lived experience. Therefore, rather than constitute "safe spaces," or spaces in which Black migrants may simply substitute an "urbanized version" of Black folk culture, these spatial formations reveal a more dynamic portrait of Black urban experience based on contested conceptions of race and place.[2] In short, they constitute spaces of both identity formation and internecine urban struggle.

Since the publication of the first Black migration novel, Paul Laurence Dunbar's *Sport of the Gods* (1902), the critical project of Black migration novelists has been distinctive in its (re)considerations of Black subjectivity and racial community. As I discussed in chapter 1, the flourishing of the Black migration novel form in the 1920s coincided with the New Negro movement of the Harlem Renaissance, thereby appropriating many of the same themes and motifs that promoted Black subjectivity and self-determination. However, Black migration novels conveyed a more complex portrait of Black urban experience; these novels complicated the racialist discourse of the New Negro movement, as they revealed in their portrayals of displaced migrant characters the cultural conflict(s) and regional tension that underlie conceptions of racial identity and Blackness. In other words, these novels presented a much more slippery conception of Black subjectivity than the discourse of the New Negro; one that could be conceived as neither rural nor urban in its connotation, but rather constituting a more dynamic figuration of identity.[3] Indeed, the Black migration novelists considered here forged a new discursive field of representation that expanded definitions of race and place. While the emergent figure of the New Negro in African American literary consciousness questioned prevailing notions of race and Blackness, the figure of the displaced migrant character forever transformed conceptions of both race and place. Unlike the proverbial New Negro, who was a distinct product of the city, the displaced Black migrant straddled two worlds, and in doing so, transformed in practice Southern and Northern—rural and urban—lived experiences. As a liminal figure oscillating between rural and urban modes of experience, the Black migrant came to signify the full complexity of African American lived experience, forever dispelling the notion that Black subjectivity could be defined solely in terms of one place or one set of ideas.

For this reason, the displaced Black migrant can be read as a progressive trope in the African American literary tradition. Just as the trope of the tragic mulatto (or "passing figure") signified the instability of racial categories in nineteenth-century American society, the figure of the displaced Black migrant signifies the dialectical quality of Black urban experience after the Great Migration(s) of the twentieth century. These novels marked an important progression in African American literature as they posited a conception of Black subjectivity that was no longer place bound. The figure of the displaced migrant symbolized the enduring quality of Black migrant experience—an experience for which the forging of place and identity was sine qua non. The displaced Black migrant is represented in these novels as having to forge an alternative space of Black subjectivity that revises the conceptual boundaries of North and South; rural and urban. It may even be argued that these representations revised the conceptual boundaries between "white" and "Black" insofar as they revealed the ideological terms that underwrote these racial categories. In effect, the displaced Black migrant is figured in these novels as a Black subject par excellence whose experience foregrounds the conflicts, contradictions, and ambiguities that form conceptions of race and Blackness.

The figure of the displaced Black migrant can also be read also as forging a unique concept of place that fundamentally expanded definitions of what constitutes Black community. The problem of displacement required Black migration novelists to imagine communal spaces in the Northern city that represent alternative conceptions of Black settlement and community. As my readings have shown, the representation of these spaces in the literature reveals the dialectical relationship between rural and urban modes of experience. Rather than figure "rural" and "urban" as mutually exclusive concepts, the novels considered here represent them as dynamic, interrelated social constructs. Thus, the representation of Black migrant experience in these novels figures a relationship between both concepts that reveals new possibilities for imagining Black settlement spaces. In his seminal work, *The Country and the City*, Raymond Williams describes the relationship between rural and urban modes of experience. Williams writes, "The country and the city are changing historical realities, both in themselves and in their interrelations. Moreover, in our own world, they represent only two kinds of settlement. Our *real social experience* is not only of the country and the city, in their most singular forms, but of many kinds of intermediate and new kinds of social and physical organization" [emphasis mine].[4] Applying Williams's formulation, the experience of the displaced black migrant represents the "real social experience" of Black folk in this country—an experience that embodies the confluence (and conflict) of rural and urban modes of experience. In this regard, Williams's formulation describes both the promise and the problem of Black migration novels.

The promise of Black migration held out the possibility of (re)creating Black cultural identity and community at the nexus of rural and urban consciousness. Alain Locke's concept of the new negro as "straddling both worlds" while figuring a distinctive cultural experience in the northern city was the articulation of that promise. The symbol of Harlem as its cultural epicenter, a proverbial shining city on a hill, was the material realization of that promise. Both were potent signifiers of Black community in the decade of Harlem Renaissance. However, what defined "Black community" in the years and decades to follow centered on the social and economic struggles of Black people after the failures of Black migration. Black communities in Northern cities would increasingly be defined by the conditions of economic deprivation and social neglect as the inner city became synonymous with joblessness and crime.[5] The image of the Black community suffered as well. Just as the Harlem Renaissance fostered a positive ideal of urban Black culture, the slow decline of Black urban communities in the North produced an equally negative conception of Black urban spaces in particular and Black people in general.

The defining literary debate of this period around the issue of black community involved a critical triangulation of three Black authors. Richard Wright emerged in the 1940s as the literary spokesperson for Black liberation and direct political action. His novel *Native Son* tested the limits of protest fiction as it portrayed a Black antihero in Bigger Thomas. Bigger was a radical departure from the Black characters of migration novels in that he was a definitive product of the Northern city having migrated there with his family at a very young age. We are not given that history in detail in Wright's novel. What we are given is a violent account of an urban Black youth whose life is stunted by poverty and racism. Wright's novel made a powerful polemical statement about the effects of systematic racism and the challenge of sustaining Black community in places like Chicago. Wright exposed the economic and legal structures of the former while revealing the associated realities of the latter. The idea of Black community for Wright was fraught with the realities of economic deprivation, social neglect, and internalized racism.

His novel and his nonfiction highlighted these problems in ways that made him a celebrity in literary and political circles.

Yet, Wright was not without his detractors. Ralph Ellison offered another vision of Black community that emphasized among other things the interrelatedness of Black shared experience and socioeconomic deprivation. Wright believed Black folk were largely deprived of traditions and shared experience because of their shared condition of poverty and deprivation.[6] For Ellison, however, Black people were able to fashion a shared experience informed by an enduring tradition precisely because of and in response to their collective struggle. Ellison offered the view that Black people "live nevertheless as they have to live" in his essay "Harlem in Nowhere," despite the racism and social neglect that stemmed from the larger society.[7] For Ellison, Black culture was rooted in a tradition of "containing pain" that would otherwise make it difficult, if not impossible, to mentally survive on a daily basis.[8] Wright's angst ridden novel, as well as his general message of social protest, was in Ellison's view an overstatement of the psychological turmoil that gripped the lives of Black people. Indeed, Ellison would pit himself directly against Wright's legacy in his famous declaration of artistic autonomy, his essay "The World and the Jug." Ellison responds to cultural critic Irving Howe's claim in the essay that he and other Black authors (including Baldwin) had betrayed Wright's literary vision. Howe believed that both younger writers did not (perhaps, could not) adequately express the struggle of Black people in the way that Wright had a decade earlier. Ellison's response is exquisite both as a rejoinder to Howe's intellectual arrogance and as an articulation of what "counts as" an authentic representation of Black lived experience:

> One unfamiliar with what Howe stands for would get the impression that when he looks at a Negro he sees not a human being but an abstract embodiment of living hell. He seems never to have considered that American Negro life is . . . , for the Negro who must live it, not only a burden . . . but also a *discipline*—just as any human life which has endured so long is a discipline teaching its own insights into the human condition, its own strategies of survival. There is a fullness, even a richness here; and here *despite* the realties of politics, perhaps, but nevertheless here and real. Because it is *human* life. [original italics][9]

Indeed, for Ellison, the collective struggle of Black people in America did not discount the possibility of their fashioning a meaningful existence for themselves on the margins of society. Such struggle did not permanently stunt them as a people nor did it relegate them to a veritable hell nor, as Wright would put it, did it signify the "essential bleakness of black life in America."[10] Instead, the enduring quality of Black life was precisely its ability to endure and, to paraphrase Ellison, live as one must despite the incongruities and contradictions that shape the experience of Blackness. It is, therefore, the tacit goal of Black people to fashion out of their unique experience a way of life that can become the basis for place and community.

James Baldwin, another important voice in this critical debate, would marshal his own formulation of urban Black community in an essay entitled "Many Thousands Gone" (1951), an essay that anticipates the major themes that would eventually shape his own migration novel, *Go Tell It on the Mountain* (1953). Baldwin's essay responds to the earlier promise of Black migration and the problems of Black communities in the North. Published the year after Ellison's novel, Baldwin's novel extends his central claim in "Many Thousands Gone." In that essay, he writes "It means something to be a Negro, as it means something to have been born in Ireland or in China, to live where one sees space and sky or to live where one sees nothing but rubble or nothing but high buildings."[11] Baldwin argues that the so-called protest literature of the preceding decade—exemplified most notably in Richard Wright's novel *Native Son* (1940)—obscured the cultural relations that defined what it meant to be a Negro in America. He devotes much of his essay to assailing Wright's novel for its limited view of urban Black life, arguing that in the novel "a necessary dimension has been cut away; this dimension being the relationship that Negroes bear to one another, that depth of involvement and unspoken recognition of shared experience which creates a way of life."[12] Devoid of the mutual recognition acknowledging an entire "way of life" that is distinctly Black, Wright's novel is for Baldwin a misrepresentation of the very struggle it sets out to articulate in progressive terms. For this reason, the novel fails not only because it portrays Bigger as a flattened out racial stereotype, but also because it does not imagine the possibility of anything else emanating from his experience as a Black boy growing up on the South Side of Chicago.

Baldwin's response to Wright's artistic vision in *Native Son* extended to his own fiction as well. Baldwin subsequently marshals the form of the black migration novel in *Go Tell It on the Mountain*, a novel based in part on his own life. His marshaling of the Black migration literary form can be read as an attempt to represent the "necessary dimension" of Black life he believed was absent in Wright's novel. Echoing Ellison's observations of Black urban life and experience, Baldwin's novel undertakes the task of revealing the symbolic forms and practices that give shape and meaning to the urban spaces where Black folk reside in the northern city. A brief consideration of the novel reveals how Baldwin attempts to adjudicate the problem of Black urban displacement through the novel's symbolically charged recounting of the past Southern experiences of his Black migrant characters. His protagonist, John Grimes, resembles Ellison's nameless protagonist in that he too must figure a space for himself—a space that exists somewhere between the restrictive spaces of both the Black church and Harlem. The "threshing floor" of the church, like the invisible man's lighted hole, becomes for Baldwin's protagonist a liminal space that signifies "infinite possibilities." It is from this space of religious initiation that Baldwin's novel reveals the past of his migrant characters, thereby initiating a symbolic journey back to the South and to the source of conflict that continues to shape the lives of his migrant characters.

Baldwin's "threshing floor" scene approaches the problem of cultural displacement at the center of the ghetto pastoral mode in a unique way. Baldwin marshals the alter of the church, otherwise figured as a "safe space" of spiritual renewal and awakening, as a place of reckoning for his migrant saints. It is here that Baldwin's characters bear witness to and take tacit part in John's spiritual/secular journey toward self-realization. Baldwin certainly utilizes this scene as a framing device for the novel, but he accomplishes much more than that. Indeed, he disrupts the narrative of racial identity that was at the center of Black migration novels. That narrative rested on the assumption that an ancestral past rooted in the South was a necessary component of fashioning an identity for oneself in the North, even (or especially) if such cultural memory produced a sense of cultural displacement in the "promised land" of Northern cities. That Black migrants had to reconcile these competing terms of their identity (rural and urban; North and South) was the common thread in these novels of Black migration. However, Baldwin represents this thematic conflict in a different way than previous authors. Indeed, he represents the Southern past through the collective memory of his "Saints," signifying their repressed trauma and the veritable *original sin* of their former lives. John Grimes becomes in this sense a messianic figure whose tarrying on the threshing floor of the church functions as a symbolic gesture of suffering and sacrifice for the sins of his immediate family. John becomes then an important figure of transition in the Black vernacular tradition, the figure standing at the crossroads linking one generation to the next—thereby establishing a critical linkage to proceeding representations of Black culture and lived experience, an experience for him that is no longer inextricably bound in place and time to a Black vernacular tradition rooted in the Deep South. Baldwin, through the messianic figure of John, *makes all things new,* and this is precisely the critical shift in perspective that establishes the novel as a seminal text in the genre.

Baldwin marshals in *Go Tell It on the Mountain* a unique conception of black community as an alternative to Wright's more deterministic and bleaker view of urban black life. In one sense, the novel is an artistic real-ization of the argument Baldwin set forth in "Many Thousands Gone."[13] Baldwin's conception of black urban life reflects the varied aspects, contin-gencies, and contradictions that define what he viewed as a complexity of shared experience.[14] Keith Clark writes of Baldwin, "as a writer whose life and art reflected so many conflicting and sometimes binary oppositions . . . [Baldwin] experienced conflicts as an isolated artist who simultaneously craved community."[15] Clark refers to this perspective in Baldwin's fiction as reflecting a "paradox of communitas."[16] Baldwin's self-imposed cultural isolation, his decision to leave the Black church and, ultimately, his expa-triation to Europe, are cited by Clark as evidence of Baldwin's paradoxical perspective given the value the author ascribed to the ideal of racial com-munity despite his self-imposed position outside of it.[17] Clark's assessment is useful in tracking the ideal of racial community in Baldwin's migration novel, precisely the extent to which his representation of racial community reflects the sort of conflict(s) that Clark ascribes to Baldwin himself. Yet, as my specific reading will show, Baldwin's representation of urban community in the novel reflects the *inherent* conflicts and contradictions (i.e., rural and urban conflict) attendant to Black migrant spaces in the city.

Baldwin figures Black migrant spaces in the novel as contested sites, defined by the contingencies of race, religion and collective memory. Draw-ing on religious signifiers, such as rituals of worship and gospel verse, the novel posits an ideal of Black urban community based in Black vernacular and religious forms of expression. Yet, in marshaling these forms of expres-sion as a basis for urban community, all of them rooted in a Southern folk tradition, the novel necessarily complicates this ideal of urban community and place in the city. The representation of racial community in the novel reflects the contested nature of ghetto pastoral, Black migrant spaces in the city. The liminal space of the Black church foregrounds this conflict in the novel. The social discourses of past and present; rural and urban; secular and sacred—are symbolically framed in the space of the church. It is against these competing discourses that Baldwin's Black migrants must negotiate a sense of place and identity.

The novel opens in the vibrant streets of Harlem but immediately shifts its focus to the small storefront church that functions as its immediate setting. Figuring it as a distinctive urban space, Baldwin sets his storefront church in sharp relief to the streets and avenues of Harlem. In making their way to the church, the Grimes family must walk a perceived gauntlet of sin and perdition, "as sinners along the avenue watched them" (4), before reaching the presumed safety of the church.[18] In contrast, the space of the church represents an escape from the irreverent secular/urban life of Harlem. It is also figured in this sense as a symbolic space imbued with the power of the Holy Spirit. Once inside the church, the perspective shifts to John as he takes in the emotive scene: "On Sunday mornings the women all seemed patient, all the men seemed mighty. While John watched, the Power struck someone, a man or woman; they cried out, a long, wordless crying, and, arms outstretched like wings, they began the Shout. Someone moved a chair a little to give them room, the rhythm paused, the singing stopped, only the pounding feet and the clapping hands were heard; then another cry, another dancer; then the tambourines began again, and the voices rose again, and the music swept on again, like fire, or flood, or judgment" (7–8).

John is portrayed as a displaced figure from the outset. Baldwin represents this displacement in religious terms. John is an interloper in this spiritual community of "saints" because his "heart was hardened against the Lord" (14). However, John's anger toward God is misplaced; his real aversion is for his stepfather, Gabriel Grimes. As Baldwin writes, "His father was God's minister, the ambassador of the King of Heaven, and John could not bow before the throne of grace without first kneeling to his father. On his refusal to do this had his life depended, and John's secret heart had flourished in its wickedness until the day his sin first overtook him" (14).

Gabriel's storefront church and the ideal of place it represents is not immediately available to John. Ironically, while the church is set apart from the city as a kind of "safe space," it is also the space that symbolizes the conflict between John and his father. In this sense, the church symbolizes the promise of community, although it reflects also the conflict(s) that defines John's spiritual (and psychological) struggle to attain that goal. As Albert J. Raboteau points out, black churches in the city were the cornerstones of burgeoning black communities in the North. Raboteau writes of the social function of these religious institutions in providing a place of belonging for newly arrived Black migrants in the city: "Facing an unfamiliar urban environment, country-raised migrants looked to the churches to reaffirm the traditional values and community ties that had always given them a sense of social location back home. In some instances they joined already-established churches; in others they founded new ones of their own."[19]

Baldwin's representation of this ideal of racial community, however, reveals the vestiges of a Southern past that always rises to contest it. The conflict associated with this past is brought to bear in the figure of John's father. Having buried a son in the South and failed another in the North, Gabriel now looks upon his stepson John with envious scorn. Consequently, John must bear the past sins of his father who tries to deny him his rightful place in this community. For this reason, John finds himself torn between the paths of righteousness—ostensibly, his father's path—and the path that is the "way of the world." "In a narrow way, the way of the cross, there awaited him only humiliation forever; there awaited him, one day, a house like his father's house, and a church like his father's, and a job like his father's, where he would grow old and black with hunger and toil" (28).

Instead of resigning himself to his "father's place," John is tempted to make a place for himself in the irreverent spaces of the city "where the buildings contested God's power" (28). John resembles Christ in his moment of temptation as he stands atop a hill overlooking Harlem, tempted by the city below "to hurl away, for a moment of ease, the glories of eternity" (28). However, unlike Christ who resisted Satan's temptation to hurl himself from the high precipice, John descends into the city comforted by the thought "I can climb back up. If it's wrong, I can always climb back up" (28). Eventually he goes to the cinema, where he becomes so enthralled with the portrayal of a heroine who possesses "neither kindness, nor scorn, nor hatred, nor love," that he decides "he wanted be like her, only more powerful, more thorough, and more cruel" (33). His close identification with a moral villain reflects for him one extreme on the broad scale of human possibilities. Yet, John can only imagine such extremes as he struggles "to find a compromise between the way that led to life everlasting and the way that ended in the pit" (34). Concluding that no such compromise exists, John consigns himself to a liminal place between his "father's church" and the "wicked" spaces of the city.

John's displaced status reveals the competing ideals and contested spaces that comprise the urban cityscape in the novel. Henri Lefebvre, in his seminal work *The Production of Space*, describes the contradictory nature of urban space itself, pointing out that what one finds there is not a tabula rasa, but rather a space inscribed with multiple meanings. He writes, "Both natural and urban spaces are, if anything, 'over-inscribed': everything therein resembles a rough draft, jumbled and self-contradictory. Rather than signs, what one encounters here are directions—multifarious and overlapping instructions. If there is indeed text, inscription or writing to be found here, it is in a context of conventions, intentions and order" (Lefebvre 142).[20]

The "conventions, intentions and order" that define urban spaces in the novel also conveys a "jumbled and self-contradictory" image. For instance, while the church signifies place and community, it also foregrounds the competing terms of Black migrant experience (i.e., rural and urban, past and present). Similarly, while the Grimes home marks the domestic setting in the novel, it is also figured as a physically (and spiritually) abject space: "The room was narrow and dirty; nothing could alter its dimensions, no labor could ever make it clean. Dirt was in the walls and the floorboards, and triumphed beneath the sink where roaches spawned; was in the fine ridges of the pots and pans, scoured daily, burned black on the bottom, hanging above the stove; was in the wall against which they hung, and revealed itself where the paint had cracked and leaned outward in stiff squares and fragments, the paper-thin underside webbed with black" (14).

This dialectical construction of urban spaces in the novel attests to the competing terms of Black migrant experience, which is defined by the conflict of rural and urban modes of experience. This conflict of rural and urban experience is vividly represented in both the church and the Grimes home by the frequent invocations of the past in those places. In one scene, John consciously transforms the weathered face of his mother into the youthful face he had once seen in an old photograph: "Her face became the face that he gave her in his dreams, the face that had been hers in a photograph he had seen once, long ago, a photograph taken before he was born" (15). However, John's vision does not generate a wistful nostalgia for the past but instead reveals the contested status of both images: "Between the two faces there stretched a darkness and a mystery that John feared, and that sometimes caused him to hate her" (15). The dialectical nature of things inside the Grimes home so disorients Baldwin's protagonist that he feels "a need to touch things, the table and chairs and the walls of the room, to make certain that the room existed and that he was in the room" (15).

Similarly, in the second section of the novel, "The Prayers of the Saints," the church is represented as another dialectical space in which the competing terms of rural and urban experience find expression for the novel's Black migrant characters. Told from the perspectives of three characters—Florence, Gabriel, and Elizabeth—the interrelated narratives comprising this section reveal the conflicts and ambiguities—past and present; rural and urban; secular and sacred—that mark the lives of these characters. The intersection of these perspectives in the space of the church reveals the complex and contested relationship that Baldwin's characters bear to one another. Their "prayers" then express both a tenuous ideal of racial community as well as the competing terms of the past that always contest it.

Florence's prayer initiates the stories of migration that comprise the second section of the novel, as it recalls memories of her past that are for her a constant source of guilt. Her prayer in the church evokes a painful montage of images from her Southern past. Florence's past looms before her like the figure of death that had appeared to her in a dream: "And after death's first silent vigil her life came to her bedside to curse her with many voices. Her mother, in rotting rags and filling the room with the stink of the grave, stood over her to curse the daughter who had denied her on her deathbed" (62).

Florence's vision evokes the pain of guilt for all those she has transgressed in her life. Her mother appears in "rotting rags," recalling Florence's decision to leave her dying mother and migrate to the North. She then envisions an image of her brother Gabriel, who appears before her "to curse the sister who had held him to scorn and mocked his ministry." Finally, she envisions her first husband Frank; "even he," who left her for another woman, evokes in her a sense of guilt. And yet, while this invocation of the past foregrounds the conflict that continues to daunt her, it does not provide an immediate resolution to it: "Of them all she would have begged forgiveness, had they come with ears to hear. But they came like many trumpets; even if they had come to hear and not to testify it was not they who could forgive her, but only God" (62).

Similarly, "Gabriel's prayer" evokes an image of the past as a constant source of guilt. In response to a momentary silence that falls over the church, Gabriel's past comes rushing over him like a torrent of guilt: "This silence, continuing like a corridor, carried Gabriel back to the silence that had preceded his birth in Christ. Like a birth indeed, all that had come before this moment was wrapped in darkness, lay at the bottom of the sea of forgetfulness, and was not now counted against him, but was related only to that blind, and doomed, and stinking corruption he had been before he was redeemed" (88).

Gabriel, displaced also by his "sins of the past," must resign himself to the "silence" of his own voice, as he is unable to preach God's word in his own church. While he was a minister in the South, Gabriel committed the sin of adultery, fathering the illegitimate child of a woman with whom he worked. Haunted by the final words of his scorned lover—"I don't know when and I don't know how, but I know you going to be brought low one of these fine days"—Gabriel cannot bear the burden of his sin (134). For him, "there was peace nowhere, and healing nowhere, and forgetfulness nowhere" (134). As a result, he cannot bring forth God's salvation without also bringing forth God's judgment on himself: "When souls came weeping to the altar he scarce dared to rejoice, remembering that soul who had not bowed, whose blood, it might be, would be required of him at judgment" (134). The conflict that attends Gabriel's experience is indefinite and unceasing, as is his perpetual sense of displacement in the small storefront church where he, "God's minister," is reduced to the status of deacon.

As the last story of this section, "Elizabeth's prayer" establishes the link between John's experience and the conflict that has shaped the lives of the novel's Black migrant characters. The past is also for her a constant source of guilt; remorsefully, Elizabeth "wondered if she had not been wrong; if there had not been something that she had overlooked, for which the Lord had made her suffer" (156). Realizing the nature of her sin, she wonders if there is any way to convey this moral hindsight to her son, John: "But, yes—there was something she had overlooked. *Pride goeth before destruction; and a haughty spirit before a fall.* She had not known this: she had not imagined that she could fall. She wondered, tonight, how she could give this knowledge to her son; if she could help him to endure what could now no longer be changed; if while life ran, he would forgive her—for her pride, her folly, and her bargaining with God!" (157). The thing that "could now no longer be changed" is the past itself; her decision to come to this "city of destruction;" its real destruction of John's biological father, Richard; her subsequent marriage to Gabriel Grimes; for all these things Elizabeth searches for forgiveness and redemption through the experience of her son John.

John's conversion on the "threshing floor" of the church then becomes a symbol of redemption for the novel's Black migrant characters. Again, Baldwin recasts the problem of urban displacement in religious terms; his migrant characters are displaced by their own guilt, and as such, must find a source of forgiveness if they are to make a place for themselves in the city. Subsequently, John's spiritual ordeal, as he is "laid low" before the church alter, evokes the scene of Christ's suffering and sacrifice for the sins of mankind; his father Gabriel is figured as a demagogue who (unlike the God of the New Testament) has selfishly forsaken his son. Conversely, the "praying saints," Baldwin's Black migrant characters, appear as sinners who seek a kind of spiritual and social redemption through John's spiritual awakening. In this sense, John is figured as a messianic figure whose spiritual ascent reflects the promise of Black migration and urban ascent that has eluded the novel's adult characters.

The spiritual change that comes over John when he is "baptized in the spirit" is made apparent when he steps out of the church and walks onto Lenox Avenue. His conversion has given him a symbolic perspective with which he now sees the avenue and, by extension, the city itself with new eyes. Evoking the Christian tradition of redemptive suffering, Baldwin's protagonist has endured the "storm" only now to be renewed in the calm that follows it:

Now the storm was over. And the avenue, like any landscape that has endured a storm, lay changed under Heaven, exhausted and clean, and new. Not again, forever, could it return to the avenue it once had been. Fire, or lightning, or the latter rain, coming down from these skies which moved with such pale secrecy above him now, had laid yesterday's avenue waste, had changed it in a moment, in the twinkling of an eye, as all would be changed on the last day, when the skies would open up once more to gather up the saints. (220)

John's spiritual ascent is represented here as an urban ascent as well. Baldwin's protagonist can now locate himself in an urban environment that has not physically changed but that somehow now no longer appears to him as it had before the loss of his "innocence and anger." The displacement he once felt on this avenue, and in the various urban spaces of the city, is replaced with an enduring sense of belonging: "He was in battle no longer, this unfolding Lord's day, with this avenue, these houses, the sleeping, staring, shouting people, but had entered into battle with Jacob's angel, *with the princes and the powers of the air*" (221). He resembles in this moment the apostle Paul who declared himself a "prisoner of God" despite his being held captive in a *real* earthly prison.[21] Similarly, Baldwin's protagonist has revised the terms of his place in the city, instead figuring for himself a symbolic place that transcends both the church of "praying saints" and the avenue of "sinners." John embodies the mediation of these seemingly disparate urban spaces, for "the light and darkness had kissed each other, and were married now, forever, in the life and the vision of John's soul" (207).

This is the "moment of arrival" for Baldwin's protagonist, who can now make his place in the city. Like Ellison's displaced protagonist, Baldwin portrays his protagonist as having to marshal the symbolic forms and practices of Black vernacular culture in order to mitigate the competing terms of his urban displacement. Also like Ellison's *Invisible Man*, Baldwin's novel does not foreclose the conflict and ambivalence that define in the last instance the experience of his protagonist. John's urban (and spiritual) ascent is only temporary; like the other "sinners" and Black migrants, his life will be an endless struggle of reconciling the competing terms (i.e., rural and urban, secular and sacred) of his existence. Baldwin admits that his protagonist "would weep again, his heart insisted, for now his weeping had begun; he would rage again, said the shifting air, for the lions of rage had been unloosed; he would be in darkness again, in fire again, now that he had seen the fire and he darkness" (221).

John's sense of place, both in the city and in his "father's house," is finally confirmed by Elisha, who functions in the novel as a kind of surrogate father for John. When John returns to his father's house after his spiritual conversion, he appeals to Elisha to affirm his new sense of place and identity:

> John looked at his father and moved from his path, stepping down into the street again. He put his hand on Elisha's arm, feeling himself trembling, and his father at his back.
>
> "Elisha," he said, "no matter what happens to me, where I go, what folks say about me, no matter what *any*body says, you remember— please remember—I was saved. I was *there*." (225)

Elisha then seals John's transformation with a "holy kiss," an act of anointing that confers on John an "ineffaceable" sense of self-identity. "Smiling," John now turns to face his father and sees that Gabriel "did not smile," indicating the irrevocable gulf that continues to exist between them. As this final scene demonstrates, Baldwin's novel does not foreclose the conflict that shapes the lives of his Black migrant characters but rather embodies in the figure of John a means of negotiating a viable albeit tenuous sense of place and identity in the city for each of them.

Baldwin's novel does not settle the debate over urban Black community that Black migration novelists began three decades prior to its publication. These authors posed the perennial question: Can urban Black communities in the North provide a place of belonging for displaced Black migrants? Instead of providing a definitive answer, Baldwin's novel offers the possibility that the city itself can transform what it means to be Black. That is, the city as liminal space, as ghetto pastoral space, can be made to (re)interpret the cultural terms that underwrote Blackness in the South. In so doing, even if Black migrants could not change the city, even if they could not overcome the material realities of racial segregation and economic exploitation, perhaps their experience of the promised land could change them for the better. Perhaps the image of Black folk trapped in a jug, presumably representing the stunted life of places like Harlem, was really, as Ralph Ellison believed, an image denoting not merely limitation but rather circumscribed possibility. As Ellison famously put it, "if [Black people] are in a jug, it is *transparent*, not *opaque*, and one is allowed not only to see outside but to read what is going on."[22]

NOTES

Introduction: "A Glory to the Grandeur of Space": The Ghetto Pastoral Mode and the Politics of Place

1. Claude McKay, *A Long Way from Home* (Rutgers University Press, 1975), 79.

2. Isabel Wilkerson, *The Warmth of Other Suns: The Epic Story of America's Great Migration* (Vintage, 2011).

3. Alaine Locke, "The New Negro," in *The New Negro: Voices of the Harlem Renaissance*, ed. Alain Locke, 1st Touchstone Edition (Simon and Schuster, 1993), 6.

4. Michael Denning, *The Cultural Front: The Laboring of American Culture in the Twentieth Century* (Verso, 1996). Denning describes the "ghetto pastoral" mode as a variant of urban pastoralism. As such, it provides a conceptual context for imagining the lives of European immigrants as they made the leap from old world culture and societies to the industrial cities of North America.

5. Denning, *The Cultural Front*, 231.

6. My major point of contention with recent scholarship is what has been its focus on the relative stability of racial representation in Black migration novels. In other words, important scholars of the genre necessarily emphasize the ways in which these novels recreate the cultural terms of Blackness in depicting the migration of Black characters from the South to the North. For some, this means reinscribing Black Southern vernacular culture in the North. For others, it has meant establishing pockets of Black cultural affirmation in the North, what Farah Griffin has termed "safe spaces" in her seminal study of Black migration novels, *"Who Set You Flowin'?": The African-American Migration Narrative* (Oxford University Press, 1995). I hope to destabilize such readings by positing an alternative view of Black subjectivity in these in novels—one that emphasizes the fluidity of Black cultural experience and racial identity in Black migration novels.

7. See Noel Ignatiev's discussion of how Irish immigrants approximated whiteness through their subjugation of African Americans in *How the Irish Became White* (Routledge, 2008).

8. W. E. B. Du Bois, *The Souls of Black Folk*, in *Writings*, ed. Nathan Huggins (The Library of America, 1986), 363–66.

9. Race novels set in the era of slavery and Reconstruction such as Frances Harper's *Iola Leroy* and Pauline Hopkins's *Contending Forces* centered on the important issue of racial uplift and often preached social respectability as a guiding principle for Black

people. While the Black migration novels of the twentieth century would represent Northern cities as privileged spaces for Black self-determination, this earlier Black fiction held out the possibility that the South could also provide a space for Black self-determination. The Black migration novels of this study represent a marked transition from this earlier period. The South, once a locus of African American culture, is decentered in these narratives of transition. As a result, concepts of Blackness and racial identity are radically transformed in these novels of social and cultural ascent.

10. Erin Royston Battat, *Ain't Got No Home: America's Great Migrations and the Making of an Interracial Left* (University of North Carolina Press, 2014).

11. Mary Weaks-Baxter, *Leaving the South: Border Crossing Narratives and the Remaking of Southern Identity* (University Press of Mississippi, 2018), 4.

12. Weaks-Baxter, *Leaving the South*, 5.

13. Weaks-Baxter, *Leaving the South*, 56.

14. Thomas Heise, *Urban Underworlds: A Geography of Twentieth-Century American Literature and Culture* (Rutgers University Press, 2011).

15. Heise, *Urban Underworlds*.

16. Zandria F. Robinson, *This Ain't Chicago: Race, Class, and Regional Identity in the Post-Soul South* (University of North Carolina Press, 2014), 31.

17. Robinson, *This Ain't Chicago*, 31.

18. Raymond Williams, *The Country and the City* (Oxford University Press, 1973), 165.

19. The emergence of the Black migration novel can be dated to the publication of Paul Laurence Dunbar's *The Sport of the Gods* in 1902. Often regarded as the first migration novel, Dunbar's story is a cautionary tale that ironically extols the culture of the South while warning of the dangers of the North. Dunbar's novel also reflects one of the primary motives of Black migration to the North, that is, the desire to escape the racial and (to a lesser extent in Dunbar's novel) economic oppression of the South. See Lawrence R. Rodgers's discussion of "fugitive migrants" who fled the South because of oppression and, in some cases, legal persecution in his seminal study of Black migration novels *Canaan Bound: The African American Great Migration Novel* (University of Illinois Press, 1997), 28.

20. Stewart E. Tolnay and E. M. Beck, "Rethinking the Role of Racial Violence in the Great Migration," in *Black Exodus*, ed. Alferdteen Harrison (University Press of Mississippi, 1991), 22–23.

21. See Huston Baker's discussion of the blues as a symbol of Black cultural expression in *Blues, Ideology, and Afro-American Literature: A Vernacular Theory* (University of Chicago Press, 1984), 11–14.

22. Baker's rhetorical trope of the "blues performer" acknowledges the economic conditions of Black cultural expression. For Baker, such expression must necessarily take as its "social ground" an economics of slavery and deportation. He makes clear how this legacy of slavery has shaped the contours of a modern Black aesthetic. What is unclear, however, in Baker's figuration of a Black cultural tradition is the extent to which processes such as migration and urbanization have also shaped this modern tradition. What appears to be missing in Baker's account is a sense of historical differentiation between slavery (and its enduring legacy) and modern forms of economic and social exploitation, such as sharecropping and industrial wage labor.

23. I have in mind especially post-Reconstruction novels such as Frances E. W. Harper's *Iola Leroy* (1893) and Charles W. Chesnutt's *The Marrow of Tradition* (1901), both of which are set in the post-Reconstruction South and convey traditional accounts of rural folk consciousness. Both novels turn on a romantic view of Black folk culture that is largely undifferentiated and makes social distinctions only between "mulatto" Black folk who can pass for white and "Negro" folk who cannot.

24. I use the term "New Negro" in the sense that Alain Locke deploys the term to reflect the modern and urban condition of Black folk after the Great Migration. See Locke's discussion in "The New Negro" and "The Legacy of the Ancestral Arts," both collected in *The New Negro* (Simon and Schuster, 1993), 3–18; 254–67.

25. Hazel Carby, "Ideologies of Black Folk: The Historical Novel of Slavery," *Cultures in Babylon* (Verso, 1999), 157.

26. Carby, "Ideologies of Black Folk," 147.

27. See James R. Grossman, *Land of Hope: Chicago, Black Southerners, and the Great Migration* (University of Chicago Press, 1991). Also see Nicholas Lemann, *The Promised Land: The Great Black Migration and How It Changed America* (Vintage Books, 1992); Griffin, *"Who Set You Flowin'?"*; Rodgers, *Canaan Bound*; Jacqueline Stewart, *Migrating to the Movies: Cinema and Black Urban Modernity* (University of California Press, 2005); Wilkerson, *The Warmth of Other Suns*.

28. Griffin, *"Who Set You Flowin'?,"* 9.

29. Griffin, *"Who Set You Flowin'?,"* 102.

30. Rodgers, *Canaan Bound*, 37.

31. Locke, "The New Negro," 6.

32. Locke, "The New Negro," 7.

33. See Tolnay and Beck's discussion of "push" and "pull" factors in Black rural to urban migration in "Rethinking the Role of Racial Violence," 23–24. Also see Grossman, *Land of Hope*, 14–27.

34. Mary Mcleod Bethune, "The Problems of the City Dweller," in *Up South: Stories, Studies and Letters of This Century's African-American Migrations*, ed. Malaika Adero (The New Press, 1993), 109.

35. The famous debate between Booker T. Washington and W. E. B. Du Bois regarding Black racial uplift also turned on the issue of Black migration. Washington called for racial cooperation in the South, urging Black folk to "drop your buckets where you are," in his famous, or rather infamous, "Atlanta Exposition" speech in 1895. Du Bois's pessimistic assessment of the South in *The Souls of Black Folk*, however, was more supportive of Black migration to the North. See W. E. B. Du Bois, "Of the Black Belt," in *The Souls of Black Folk* (Penguin Books, 1996), 91–110.

36. See Upton Sinclair, *The Jungle* (R. Bentley, 1972); Theodore Dresier, *An American Tragedy* (Boni and Liveright, 1925); John Steinbeck, *The Grapes of Wrath* (Viking Press, 1966).

37. Tolnay and Beck, "Rethinking the Role of Racial Violence," 22.

38. Tolnay and Beck, "Rethinking the Role of Racial Violence," 22.

39. Grossman, *Land of Hope*, 25–26.

40. Alain Locke appropriates this term in his anthology *The New Negro* (1925) as a way of describing the "modern representations" of Black people that emerged in the 1920s, and that found currency as a literary movement during the Harlem Renaissance.

41. The "push-pull" theory of the Great Migration asserts that Black Americans were primarily "pushed" by bad economic and social conditions to leave the South, and subsequently "pulled" by the economic opportunities that existed in the North. The theory rests on economic determinants as the primary cause for the Migration.

42. William Cohen, "The Great Migration as a Lever for Social Change," in *The Black Exodus: The Great Migration from the American South*, ed. Alferdteen Harrison (University Press of Mississippi, 1991), 77.

43. Grossman, *Land of Hope*, 246–58.

44. Describing the Chicago public school system, James Grossman writes "within the context of the experience of most migrants . . . Chicago's school epitomized northern opportunity" (*Land of Hope*, 248).

45. The *Chicago Defender* routinely reported incidents of mob violence against southern Black citizens. In response, the paper extolled the social advantages of life in northern cities, along with the ideal that Black folk could gain first-class citizenship in the North. These appeals to the racial and political consciousness of Black folk attended to social, not merely economic, concerns. See Grossman's discussion of the *Chicago Defender* in *Land of Hope*, 74–88.

46. Wilkerson, *The Warmth of Other Suns*, 391.

47. Cohen, "The Great Migration," 77.

48. Tolnay and Beck, "Rethinking the Role of Racial Violence," 22.

49. Lemann, *The Promised Land*, 6.

50. Arthur C. Holden, "A Northerner's View of the Negro Problem," in *Up South: Stories, Studies and Letters of This Century's African-American Migrations*, ed. Malaika Adero (Norton & Company, Inc., 1993), 165.

51. Lemann, *The Promised Land*, 277.

52. Rodgers, *Canaan Bound*, 30.

53. Rodgers, *Canaan Bound*, 33.

54. See Carole Marks, "Social and Economic Life of Southern Blacks," in *The Black Exodus: The Great Migration from the American South*, ed. Alferdteen Harrison (University Press of Mississippi, 1991), 36–49. Marks's discussion highlights the demographic patterns of early Black migration from 1890 until 1920. Marks points out that the demographic patterns of early Black migration reflected a "select" group of literate, nonagricultural workers and professionals. By the start of the Great Migration proper (anywhere between 1917 and 1920), nascent centers of Black culture and commerce were already taking shape in Northern cities due to more than two decades of migration by Black professionals and skilled laborers.

55. Locke, "The New Negro," 11.

56. Locke, "The New Negro," 4–5.

57. Locke, "The New Negro," 15.

58. Davarian L. Baldwin, *Chicago's New Negroes: Modernity, the Great Migration, and Black Urban Life* (University of North Carolina Press, 2007).

59. Baldwin, *Chicago's New Negroes*, 25.

60. Baldwin, *Chicago's New Negroes*, 25–26.

61. Denning, *The Cultural Front*, 247.

62. Denning, *The Cultural Front*, 247.

63. Blackface minstrelsy was a popular form of stage and musical entertainment in America, particularly at the turn of the twentieth century during the vaudeville era. White performers "blackened" their faces, primarily using burnt cork to make them appear as Black people. These performances signaled the most egregious racist stereotypes. They allowed white performances to push the boundaries of moral decency as their racial alter-egos could be used as cover for their lewd stage acts. Blackface minstrelsy was not solely the work of white performers either, as a number of Black performers and musicians also participated in the practice. James Weldon Johnson, who composed "Lift Every Voice and Sing," a song widely considered the "Black national anthem," wrote several popular minstrels with his brother Rosamond.

64. Stephen Nathan Haymes, *Race, Culture, and the City* (State University of New York Press, 1995), 10.

65. Haymes, *Race, Culture, and the City*, 112.

66. Haymes, *Race, Culture, and the City*, 112.

67. Haymes notes that this politics of spatial difference resulted in the "shattering of black civil society." He points out that "the white middle class has created an urban landscape at the expense of black settlement space, causing disorder within black civil society, which in turn weakens the ability of blacks to create their own public spaces" (*Race, Culture, and the City*, 71).

68. Haymes, *Race, Culture, and the City*, 114.

69. Brian McCammack, *Landscapes of Hope: Nature and the Great Migration in Chicago* (Harvard University Press, 2017), 20.

70. McCammack, *Landscapes of Hope*, 16; 20.

71. McCammack, *Landscapes of Hope*, 30.

72. McCammack, *Landscapes of Hope*, 36.

73. McCammack, *Landscapes of Hope*, 36.

74. Richard Wright, *Native Son* (abridged) (Harper Collins, 2003), 24.

75. The "Old South" of Black vernacular culture referred to here should be distinguished from the "Ole South" of the plantation tradition. The former denotes the portrayals of Black culture and lived experience as practices, beliefs, and forms that have survived enslavement, finding their vestiges in postbellum Southern life. The latter refers to romanticized depictions of Black enslavement and its later offshoots, Jim Crow segregation, sharecropping, and racial violence in the South. Toomer witnessed firsthand, and later portrayed in his novel, the inevitable tension between both portrayals of the South. He ultimately believed that the "Old South" denoting Black culture and lived experience would only continue to exist in collective memory as Black migrants left the South for social and economic opportunity in the North.

Chapter One: The Mock Pastoral Mode and the Emergence
of the Black Migration Novel

1. Plantation fiction ran the gamut between the popular folk tales of Joel Chandler
Harris and the blatantly racist fiction of Thomas Nelson Page. Harris's "Uncle Remus"
tales were made popular in *Uncle Remus: His Songs and Sayings*, published in 1880. Page's
In Ole Virginia similarly expressed a nostalgic account of antebellum Southern society replete with happy slaves and benevolent, paternalistic masters. Where Harris's "folk tales"
may be read as innocuous in their depiction of Southern Black folk culture, Page's fiction
expresses a much more diminished view of Black people. In *The Negro: The Southerner's
Problem*, his most definitive work on the subject of race, Page expresses an ideology of
white paternalism that would become the cornerstone for the plantation tradition: "None
of us knows what relation the future may produce between the two races in the South, but
possibly when the self-righteous shall be fewer than they are now and the teachings which
have estranged the races shall become more sane, the great Anglo-Saxon race, which
is dominant, and the Negro race, which is amiable, if not subservient, will adjust their
differences more in accordance with the laws which must eventually prevail, and the old
feeling of kindliness, which seems, under the stress of antagonism, to be dying away, will
once more reassert itself" (*The Negro: The Southerners Problem* [The Confederate Reprint
Company, 1904], 203–4). Indeed, the prevailing social message of plantation fiction rested
on this assumption of white supremacy and Black inferiority. Ironically, it was, according
to these authors, the acceptance of this "natural order" that would provide the only real
basis for racial reconciliation.

2. Johnson's novel was first published anonymously in 1912, but it was republished
in 1927 with the acknowledgment of Johnson as the author. After its initial publication,
some speculated that the "story" of Johnson's nameless protagonist was based on an actual
account. This was undoubtedly a ploy by the publisher to fuel the sales of the novel. The
scandalous nature of the subject matter that portrayed a Black protagonist who passes as
white, even marrying a white woman, would have piqued the interest of more than a few
readers in the early 1900s.

3. James Weldon Johnson and his brother J. Rosamond Johnson wrote several popular
minstrel songs for the vaudeville stage in the early 1900s. They included titles such as "Run,
Brudder Possum, Run" and "Roll Them Cotton Bales." The Johnsons' contribution to this
popular genre seems to contradict their prized musical work, "Lift Every Voice and Sing,"
often described as the Black national anthem. But when considered in the broader context
of African American literary and artistic expression, it would not have been an uncommon
practice for Black artists to trade on the racial stereotypes of the plantation tradition and
minstrel stage while also countering those negative representations in their other works.
Charles W. Chesnutt accomplished this through sometimes unflattering, albeit ironic,
portrayals of Black rustic types in his novels, particularly his books *The Conjure Woman*
and *The House Behind the Cedars*. Paul Laurence Dunbar demonstrated this duality in his
volumes of poetry often divided by his Black dialect poems and his standard verses.

4. See St. Clair Drake and Horace R. Cayton, *Black Metropolis: A Study of Negro Life in
a Northern City* (University of Chicago Press, 1933), 58-61. Drake and Horace discuss the

motivating factors for black migration during and after World War I, citing labor short-ages in northern cities due in part to European immigrants returning home to enlist in the war effort.

5. Leah Platt Boustan, *Competition in the Promised Land: Black Migrants in Northern Cities and Labor Markets* (Princeton University Press, 2020), 20.

6. Boustan, *Competition in the Promised Land*, 20.

7. Boustan, *Competition in the Promised Land*, 20.

8. Paul Laurence Dunbar published three novels and several short story collections prior to the publication of *Sport of the Gods*, his fourth and final novel. Dunbar's "white life novels," *The Uncalled* (1898), *The Love of Landry* (1900) and *The Fanatics* (1902) centered on the portrayals of white characters. This was not an uncommon practice for African American authors of this period. Charles W. Chesnutt is another notable example of a Black author who wrote several "white life" novels. It is significant that Dunbar's last novel focuses on the lives of Black migrants. Dunbar himself was near the end of his life and career. As a final statement of racial and cultural identity, *Sport* does the work of setting the record straight on Dunbar's tumultuous career as a Black poet writing both within and against the racist plantation tradition.

9. William Dean Howells, "Review of Majors and Minors," *Harper's Weekly*, 1896.

10. Paul Laurence Dunbar and Lida Keck Wiggins, *The Life and Works of Paul Laurence Dunbar* (J. L. Nichols & Company, 1907), 592.

11. Dunbar and Wiggins, *The Life and Works*, 620.

12. Dunbar and Wiggins, *The Life and Works*, 620.

13. Dunbar and Wiggins, *The Life and Works*, 620.

14. Dunbar and Wiggins, *The Life and Works*, 620.

15. Dunbar and Wiggins, *The Life and Works*, 29.

16. See Lawrence R. Rodgers's discussion of the "fugitive migrant" character in *Canaan Bound: The African American Great Migration Novel* (University of Illinois Press, 1997), 97–131.

17. Benjamin Brawley, *Paul Laurence Dunbar, Poet of his People* (Kennikat Press, 1936), 121.

18. Rodgers, *Canaan Bound*, 54.

19. Rodgers, *Canaan Bound*, 54.

20. Thomas L. Morgan, "The City as Refuge: Constructing Urban Blackness in Paul Laurence Dunbar's *The Sport of the Gods* and James Weldon Johnson's *The Autobiography of an Ex-Colored Man*," *African American Review* 38, no. 2 (Summer 2004): 214.

21. Morgan, "The City as Refuge," 219.

22. Gregory L. Candela, "We Wear the Mask: Irony in Dunbar's *The Sport of the Gods*," *American Literature* 48, no. 1 (1976): 61.

23. Candela, "We Wear the Mask," 61.

24. Candela, "We Wear the Mask," 71.

25. Gene Andrew Jarrett, *Paul Laurence Dunbar: The Life and Times of a Caged Bird* (Princeton University Press, 2023), 12.

26. Jarrett, *Paul Laurence Dunbar*, 3.

27. Donna Campbell, "Paul Laurence Dunbar: 'When Malindy Sings,' the Sport of the Gods, and Black Lives Matter," *American Literary Realism* 53, no. 2 (2020): 109.

28. Campbell, "Paul Laurence Dunbar," 110.

29. Cameron C. Nickels, "Federalist Mock Pastorals: The Ideology of Early New England Humor," *Early American Literature* 17, no. 2 (1982): 141.

30. Nickels, "Federalist Mock Pastorals," 141.

31. William Shakespeare, *King Lear*. In *The Complete Signet Classic Shakespeare*, ed. Sylvan Barnet (Harcourt Brace Jovanovich Publishers, 1963), 4.1.36.

32. William Andrews, "Introduction." In *The Sport of the Gods*, by Paul Laurence Dunbar (New American Library, 1999), vi.

33. In 1900, Dunbar was diagnosed with tuberculosis, which became progressively worse until his eventual death in 1906. His doctor proscribed whisky as a remedy to his unremitting cough. This unfortunate prescription proved worse than the disease itself. Dunbar was soon abusing alcohol, which led to his physical abuse of Alice Ruth Dunbar, his wife of eight years. The couple separated in 1902 after frequent occurrences of alcohol-induced domestic violence. Dunbar was only thirty-three years old at the time of his death.

34. In his oft quoted poem *Sympathy*, Paul Laurence Dunbar evokes the ubiquitous image of the caged songbird that sings and beats its wings against the bars, not as an expression of joy but rather as indication of its imprisoned, tortured existence. This has become an apt metaphor for describing Dunbar's artistic and philosophical dilemma as a Black artist forced to trade in the racist stereotypes of the plantation tradition.

35. William Dean Howells, "Review of *Majors and Minors*" (*Harper's Weekly* 27, June 1896) quoted in Addison Gayle Jr., *Oak and Ivy: A Biography of Paul Laurence Dunbar* (Doubleday, 1971), 54.

36. Howells, "Review of *Majors and Minors*," 54.

37. See Henry Louis Gates's *The Signifying Monkey: A Theory of Afro-American Literary Criticism* (Oxford University Press, 1988). Also see Houston Baker's *Workings of the Spirit* (University of Chicago Press, 1991).

38. Paul Laurence Dunbar, "Sympathy," in *The Collected Poetry of Paul Laurence Dunbar*, ed. Joanne M. Braxton (University of Virginia Press, 1993), 102.

39. Benjamin Brawley, *Poet of His People* (Kennikat Press, 1936), 9.

40. See Alain Locke's description of the "New Negro," in *The New Negro*, ed. Alain Locke (Simon & Schuster, 1997), 5–25. Locke's view of urban Black culture acknowledged its indebtedness to Black vernacular culture in the South. Therefore, he posits the ideal of the "New Negro" as a liminal concept standing betwixt and between rural and urban spaces and places. But the Great Migration hailed for Locke an opportunity for Black folk culture, albeit rooted in the South, to find definitive expression in the North. He writes, "Negroes have been a race more in name than in fact, or to be exact, more in sentiment than in experience. The chief bond between them has been that of a common condition rather than a common consciousness; a problem in common rather than a life in common. In Harlem, Negro life is seizing upon its first chances for group expression and self-determination. It is—or promises at least to be—a race capital" (7). Locke's belief in the symbolic potency of Harlem to provide the material and intellectual conditions for Black expression and self-determination is based on a ghetto pastoral conception of Black

artistic expression during this important period in Black literary history. In this view, not just the Northern city itself but also the promise of the North constituted a viable framework for Black expression and self-determination.

41. Paul Laurence Dunbar, "The Deserted Plantation." In *The Collected Poetry of Paul Laurence Dunbar*, ed. Joanne M. Braxton (University of Virginia Press, 1993), 67.

42. Dunbar, "The Deserted Plantation," 68.

43. Dunbar, "The Deserted Plantation," 68.

44. Paul Laurence Dunbar, *The Sport of the Gods* (New American Library, 1999)

45. Jillmarie Murphy, "Chains of Emancipation: Place Attachment and the Great Northern Migration in Paul Laurence Dunbar's the Sport of the Gods," *Studies in American Naturalism* 8, no. 2 (2013): 157.

46. Murphy, "Chains of Emancipation," 157.

47. See Madhu Dubey's *Signs and Cities: Black Literary Postmodernism* (University of Chicago Press, 2003). Dubey describes the complex pastoralism that defines much of African American literature. Also see Farah J. Griffin's *"Who Set You Flowin'?": The African American Migration Narrative* (Oxford University Press, 1995). Griffin describes the symbolic figuration of African American folk culture in migration novels.

48. Bridget Harris Tsemo, "The Politics of Self-Identity in Paul Laurence Dunbar's *The Sport of the Gods*," *Southern Literary Journal* 41, no. 2 (2009): 24.

49. Carl Van Vechten, "Introduction to Mr. Knopf's New Edition" in *The Autobiography of an Ex-Coloured Man*, First Vintage Books Edition (Vintage Books, 1989), xxxiii–xxxviii.

50. The historical timeline for the Great Migration ranges from 1910 to 1940, though some historians place the start of the migration in 1915 after the end of the First World War and extending as far as 1970.

51. I have in mind authors like Frances E. W. Harper, whose "novel of passing," *Iola Leroy*, touches on themes of Black racial uplift and the central importance of the passing figure whose liminal status as a biracial individual challenged prevailing assumptions of white racial superiority. Other examples include Charles W. Chesnutt's race novels *The House Behind the Cedars* and *The Marrow of Tradition*.

52. See Donald M. Shaffer Jr.'s discussion of Charles W. Chesnutt's "racial project" in "African American Folklore as Racial Project in Charles W. Chesnutt's *The Conjure Woman*," *The Western Journal of Black Studies* 36, no. 4 (Winter 2012): 325. Also see Donald M. Shaffer, "Charles W. Chesnutt, Whiteness, and the Problem of Citizenship," in *The Construction of Whiteness*, eds. Stephen Middleton, David Roediger and Donald Shaffer (University Press of Mississippi, 2016), 129–49.

53. James Weldon Johnson, *Along This Way: The Autobiography of James Weldon Johnson* (Penguin, 1990), 238.

54. Johnson, *Along This Way*, 238.

55. Johnson, *Along This Way*, 239.

56. Johnson, *Along This Way*, 239.

57. Johnson, *Along This Way*, 380.

58. Johnson, *Along This Way*, 380.

59. Johnson, *Along This Way*, 47.

60. Johnson, *Along This Way*, 47.

61. Perhaps the best example of this contradiction is the famous Cotton Club in Harlem, New York, whose policy prohibited Black people from entering the establishment except as workers or performers. For this reason, the Cotton Club came to symbolize both the dehumanizing nature of Jim Crow segregation and the unique contradiction it posed in spaces of Black cultural expression.

62. James Weldon Johnson, "The Dilemma of the Negro Author" in *The Essential Writings of James Weldon Johnson*, ed. Rudolph P. Byrd (Modern Library Classics, 2008), 203.

63. Johnson, "The Dilemma of the Negro Author," 203.

64. Johnson, "The Dilemma of the Negro Author," 203.

65. Johnson, "The Dilemma of the Negro Author," 208.

66. James Weldon Johnson, *The Autobiography of an Ex-Coloured Man* (Vintage Books, 1989)

67. Henry Louis Gates, "Introduction," to the Vintage Edition of *The Autobiography of an Ex-Coloured Man* (Vintage Books, 1989), v–xxiii.

68. Gates, "Introduction," xxi.

69. M. Giulia Fabi, *Passing: And the Rise of the African American Novel* (University of Illinois Press, 2001), 40.

70. Kenneth Mostern, *Autobiography and Black Identity Politics* (Cambridge University Press, 1999), 88.

71. Mostern, *Autobiography and Black Identity Politics*, 88.

72. John Lowe, "Humor and Identity in Ethnic Autobiography: Zora Neale Hurston and Jerre Mangione," in *Cultural Difference & the Literary Text*, eds. Winfried Siemerling and Katrin Schwenk (University of Iowa Press, 1996), 77.

73. Rodgers, *Canaan Bound*, 63.

74. Rudolph Fisher, "The Caucasian Storms Harlem," in *Voices from the Harlem Renaissance*, ed. Nathan Irvin Huggins (Oxford University Press, 1995), 81.

75. Fisher, "The Caucasian Storms Harlem," 81.

76. Fisher, "The Caucasian Storms Harlem," 81.

77. Fisher, "The Caucasian Storms Harlem," 81.

78. W. E. B Du Bois writes in *The Souls of Black Folk* that it should be the goal of Black folk to become "co-workers in the Kingdom of Culture" (*Souls*, 135). Du Bois's integrationist model of cultural production is reflected in the ex-colored man's desire to transform the "raw materials" of Negro folk culture into "classical art." Although he ultimately fails in this endeavor, it is unclear what Johnson's sympathies were regarding Du Bois's model of cultural production.

79. See Jean Toomer's *Cane*. In the story "Blood Burning Moon," Tom Burwell is burned alive at the stake for killing a white man. I argue in chapter 3 that Burwell's death represents the subversion of pastoral imagery and symbolism in the initial Southern section of the novel.

80. See Ralph Ellison, "Harlem Is Nowhere," in *Shadow and Act* (Vintage International, 1995), 294–302.

Chapter Two: "When the Sun Goes Down": The Ghetto Pastoral Mode in Jean Toomer's *Cane*

1. Stewart E. Tolnay and E. M. Beck, "Rethinking the Role of Racial Violence in the Great Migration." In *Black Exodus*, ed. Alferdteen Harrison (University Press of Mississippi, 1991), 22–23. Also see James Grossman, *Land of Hope, Chicago, Black Southerners, and the Great Migration* (University of Chicago Press, 1989), 1–9.

2. For a discussion of this, see Robert Bone, *The Negro Novel in America* (New Haven Press, 1958), 81. Also see Nathan Irvin Huggins, *Harlem Renaissance* (Oxford University Press, 1971), 180.

3. Tolnay and Beck, "Rethinking the Role of Racial Violence," 22–23.

4. These thematic concerns generally include the formation of an urban Black aesthetic, a revisioning of Southern Black "folk" culture, and the possibility of racial progressivism in the Northern city.

5. Lee Baker points out that the notorious "red riots" of this period provided the ideological conditions for political resistance and self-determination among urban Black populations: "Instead of [urban Black people] knowing their *place*, uplifting the race, or fighting from being kept down, African Americans organized proactive institutions with increased vigor" (*From Savage to Negro: Anthropology and the Construction of Race, 1896–1954* [University of California Press, 1998], 139).

6. See Michael Denning's discussion of the "ghetto pastoral" mode in *The Cultural Front: The Laboring of American Culture in the Twentieth Century* (Verso Press, 1996).

7. Denning, *The Cultural Front*, 231.

8. Denning, *The Cultural Front*, 239.

9. Denning, *The Cultural Front*, 239.

10. Laurence Rodgers argues that the primary goal of the characters of Black migration fiction is to establish an "authentic reattachment" to rural folk culture in the city (*Canaan Bound: The African American Great Migration Novel* (University of Illinois Press, 1997), 37).

11. Darwin Turner, *In a Minor Chord* (Southern Illinois University Press, 1971), 207.

12. Bernard Bell, "Portrait of the Artist as High Priest of Soul: Jean Toomer's *Cane*," *Black World*, September 1974, 13.

13. Lucinda MacKethan, "Jean Toomer's *Cane*: A Pastoral Problem," *Mississippi Quarterly* 35 (1975): 425.

14. Leo Marx, *The Machine in the Garden* (Oxford University Press, 2000), 362–63.

15. Denning, *The Cultural Front*, 247.

16. See Nathan Huggins, *Harlem Renaissance* (Oxford University Press, 1971), 180. Also see Robert Bone, *The Negro Novel in America* (New Haven Press, 1958), 81.

17. David Nicholls, *Conjuring the Folk: Forms of Modernity in African America* (University of Michigan Press, 2000), 21.

18. William Ramsey, "Jean Toomer's Eternal South," *Southern Literary Journal* 36 (Fall 2003): 74.

19. Ramsey, "Jean Toomer's Eternal South," 76.

20. Ramsey, "Jean Toomer's Eternal South," 76.

21. Nicholls, *Conjuring the Folk*, 25.

22. Nicholls, *Conjuring the Folk*, 25.

23. Nicholls, *Conjuring the Folk*, 26.

24. Jean Toomer, "Letter to Waldo Frank," in *The Jean Toomer Reader*, ed. Frederik L. Rusch (Oxford University Press, 1993), 23.

25. Jean Toomer, quoted in Charles Larsen, *Invisible Darkness: Jean Toomer & Nella Larsen* (University of Iowa Press, 1993), 22.

26. Jean Toomer, quoted in Larsen, *Invisible Darkness*, 22.

27. Jean Toomer, "Letter to James Weldon Johnson," in *The Jean Toomer Reader*, 106.

28. Larsen, *Invisible Darkness*, 13–17.

29. Jean Toomer, quoted in Larsen, *Invisible Darkness*, 16.

30. Alain Locke, "The New Negro." In *The New Negro*, ed. Alain Locke, 1st Touchstone Edition (Simon and Schuster, 1993), 15.

31. Richard Wright, "The Blue Print for Negro Writing," in *The Norton Anthology of African American Literature*, eds. Henry Louis Gates Jr. and Nellie Y. McKay (W. W. Norton & Company, 2004), 1403.

32. "Sugar Production," *The Handbook of Texas Online*. November 2000. Web. 20 August 2000.

33. Charlene Gilbert and Eli Quinn, *Homecoming: The Story of African-American Farmers* (Beacon Press, 2000), 71–78.

34. Jean Toomer, *Cane* (The Modern Library, 1994).

35. Farah J. Griffin, *"Who Set You Flowin'?": The African-American Migration Narrative* (Oxford University Press, 1995), 8.

36. Nicholls, *Conjuring the Folk,* 26.

37. Toomer, "Letter to Waldo Frank," 25.

38. Jean Toomer, "Letter to *The Liberator*," in *The Jean Toomer Reader*, 16.

Chapter Three: The Ghetto Pastoral and Domestic Spaces
of Black Female Desire in the City

1. W. E. B. Du Bois, "The Browsing Reader: Review of Two Novels," *The Crisis* 35, no. 6 (1928): 202.

2. Du Bois, "The Browsing Reader," 202.

3. Ronald Takaki, *A Different Mirror* (Little, Brown and Company, 1993), 56.

4. Du Bois, "The Browsing Reader," 202.

5. See Carl Van Vechten, *Nigger Heaven* (University of Illinois Press, 2000). Van Vechten's novel valorizes the racial exoticism of Harlem as signifying an essential aspect of Black experience that its protagonist (and presumably everyone) must cultivate. The racial essentialism of Van Vechten's descriptions parallels that of his protagonist. Van Vechten posits in this primitive image of Harlem a sexual vitality that is absent in the larger society. Although the novel figures this racial exoticism as positive value, its perspective narrowly views Black experience as something that emanates solely from Harlem's culture industry.

6. Lisa Krissoff Boehm, *Making a Way Out of No Way: African American Women and the Second Great Migration* (University Press of Mississippi, 2010), 5.

7. Boehm, *Making a Way Out of No Way*, 5.

8. Rudolph Fisher, "The Caucasian Storms Harlem." In *Voices from the Harlem Renaissance*, ed. Nathan Irvin Huggins (Oxford University Press, 1995), 74–82.

9. Peter M. Rutkoff and William B. Scott, *Fly Away: The Great African American Cultural Migrations* (Johns Hopkins University Press, 2016), 61.

10. Takaki, *A Different Mirror*, 353–69.

11. Gilbert Osofsky, *Harlem: The Making of a Ghetto* (New York, Harper & Row, 1966), 103–4.

12. Charles Scruggs, quoted in Maria Balshaw, *Looking for Harlem* (Pluto Press, 2000), 5.

13. The Cotton Club is one famous example of Harlem's nightclubs that instituted "white only" policies. These segregated spaces were ironic instances of the paradoxical quality of the color line in the heart of the "Negro Mecca."

14. Osofsky, *Harlem*, 38.

15. Amiri Baraka discusses themes of primitivism and minstrelsy in *Blues People* (William Morrow and Company, 1963), 83. Also see George Hutchinson's discussion of Harlem's dual character in *The Harlem Renaissance in Black and White* (Belknap Press of Harvard University Press, 1995), 14–28.

16. Langston Hughes discusses this dual aspect of Harlem, especially as it relates to black artistic production, in *The Big Sea* (A. A. Knopf, 1940), 233–41.

17. Kelly Miller, "Where Is the Negro's Heaven?" In *The Opportunity Reader*, ed. Sondra Kathryn Wilson (Random House, 1999), 422.

18. Miller, "Where Is the Negro's Heaven?," 429.

19. Miller, "Where Is the Negro's Heaven?," 429.

20. Hughes famously admits in his autobiography, *Big Sea*, that if there had been a renaissance in Harlem, common Black folk knew nothing about it because "it had not raised wages any." His observation is taken by some scholars, most notably Nathaniel Huggins, that the Harlem Renaissance involved primarily the interests of a small cadre of Black intellectuals and their white benefactors.

21. Zora Neale Hurston, "How It Feels to Be Colored Me." In *The Norton Anthology of African American Literature* (Norton & Company, 1997), 1010.

22. Brian Dorsey, *Who Stole the Soul* (Salzburg: Institut für Anglistik und Amerikanistik, Universität Salzburg, 1997), 14.

23. Dorsey, *Who Stole the Soul*, 14.

24. See Huston Baker, *Workings of the Spirit: The Poetics of Afro-American Women's Writing* (University of Chicago Press, 1991), 28–37; and Hortense J. Spillers, "Mama's Baby, Papa's Maybe: An American Grammar Book," in *Black, White and in Color* (University of Chicago Press, 2003), 203–29.

25. Claudia Tate, *Domestic Allegories of Political Desire* (Oxford University Press, 1992), 5.

26. Tate, *Domestic Allegories of Political Desire*, 9.

27. Tate, *Domestic Allegories of Political Desire*, 101.

28. Tate, *Domestic Allegories of Political Desire*, 101.

29. Sinclair Lewis, "Letter from Sinclair Lewis to Walter White," "Papers of the NAACP," Part 2, 1919–1939, Personal Correspondence of Selected NAACP Officials (University Publications of America, 1982).

30. Lewis, "Letter from Sinclair Lewis to Walter White."

31. Francis White, *A Man Called White: The Autobiography of Walter White* (Viking Press, 1948), 114–15.

32. Walter White, quoted in Janken, *White*, 95.

33. Walter White, *How Far the Promised Land* (AMS Press, 1973), 127–28.

34. Walter White, *Flight* (Louisiana State University Press, 1998), 73.

35. Helen Levy, *Fiction of the Home Place: Jewett, Cather, Glasgow, Porter, Welty, and Naylor* (University Press of Mississippi, 1992), 4.

36. Earl Lewis, "Expectations, Economic Opportunities, and Life in the Industrial Age: Black Migration to Norfolk, Virginia, 1910–1945." In *The Great Migration in Historical Perspective*, ed. Joe William Trotter Jr. (Indiana University Press, 1991), 33.

37. Darlene Clark Hine, "Black Migration to the Urban Midwest: The Gender Dimension, 1915–1945." In *The Great Migration in Historical Perspective*, ed. Joe William Trotter Jr. (Indiana University Press, 1991), 132.

38. I have in mind the "tragic mulatto" novels of such authors as Charles Chesnutt, Pauline Hopkins, and Frances E. W. Harper. Their novels typically centered on the experience of tragic mulatto turned race leaders, characters that embodied the values of their white middle-class readership.

39. Laurence Rodgers, *Canaan Bound: The African American Great Migration Novel* (University of Illinois Press, 1997), 88.

40. Charles Larsen, *Invisible Darkness: Jean Toomer & Nella Larsen* (University of Iowa Press, 1993), 184.

41. Larsen, *Invisible Darkness*, 184.

42. Larsen, *Invisible Darkness*, 185.

43. Nella Larsen, *Quicksand and Passing*, ed. Deborah E. McDowell (Rutgers University Press, 2000), 4; 17.

44. Cheryl Wall, *Women of the Harlem Renaissance* (Indiana University Press, 1995), 87.

45. Tate, *Domestic Allegories*, 63.

46. See Juda Benett's discussion of the trope of the "tragic mulatto" in *The Passing Figure: Racial Confusion in Modern American literature* (Peter Lang, 1996).

Chapter Four: "Harlem Is Nowhere": Blues Expression and the Ghetto Pastoral Mode in Ralph Ellison's *Invisible Man*

1. David Margolick, *Strange Fruit: Billie Holiday, Café Society, and an Early Cry for Civil Rights* (Running Press, 2000).

2. Margolick, *Strange Fruit*.

3. Lewis Allen (Abel Meeropol), *Strange Fruit* (Vocalian Records, 1939), Lyricfind.com.

4. Allen, *Strange Fruit*.

5. Ralph Ellison, "Richard Wright's Blues." In *The Collected Essays*, ed. John F. Callahan (Modern Library, 1995), 129.

6. See Horace Porter, *Jazz Country: Ralph Ellison in America* (University of Iowa Press, 2001). Also See Michael Magee, "Ralph Ellison: Pragmatism, Jazz and the American Vernacular," *Transactions of the Charles S. Peirce Society* no. 39 (2003): 227–58.

7. Ken Warren, *So Black and Blue* (University of Chicago Press, 2003), 2.

8. Ralph Ellison, "Harlem Is Nowhere," in *Shadow and Act* (Vintage International, 1964), 296.

9. See Gilbert Osofsky, *Harlem; The Making of a Ghetto; Negro New York, 1890–1930* (Harper & Row, 1966), 127–48. Also see Monique M. Taylor, *Harlem Between Heaven and Hell* (University of Minnesota Press, 2002), 17–26.

10. Ellison, "Harlem Is Nowhere," 300.

11. The overarching theme of most Black migration novels is the importance of imagining spaces that can reflect both the past cultural experience of the South, as well as the unique urban experience of the North. These spaces are necessarily dialectical in that they do not privilege rural or urban meanings, but rather foreground a ghetto pastoral experience that becomes the basis for the postmigration, urban identity of Black migrant characters. Black musical forms, particularly the blues, constitute one of the important cultural elements at work in these urban spaces. Therefore, the blues functions as a mediational cultural form that reflects the past and the present—the rural experience of the South and urban experience of the North. In this sense, the blues most closely reflects the ghetto pastoral ideal that is the thematic basis for the central complication posed by Black migrant characters struggling to establish a sense of belonging in Northern cities.

12. Ellison, "Harlem Is Nowhere," 300.

13. Ellison, "Harlem Is Nowhere," 300.

14. See Kenneth Warren, *So Black, So Blue* (University of Chicago Press, 2003), 26. Also see Lawrence Jackson, *Ralph Ellison: Emergence of Genius* (John Wiley & Sons, 2002), 152–54.

15. Porter, *Jazz Country*, 74.

16. Farah Griffin, *"Who Set You Flowin'?": The African-American Migration Narrative* (Oxford University Press, 1995), 55.

17. Ralph Ellison, "The World and the Jug," *Shadow and Act*, 112.

18. Henri Lefebvre, *The Urban Revolution* (University of Minnesota Press, 2003), 118–19.

19. In the previous chapter, I described the earlier housing crisis of the 1920s as a social factor that influenced the representation of domestic spaces in the migration novels of the Harlem Renaissance.

20. Manning Marable, *Race, Reform, and Rebellion: The Second Reconstruction in Black America, 1945–1990* (University Press of Mississippi, 1991), 41–60.

21. Marable, *Race, Reform, and Rebellion*, 38.

22. See Alan Spear, *Black Chicago: The Making of a Negro Ghetto, 1890–1920* (University of Chicago Press, 1967), 129–222.

23. Stephen Nathan Haymes discusses the "racialization" of urban space in *Race, Culture and the City: A Pedagogy for Black Urban Struggle* (State University of New York Press, 1995), 116–17.

24. Barbara Foley defines "social protest fiction" and the "proletarian novel" in her seminal work, *Radical Representations: Politics and Form in U.S. Proletarian Fiction* (Duke University Press, 1993), 86–127. There she writes, "The definition of proletarian literature as literature treating the subject matter of working-class experience was perhaps the most commonly invoked criterion for determining whether or not a text should be defined

as proletarian (109)." Also see James F. Murphy's *The Proletarian Moment* (University of Illinois Press, 1991), 21–35.

25. The social realist movement in literature was embraced by these novelists who considered themselves (if not full-fledged members of the Communist party) so-called "fellow travelers" in the class struggle. It is worth noting that many of them were at some point in their careers affiliated with the communist party. Wright officially broke with the communist party in 1940, although he (like many other writers of the period) would maintain a commitment to Marxist and socialist ideals. See Michael Denning, *The Cultural Front: The Laboring of American Culture in the Twentieth Century* (Verso, 1996), 4–20.

26. Ralph Ellison, "Blues People," *Shadow and Act*, 256.

27. I define the "trope of displacement" as the central thematic feature of early Black migration novels and a defining aspect of Black migrant characters as it represents them as permanently displaced in an urban environment that has evolved not adequate place for them.

28. The "Battle Royal" was published separately in 1946 and became the basis for the longer manuscript of the novel by then a work in progress.

29. Ralph Ellison, *Invisible Man*, Second Vintage International Edition (Vintage Books, 1995), 16.

30. Clyde Woods writes: "The blues emerge immediately after the overthrow of Reconstruction. During this period, unmediated African American voices were routinely silenced through the imposition of a new regime of censorship based on exile, assassination and massacre. The blues became an alternative form of communication, analysis, moral intervention, observation, celebration for a new generation that had witnessed slavery, freedom, and unfreedom in rapid succession between 1860 and 1875" (*Development Arrested: Race, Power, and the Blues in the Mississippi Delta* [Verso, 1998], 36).

31. Huston Baker Jr., *Blues, Ideology, and Afro-American Literature: A Vernacular Theory* (University of Chicago Press, 1984), 190.

32. LeRoi Jones describes the "Peatie Wheatstraw blues" in *Blues People: Negro Music in White America* (Morrow Quill Paperbacks, 1963), 67.

33. Charles Keil, *Urban Blues* (University of Chicago Press, 1966), 76.

34. Mary's apartment reflects the representations of "domestic spaces" in two Black migration novels of the 1920s, Walter White's *Flight* and Nella Larsen's *Quicksand*. Larsen's protagonist, Helga Crane, strives for an elusive ideal of domesticity, seeing in the Black middle-class homes of Harlem a potential model of her own future. Like other Black migrant characters in this tradition, she seeks a place to call home in the city. Similarly, White's novel centers on the experience of a Black female migrant, Mimi Daquin, whose "flight" to the city has as its goal the establishment of a domestic place of belonging in the city. Ellison riffs on this important thematic goal of the migration novel by introducing his protagonist to a domestic space in the city replete with the conflict and contradictions that mark his existence as an "invisible man." In other words, this domestic space of belonging is also a blues space located at the proverbial crossroads of racial meaning and cultural understanding.

35. This passage wonderfully recalls a similar passage in *The Sport of the Gods* (1902) in which Paul Laurence Dunbar comments on the dilemma of the city dweller who

must choose between the domestic values of home and the allure of the city streets (Paul Laurence Dunbar, *The Sport of the Gods* in *Three Negro Classics* [Avon Books 1965], 507–8).

36. Lawrence R. Rodgers, *Canaan Bound: The African American Great Migration Novel* (University of Illinois Press, 1997), 37.

37. Ralph Ellison, "The Little Man at Chehaw Station." In *The American Scholar* 47, no. 1 (Winter 1978): 29.

38. Ellison, "The Little Man at Chehaw Station," 29.

39. Ellison, "The Little Man at Chehaw Station," 29.

40. Ellison, "The Little Man at Chehaw Station," 30.

41. Ellison, "The Little Man at Chehaw Station," 30.

Conclusion: Where Is the Promised Land?

1. Claude Brown, *Manchild in the Promised Land*, 1st Touchstone Edition (Simon and Schuster, 1999), 1.

2. I argued in chapter 1 that Laurence Rodgers and Farah Griffin valorize notions of the folk, thereby positing a "rural ideal" as the basis for Black migrant ascent in the city. Both locate an "urbanized" version of the folk in these novels that serves as an immediate point of reference and initiation for the displaced Black migrant. I counter with a reading that emphasizes the inevitable (and disruptive) rural and urban conflict that necessarily complicates this version of Black migrants' urban ascent.

3. The New Negro movement of the 1920s understood Black racial identity as a fluid construct formed in the crucible of Black migration, industrialism and urban displacement. But New Negro authors and intellectuals such as Alain Locke believed that Black folk had "leaped several generations" in their migrant aspirations in the Northern city. In other words, they had become new creations in the urban spaces of cities like Harlem and Detroit. The optimism of the New Negro movement, however, was undercut by the reality of life in those Jim Crow Northern cities. Also undercutting the New Negro idealism was the inevitable tension between rural and urban modes of cultural experience—both exerting tremendous influence on how authors depicted Black communities in the North. While Locke clearly understood that the New Negro was really neither wholly a product of the South nor of the North, he and others were hard pressed to precisely define the New Negro. It may well be conjectured that the New Negro is the Black migrant herself, torn as it were between two cultural locales, with her feet tenuously in both.

4. Raymond Williams, *The Country and the City* (Oxford University Press, 1973), 289.

5. See William Julius Wilson, *When Work Disappears* (Alfred A. Knopf, 1996).

6. See Richard Wright's discussion of Black community in *Black Boy* (HarperCollins Books, 1998). There he writes, "I began to marvel at how smoothly the black boys acted out roles that the white had mapped out for them. Most of them were not conscious of living a special, separate, stunted way of life" (196–97).

7. Ralph Ellison, "Harlem Is Nowhere." In *Shadow and Act*, First Vintage International Edition (Vintage Books, 1995), 301.

8. Ralph Ellison, "The World and the Jug." In *Shadow and Act*, First Vintage International Edition (Vintage Books, 1995), 111.

9. Ellison, "The World and the Jug," 112.

10. Richard Wright, *Black Boy* (Alfred Knopf, 1996), 37.

11. James Baldwin, "Many Thousands Gone." In *The Price of the Ticket* (St. Martin's Press, 1985), 67.

12. Baldwin, "Many Thousands Gone," 72.

13. Baldwin argues in the essay for a complexity of shared experience among Black people that Wright's novel either obscures in its generalizing Marxist analysis of social relations or jettisons altogether in its stereotypical portrayal of Bigger Thomas as a "social symbol" (Baldwin, "Many Thousands Gone," 66). In many ways, Baldwin's novel is an attempt to move beyond the extremes of racial stereotyping—the racist "step and fetch it" Negro caricatures of a previous generation *and* the tendentious race men (and women) of the Harlem Renaissance. Indeed, writes Baldwin, "Aunt Jemimah and Uncle Tom are dead, their places taken by a group of amazingly well-adjusted young men and women, almost as dark, but ferociously literate, well-adjusted and scrubbed, who are never laughed at, who are not likely ever to set foot in a cotton or tobacco field or in any but the most modern of kitchens" (Baldwin, "Many Thousands Gone," 67).

14. Baldwin, "Many Thousands Gone," 72.

15. Keith Clark, "Baldwin, Communitas, and the Black Masculinist Tradition." In *New Essays on "Go Tell It on the Mountain,"* ed. Trudier Harris (Cambridge University Press, 1996), 127.

16. Clark, "Baldwin, Communitas, and the Black Masculinist Tradition," 129.

17. Clark, "Baldwin, Communitas, and the Black Masculinist Tradition," 129.

18. James Baldwin, *Go Tell It on the Mountain* (Dell Publishing, 1981), 4.

19. Albert J. Raboteau, *Canaan Land: A Religious History of African Americans* (Oxford University Press, 2001), 84.

20. Henri Lefebvre, *The Production of Space*, trans. Donald Nicholson-Smith (Blackwell Publishers Ltd., 1991), 142.

21. Eph. 3:1 (New International Version): "For this reason I, Paul, the prisoner of Christ Jesus for the sake of you Gentiles."

22. Ellison, "The World and the Jug," 116.

BIBLIOGRAPHY

Allen, Lewis (Abel Meeropol). *Strange Fruit*. Vocalian Records, 1939. Lyricfind.com.

Andrews, William. "Introduction." *Sport of the Gods*. By Paul Laurence Dunbar. New American Library, 1999.

Bachelard, Gaston. *The Poetics of Space*. Trans. Maria Jolas. Beacon Press, 1994.

Baker, Huston, Jr. *Afro-American Poetics: Revisions of Harlem and the Black Aesthetic*. University of Wisconsin Press, 1988.

Baker, Huston, Jr. *Blues, Ideology, and Afro-American Literature: A Vernacular Theory*. University of Chicago Press, 1984.

Baker, Huston, Jr. *Long Black Song: Essays in Black American Literature and Culture*. University Press of Virginia, 1990.

Baker, Huston, Jr. *Modernism and the Harlem Renaissance*. University of Chicago Press, 1987.

Baker, Huston, Jr. *Workings of the Spirit: The Poetics of Afro-American Women's Writing*. University of Chicago Press, 1991.

Baker, Lee. *From Savage to Negro: Anthropology and the Construction of Race, 1896–1954*. University of California Press, 1998.

Bakhtin, M. M. *The Dialogic Imagination*, edited by Michael Holquist. Translated by Carl Emerson and Michael Holquist. University of Texas Press, 1981.

Baldwin, Davarian L. *Chicago's New Negroes: Modernity, the Great Migration, and Black Urban Life*. University of North Carolina Press, 2007.

Baldwin, James. "Everybody's Protest Novel." *The Price of the Ticket*. 27–33.

Baldwin, James. *Go Tell It on the Mountain*. Dell Publishing, 1981.

Baldwin, James. "Many Thousands Gone." *The Price of the Ticket*. St. Martin's Press, 1985. 65–78.

Balshaw, Maria. *Looking for Harlem*. Pluto Press, 2000.

Baraka, Amiri. *Blues People*. William Morrow and Company, 1963.

Bell, Bernard. *The Afro-American Novel and Its Tradition*. University of Massachusetts, 1987.

Bell, Bernard. "Portrait of the Artist as High Priest of Soul: Jean Toomer's *Cane*." *Black World*, September 1974, 20–29.

Benett, Juda. *The Passing Figure: Racial Confusion in Modern American Literature*. Peter Lang, 1996.

Bethune, Mary Mcleod. "The Problems of the City Dweller." In *Up South: Stories, Studies and Letters of this Century's African-American Migrations*, edited by Malaika Adero, 109–15. The New Press, 1993.

Boehm, Lisa Krissoff, *Making a Way Out of No Way: African American Women and the Second Great Migration*. University Press of Mississippi, 2010.

Bone, Robert. *The Negro Novel in America*. Yale University Press, 1958.

Boustan, Leah Platt. *Competition in the Promised Land: Black Migrants in Northern Cities and Labor Markets*. Princeton University Press, 2020.

Brawley, Benjamin. *Paul Laurence Dunbar, Poet of His People*. Kennikat Press, 1936.

Bremer, Sidney H. *Urban Intersections: Meetings of Life and Literature in United Stats Cities*. University of Illinois Press, 1992.

Brown, Claude. *Manchild in the Promised Land*. 1st Touchstone Edition. Simon and Schuster, 1999.

Campbell, Donna. "Paul Laurence Dunbar: 'When Malindy Sings,' the Sport of the Gods, and Black Lives Matter." *American Literary Realism* 53, no. 2 (November 23, 2021): 106–11.

Candela, Gregory L., "We Wear the Mask: Irony in Dunbar's *The Sport of the Gods*." *Literature* 48, no. 1 (March, 1976): 60–72.

Carby, Hazel A. *Cultures in Babylon*. Verso, 1999.

Chesnutt, Charles W. *The Conjure Woman*. Duke University Press, 1993.

Chesnutt, Charles W. *The House Behind the Cedars*. Penguin Group, 1993.

Clark, Keith. "Baldwin, Communitas, and the Black Masculinist Tradition." In *New Essays on "Go Tell It on the Mountain,"* edited by Trudier Harris, 127–56. Cambridge University Press, 1996.

Cohen, William. "The Great Migration as a Lever for Social Change." In *The Black Exodus: The Great Migration from the American South*, edited by Alferdteen Harrison, 72–82. University Press of Mississippi, 1991.

Cruz, Jon. *Culture on the Margins: The Black Spiritual and the Rise of American Cultural Interpretation*. Princeton University Press, 1999.

Denning, Michael. *The Cultural Front: The Laboring of American Culture in the Twentieth Century*. Verso, 1996.

Dorsey, Brian. *Who Stole the Soul*. Institut für Anglistik und Amerikanistik, Universität Salzburg, 1997.

Drake, St. Clair and Cayton, Horace. *Black Metropolis: A Study of Negro Life in a Northern City*. University of Chicago Press, 1993.

Dreiser, Theodore. *An American Tragedy*. Boni and Liveright, 1925.

Dubey, Madhu. *Signs and Cities: Black Literary Postmodernism*. University of Chicago Press, 2003.

Du Bois, W. E. B. "The Browsing Reader: Review of Two Novels." *The Crisis* 35, no. 6 (June 1928): 202.

Du Bois, W. E. B. "Criteria of Negro Art." Sundquist 324–28.

Du Bois, W. E. B. "The Migration of Negroes." June 1917. In *Black Protest and the Great Migration: A Brief History with Documents*, edited by Eric Arnesen, 46–50. Beford/St. Martin's, 2003.

Du Bois, W. E. B. "The Negro and the Warsaw Ghetto." In *The Oxford W. E. B. Du Bois Reader*, edited by Eric Sundquist, 469–73. Oxford University Press.

Du Bois, W. E. B. *The Souls of Black Folk*. In *Writings*, edited by Nathan Huggins, 357–547. Library of America, 1987.

Dunbar, Paul Laurence. "The Deserted Plantation." Braxton. 67.

Dunbar, Paul Laurence. *Lyrics of Lowly Life*. Carol Publishing Group, 1997.

Dunbar, Paul Laurence. *The Sport of the Gods*. New American Library, 1999.

Dunbar, Paul Laurence. "Sympathy." In *The Collected Poetry of Paul Laurence Dunbar*, edited by Joanne M. Braxton, 102. University of Virginia Press, 1993.

Dunbar, Paul Laurence, and Lida Keck Wiggins. *The Life and Works of Paul Laurence Dunbar*. J. L. Nichols & Company, 1907.

Ellison, Ralph. "Blues People." In *Shadow and Act*, 247–58. Vintage International, 1964.

Ellison, Ralph. "Harlem Is Nowhere." In *Shadow and Act*, 294–302. Vintage International, 1964.

Ellison, Ralph. *Invisible Man*. Second Vintage International Edition. Vintage Books, 1995.

Ellison, Ralph. "The Little Man at Chehaw Station." *The American Scholar* 47, no. 1 (Winter 1978): 25–48.

Ellison, Ralph. "Richard Wright's Blues." In *The Collected Essays of Ralph Ellison*, edited by John F. Callahan, 128–45. Modern Library, 1995.

Ellison, Ralph. "The World and the Jug." In *Shadow and Act*, 107–43. Vintage International, 1964.

Fabi, M. Giulia. *Passing: And the Rise of the African American Novel*. University of Illinois Press, 2001.

Favor, J. Martin. *Authentic Blackness: The Folk in the New Negro Renaissance*. Duke University Press, 1999.

Fisher, Rudolph. "The Caucasian Storms Harlem." In *Voices from the Harlem Renaissance*, edited by Nathan Irvin Huggins, 74–82. Oxford University Press, 1995.

Fisher, Rudolph. "The City of Refuge." In *The City of Refuge: The Collected Stories of Rudolph Fisher*, edited by John McCluskey Jr., 35–47. University of Missouri Press, 1987.

Foley, Barbara. *Radical Representations: Politics and Form in U.S. Proletarian Fiction, 1929–1941*. Duke University Press, 1993.

Gates, Henry Louis. Introduction to *The Autobiography on an Ex-Coloured Man* by James Weldon Johnson, v–xxiii. Vintage edition. Vintage Books 1989.

Gates, Henry Louis. *The Signifying Monkey: A Theory of Afro-American Literary Criticism*. Oxford University Press, 1988.

Gayle, Addison. *Oak and Ivy: A Biography of Paul Laurence Dunbar*. Doubleday, 1971.

Gilbert, Charlene, and Eli Quinn. *Homecoming: The Story of African American Farmers*. Beacon Press, 2000.

Gilbert, James Burkhart. *Writers and Partisans: A History of Literary Radicalism in America*. John Wiley and Sons, Inc., 1968.

Griffin, Farah. *"Who Set You Flowin'?": The African-American Migration Narrative*. Oxford University Press, 1995.

Grossman, James. *Land of Hope: Chicago, Black Southerners, and the Great Migration*. University of Chicago, 1989.

Harper, Frances E. W. *Iola Leroy*. Dover Publications, 2010.

Harris, Joel Chandler. *Uncle Remus: His Songs and Sayings*. Penguin Group, 1982.

Haymes, Stephen Nathan. *Race, Culture, and the City*. State University of New York Press, 1995.

Haynes, George E. "Negro Migration: Its Effect on Family and Community Life in the
    North." (1924). In *Black Protest and the Great Migration: A Brief History with Documents*,
    edited by Eric Arnesen, 193–98. Beford/St. Martin's Press, 2003.
Herskovits, Melville J. *The Myth of the Negro Past*. Beacon Press, 1990.
Hine, Darlene Clark. "Black Migration to the Urban Midwest: The Gender Dimension,
    1915–1945." In *The Great Migration in Historical Perspective*, edited by Joe William
    Trotter Jr., 127–46. Indiana University Press, 1991.
Holden, Arthur C. "A Northerner's View of the Negro Problem." In *Up South: Stories,
    Studies and Letters of This Century's African-American Migrations*, edited by Malaika
    Adero, 165–68. Norton & Company, Inc., 1993.
Hopkins, Pauline. *Contending Forces*. Oxford University Press, 1991.
Huggins, Nathan Irvin. *Harlem Renaissance*. Oxford University Press, 1971.
Hughes, Langston. *The Big Sea*. A. A. Knopf, 1940.
Hughes, Langston. "The Negro and the Racial Mountain." In *The Norton Anthology of
    African American Literature*, edited by Henry Louis Gates Jr. and Nellie Y. McKay,
    1211–1314. W. W. Norton & Company, 1997.
Hughes, Langston. "Songs Called the Blues." In *Write Me a Few of Your Lines*, edited by
    Steven C. Tracy, 391–93. University of Massachusetts Press, 1999.
Hurston, Zora Neale. "How It Feels to Be Colored Me." In *The Norton Anthology of African
    American Literature*, edited by Henry Louis Gates Jr. and Nellie Y. McKay, 1030–33.
    W. W. Norton & Company, 1997.
Hutchinson, George. *The Harlem Renaissance in Black and White*. The Belknap Press of
    Harvard University Press, 1995.
Jackson, Lawrence. *Ralph Ellison: Emergence of Genius*. John Wiley and Sons Inc., 2002.
Janken, Keneth Robert. *White: The Biography of Walter White, Mr. NAACP*. New York
    Press, 2003.
Johnson, Charles S. "How Much Is the Migration a Flight from Persecution." (September
    1923). In *Black Protest and the Great Migration: A Brief History with Documents*, edited
    by Eric Arnesen, 54–58. Beford/St. Martin's Press, 2003.
Johnson, James Weldon. *Along This Way: The Autobiography of James Weldon Johnson*.
    Penguin Books, 1990.
Johnson, James Weldon. *The Autobiography of an Ex-Coloured Man*. In *Three Negro Classics*.
    Avon Books 1965.
Johnson, James Weldon. *Black Manhattan*. Da Capo Press, 1991.
Johnson, James Weldon. "The Dilemma of the Negro Author" in *The Essential Writings of
    James Weldon Johnson*, ed. Rudolph P. Byrd. Modern Library Classics, 2008.
Jones, Leroi. *Blues People: Negro Music in White America*. Morrow Quill Paperbacks, 1963.
Keil, Charles. *Urban Blues*. University of Chicago Press, 1966.
Kotlowitz, Alex. *There Are No Children Here*. Anchor Books, 1992.
Larsen, Charles. *Invisible Darkness: Jean Toomer & Nella Larsen*. University of Iowa
    Press, 1993.
Larsen, Nella. *Quicksand and Passing*, edited by Deborah E. McDowell. Rutgers University
    Press, 2000.

Lefebvre, Henri. *The Production of Space*. Translated and edited by Donald Nicholson-Smith. Blackwell Publishers Ltd., 1991.

Lefebvre, Henri. *The Urban Revolution*. University of Minnesota Press, 2003.

Lefebvre, Henri. *Writings on Cities*. Translated and edited by Eleonore Kofman and Elizabeth Lebas. Blackwell Publishers Ltd, 1996.

Lehan, Richard. *The City in Literature: An Intellectual and Cultural History*. University of California Press, 1998.

Lemann, Nicholas. *The Promised Land: The Great Black Migration and How It Changed America*. A. A. Knopf, 1991.

Levine, Lawrence. *Black Culture and Black Consciousness: Afro-American Folk Thought from Slavery to Freedom*. Oxford University Press, 1977.

Levy, Helen. *Fiction of the Home Place: Jewett, Cather, Glasgow, Porter, Welty, and Naylor*. University Press of Mississippi, c1992.

Lewis, Earl. "Expectations, Economic Opportunities, and Life in the Industrial Age: Black Migration to Norfolk, Virginia, 1910–1945." In *The Great Migration in Historical Perspective*, edited by Joe William Trotter Jr., 22–45. Indiana University Press, 1991.

Lewis, Sinclair. "Letter from Sinclair Lewis to Walter White." In *Papers of the NAACP. Part 2. 1919–1939. Personal correspondence of selected NAACP officials.* [Microform] University Publications of America, 1982.

Locke, Alain. *The New Negro*, edited by Alain Locke. 1st Touchstone Edition. Simon and Schuster, 1993.

Logan, John R., and Harvey L. Molotch. *Urban Fortunes: The Political Economy of Place*. University of California Press, 1987.

Lowe, John. "Humor and Identity in Ethnic Autobiography: Zora Neale Hurston and Jerre Mangione." In *Cultural Difference & the Literary Text*, edited by Winfried Siemerling and Katrin Schwenk, 75–99. University of Iowa Press, 1996.

Machor, James L. *Pastoral Cities: Urban Ideals and the Symbolic Landscape of America*. University of Wisconsin Press, 1987.

MacKethan, Lucinda. "Jean Toomer's *Cane*: A Pastoral Problem. *Mississippi Quarterly* 35 (Fall 1975): 423–34.

Magee, Michael. "Ralph Ellison: Pragmatism, Jazz and the American Vernacular." *Transactions of the Charles S. Peirce Society*, no. 39 (2003): 227–58.

Marable, Manning. *Race, Reform, and Rebellion: The Second Reconstruction in Black America, 1945–1990*. University Press of Mississippi, 1991.

Margolick, David. *Strange Fruit: Billie Holiday, Café Society, and an Early Cry for Civil Rights*. Running Press, 2000.

Marks, Carole. "The Social and Economic Life of Southern Blacks During the Migration." In *The Black Exodus: The Great Migration from the American South*, edited by Alferdteen Harrison, 36–50. University Press of Mississippi, 1991.

Marx, Leo. *The Machine in the Garden: Technology and the Pastoral Ideal in America*. Oxford University Press, 2000.

Massey, Doreen. "Double Articulation: A Place in the World." In *Displacements*, edited by Angelika Bammer, 110–21. Indiana University Press, 1994.

Maxwell, William J. "The Proletarian as New Negro: Mike Gold's Harlem Renaissance." In *Radical Revisions: Rereading 1930s Culture*, edited by Bill Mullen and Sherry Linkon, 91–119. University of Illinois Press, 1996.

McCammack, Brian. *Landscapes of Hope: Nature and the Great Migration in Chicago.* Harvard University Press, 2017.

McKay, Claude. *Home to Harlem.* Northeastern University Press, 1987.

McKay, Claude. *A Long Way from Home.* Rutgers University Press, 1975.

Miller, Kelly. "Where Is the Negro's Heaven?" In *The Opportunity Reader*, edited by Sondra Kathryn Wilson, 421–29. Random House, Inc., 1999.

Mills, Charles. *The Racial Contract.* Cornell University Press, 1997.

Morgan, Thomas L. "The City as Refuge: Constructing Urban Blackness in Paul Laurence Dunbar's *The Sport of the Gods* and James Weldon Johnson's *The Autobiography of an Ex-Colored Man*. *African American Review* 38, no. 2 (Summer 2004): 213–37.

Mostern, Kenneth. *Autobiography and Black Identity Politics.* Cambridge University Press, 1999.

Mullen, Bill V. *Popular Fronts: Chicago and African Cultural Politics, 1935–46.* University of Illinois Press, 1999.

Murphy, James F. *The Proletarian Moment: The Controversy over Leftism in Literature.* University of Illinois Press, 1991.

Murphy, Jillmarie. "Chains of Emancipation: Place Attachment and the Great Northern Migration in Paul Laurence Dunbar's the Sport of the Gods." *Studies in American Naturalism* 8, no. 2 (January 1, 2013): 150–70.

Nicholls, David G. *Conjuring the Folk: Forms of Modernity in African America.* University of Michigan Press, 2000.

Nickels, Cameron C. "Federalist Mock Pastorals: The Ideology of Early New England Humor." *Early American Literature* 17, no. 2 (Fall, 1982): 139–51.

Osofsky, Gilbert. *Harlem: The Making of a Ghetto.* Harper & Row, 1966.

Page, Thomas Nelson. *In Ole Virginia: Or, Marse Chan and Other Stories.* Southern Classics Series. J. S. Sanders Books, 1991.

Park, Robert E., and Ernest W. Burgess. *The City: Suggestions for Investigation of Human Behavior in the Urban Environment.* University of Chicago Press, 1984.

Porter, Horace A. *Jazz Country: Ralph Ellison in America.* University of Iowa Press, 2001.

Porter, Horace A. "The South in *Go Tell It on the Mountain*: Baldwin's Personal Confrontation." In *New Essays on "Go Tell It on the Mountain*," edited by Trudier Harris, 59–75. University of Cambridge Press, 1996.

Raboteau, Albert J. *Canaan Land: A Religious History of African Americans.* Oxford University Press, 2001.

Ramsey, William. "Jean Toomer's Eternal South." *Southern Literary Journal* 36 (Fall 2003): 74–89.

Robinson, Zandria F. *This Ain't Chicago: Race, Class, and Regional Identity in the Post-Soul South.* University of North Carolina Press, 2014.

Rodgers, Lawrence R. *Canaan Bound: The African American Great Migration Novel.* University of Illinois Press, 1997.

Rotella, Carlo. *October Cities: The Redevelopment of Urban Literature.* University of California Press, 1998.

Rowley, Hazel. *Richard Wright: The Life and Times*. Henry Holt and Company, 2001.

Rutkoff, Peter M., and William B. Scott. *Fly Away: The Great African American Cultural Migrations*. Johns Hopkins University Press, 2016.

Schatzki, Theodore. *The Site of the Social: A Philosophical Account of the Constitution of Social Life and Change*. The Pennsylvania University Press, 2002.

Shakespeare, William. *King Lear. The Complete Signet Classic Shakespeare*, edited by Sylvan Barnet. Harcourt Brace Jovanovich Publishers, 1963.

Siemerling, Winfried. "Democratic Blues: Houston Baker and the Representation of Culture." In *Cultural Difference & the Literary Text*, edited by Winfried Siemerling and Katrin Schwenk, 40–48. University of Iowa Press, 1996.

Simpson, Lewis P. *The Dispossessed Garden: Pastoral and History in Southern Literature*. University of Georgia Press, 1975.

Sinclair, Upton. *The Jungle*. R. Bentley, 1972.

Spear, Alan. *Black Chicago: The Making of a Negro Ghetto, 1890–1920*. University of Chicago Press, 1967.

Spillers, Hortense J. *Black, White and in Color*. University of Chicago Press, 2003.

Steinbeck, John. *The Grapes of Wrath*. Viking Press, 1966.

Stewart, Jacqueline. *Migrating to the Movies: Cinema and Black Urban Modernity*. University of California Press, 2005.

Takaki, Ronald. *A Different Mirror*. Little, Brown and Company, 1993.

Tate, Claudia. "Allegories of Black Female Desire; or, Rereading Nineteenth-Century Sentimental Narratives of Black Female Authority." In *Changing Our Own Words*, edited by Cheryl A. Wall, 98–126. Rutgers University Press, 1991.

Tate, Claudia. *Domestic Allegories of Political Desire*. Oxford University Press, 1992.

Taylor, Monique M. *Harlem Between Heaven and Hell*. University of Minnesota Press, 2002.

Teres, Harvey. *Renewing the Left: Politics, Imagination, and the New York Intellectuals*. Oxford University Press, 1996.

Tolnay, Stewart E., and E. M. Beck. "Rethinking the Role of Racial Violence in the Great Migration." In *Black Exodus*, edited by Alferdteen Harrison, 20–35. University Press of Mississippi, 1991.

Toomer, Jean. *Cane*. The Modern Library, 1994.

Toomer, Jean. "Letter to John McClure." In *The Jean Toomer Reader*, edited by Frederik L. Rusch, 12. Oxford University Press, 1993.

Toomer, Jean. "Letter to *The Liberator*." In *The Jean Toomer Reader*, edited by Frederik L. Rusch, 16. Oxford University Press, 1993.

Toomer, Jean. "Letter to Waldo Frank." In *The Jean Toomer Reader*, edited by Frederik L. Rusch, 10–11. Oxford University Press, 1993.

Trachtenberg, Alan. *The Incorporation of America: Culture and Society in the Gilded Age*. Hill and Wang, 1997.

Trotter, Joe William, Jr. "Introduction. Black Migration in Historical Perspective: A Review of the Literature." In *The Great Migration in Historical Perspective*, edited by Joe William Trotter Jr., 1–21. Indiana University Press, 1991.

Tsemo, Bridget Harris. "The Politics of Self-Identity in Paul Laurence Dunbar's *The Sport of the Gods*." *Southern Literary Journal* 41, no. 2 (Spring 2009): 24.

Turner, Darwin. *In a Minor Cord.* Southern Illinois University Press, 1971.

Van Vechten, Carl. Introduction to *The Autobiography of an Ex-Colored Man* by James Weldon Johnson, v–xxiii. Vintage Books, 1989.

Van Vechten, Carl. *Nigger Heaven.* University of Illinois Press, 2000.

Waldron, Edward E. *Walter White and the Harlem Renaissance.* Kennikat Press, 1978.

Wall, Cheryl. *Women of the Harlem Renaissance.* Indiana University Press, 1995.

Warren, Kenneth. *So Black and Blue.* University of Chicago Press, 2003.

Waters, Mary C. *Ethnic Options: Choosing Identities in America.* University of California Press, 1990.

Weaks-Baxter, Mary. *Leaving the South: Border Crossing Narratives and the Remaking of Southern Identity.* University Press of Mississippi, 2018.

White, Francis. *A Man Called White: The Autobiography of Walter White.* Viking Press, 1948.

White, Walter. *Flight.* Louisiana State University Press, 1998.

White, Walter. *How Far the Promised Land.* AMS Press, 1973.

Williams, Raymond. *The Country and the City.* Oxford University Press, 1973.

Williams, Raymond. *Culture and Society: 1780–1950.* Columbia University Press, 1983.

Williams, Raymond. *The Sociology of Culture.* University of Chicago Press, 1995.

Wilkerson, Isabel. *The Warmth of Other Suns.* Random House, 2010.

Wilson, William Julius. *The Truly Disadvantaged: The Inner City, the Underclass, and Public Policy.* University of Chicago Press, 1987.

Wilson, William Julius. *When Work Disappears.* Alfred A. Knopf, 1996.

Woods, Clyde. *Development Arrested: Race, Power, and the Blues in the Mississippi Delta.* Verso, 1998.

Woodson, Jon. *To Make a New Race: Gurdjieff, Toomer, and the Harlem Renaissance.* University Press of Mississippi, 1999.

Wright, Richard. *Black Boy.* Alfred Knopf, 1996.

Wright, Richard. "The Blue Print for Negro Writing." In *The Norton Anthology of African American Literature,* edited by Henry Louis Gates Jr. and Nellie Y. McKay, 1403–10. W. W. Norton & Company, 2004.

Wright, Richard. *Native Son.* Harper Perennial edition. Harper Perennial, 1993.

INDEX

ABOUT THE AUTHOR

Donald Shaffer is a native of Jackson, Mississippi, where he grew up attending College Hill Missionary Baptist Church. His passion for reading was instilled at an early age by his mother, Mrs. Ruby Shaffer, who worked as a librarian in the Jackson Public School system for over thirty years. She gifted her son with the complete short stories of Edgar Allan Poe when he was ten years old. Donald's love of literature began with that collection of short stories and started him on a path that would lead him back home to Mississippi State University, where he is currently director of African American Studies and faculty mentor for the Presidential Scholars Program in the Judy and Bobby Shackouls Honors College.